This S ntence is False

This Sentence is False

An introduction to philosophical paradoxes

Peter Cave

continuum

Continuum
The Tower Building, 11 York Road, London SE1 7NX
80 Maiden Lane, Suite 704, New York, NY 10038

www.continuumbooks.com

British Library Cataloguing-in-Publication Data
A catalogue record for this book is available from the British Library.

ISBN: HB: 978-1-8470-6219-2
       PB: 978-1-8470-6220-8

Library of Congress Cataloging-in-Publication Data
A catalog record for this book is available from the Library of Congress

Typeset by Kenneth Burnley, Wirral, Cheshire
Printed and bound in Great Britain by the MPG Books Group

Contents

For Angela Joy Harvey,
Blue S., Silver S., and paradoxical lives everywhere,
within and without.

Preface

Let us be human.

When first told that the Earth both spins and orbits the Sun, we may find it paradoxical. After all, it looks as if just the Sun does the moving. When we later reflect that things would look exactly as they do, with the Earth orbiting as paradoxically claimed, we may still find its movement surprising, for we feel neither rushes of air nor sensations of dizziness – nor, for that matter, do we get anywhere. If governments tell us, 'Don't panic', paradoxically we may feel well justified in panic; and, on those few occasions when a husband brings his wife chocolates and roses wrapped with loving smiles, paradoxically she may question both husband and wrapping.

The above are not philosophical but everyday cases of paradox. They are simply instances of what at first seems unlikely, surprising or casually incongruous. Indeed, in 1616 a certain John Bullokar offered as paradox the affirmation that 'the earth doth mooue round, and the heauens stand still'. Today most people accept that the evidence is in: the Earth both spins and orbits. Most of us recognize that, human that we are, the 'Don't panic' injunctions may suggest events over which to panic – and when guilty behaviour is sensed, sensed because of chocolates and roses, the gifts paradoxically may still promote peace.

In contrast to such explicable surprises, the paradoxes of this book are nearly all philosophical – often with continuing debate over resolution. Many are classical; most are well known to the philosophical community, though a small number feature the author's own spin. They embrace all the main areas of philosophy: from metaphysics – that is, understanding the world's nature in most general terms – to reasoning and knowledge, to values within morality and more widely. Indeed, paradoxes, generously understood and unlimited to the logical, offer excellent pathways into the philosophical activity. This is not surprising: key philosophical problems can be readily seen as paradoxical or puzzling.

I use the terms 'paradox' and 'puzzle' more or less interchangeably, but when labelling I reserve 'paradox' for those traditionally known as such, with 'puzzle' or 'problem' for the rest – though this is far from definitive. To provide foci for discussion, some paradoxes are highlighted in the text – and, when not too aberrant, I have resisted adding the word 'paradox' to each name.

With many of the paradoxes, full-length books could be written – and they have. While this book covers many, many paradoxes – including virtually all the accessible key philosophical paradoxes – we journey slowly over some paradoxical terrains, yet speed across others with little more than glimpses.

Philosophical paradoxes fill this book, save that the last few thoughts of Chapters 1 and 6 outline a few probability 'paradoxes'. They are included because we are often surprised by probability assessments, treating them as paradoxical. Humans typically reach mistaken conclusions about what is more, or less, probable; yet here, once the mathematics is understood, there usually remains no dispute. Partly because controversy does not rage for those in the probability know – and they do not immediately generate more puzzles – I do not view them as philosophical, hence their relegation to little more than asides.

This is an introductory work with, I hope, lightness of touch, but also with notes to guide further and deeper reading. The aim is to encourage reflection about the paradoxes and what lies behind.

The book is loosely arranged by means of types of underlying problem in the first six chapters, with the subsequent three chapters orientated to morality, God and the self respectively. The last chapter brings together some themes, while adding further thoughts and paradoxes. In philosophy there are no sharp boundaries – 'all things conspire' is the ancient saw – so there is some arbitrariness in the groupings. There is an interweaving of concerns: later chapters sometimes loop round to problems of the earlier, and the last chapter explicitly does this. The endnotes cover more than references; they engage in a little gossip and a few additional paradoxes.

Although the book is tentative about the resolution of some paradoxes, with regard to others I quote the splendid and well-rounded John Maynard Keynes: '. . . the author must, if he is to put his point of view clearly, pretend sometimes to a little more conviction than he feels'.

To the extent that there is a theme for paradoxical resolution in this work, it is the dictum, 'Let us be human' – a dictum, in one way or another, found in philosophers as diverse as Spinoza, Hume, Kierkegaard and Wittgenstein. We often forget life's different colours and shades of grey, mistakenly seeking the black and white, the Yes/No answers. We often forget that, when applying abstract reasoning and concepts to the world, restraint is required.

We live, argue and reason on Earth, not in abstract heavens. Philosophy can offer reminders.

Acknowledgements

Many paradoxical thoughts have been played and replayed throughout time's mists. Where I have wittingly used others' examples,
remembering the sources, references occur in the notes. I thank all
such people mentioned. Paradoxically, I thank many unmentioned
who doubtless have influenced me – and also the editors of *Philosophical Investigations* and *Philosophy* for permission to use some material,
detailed in 'Further reading'.

Turning to naming personal names, my thanks to Laurence Goldstein who, many years ago, rejuvenated, and has since sustained, my
paradoxical interest – through conversation, good humour and many
papers – and to Michael Clark for his valuable *Paradoxes from A to Z*,
combined with enjoyable conversations. My paradox purveying was
originally sparked by two incisive philosophers, little known, namely
John Watling and Peter Downing, both of University College
London. Recently, Julian Mayers and Nick Romero added paradoxical sparkle with our endeavours to broadcast philosophy to the
nations, somewhat embarrassingly in my case, courtesy of Pier
Productions and BBC Radio 4.

Helpful paradoxical conversations, sometimes paradoxically helpful, have occurred over the years with Chris Belshaw, Seth Crook,
Nick Everitt, David Ferris, John Gingell, Ossie Hanfling (now, sadly
deceased), Ross Harrison, Martin Holt, Derek Matravers/Maltravers,
Nicholas Shackel, John Shand, Jerry Valberg, Arnold Zuboff – and
many students of Britain's The Open University and of City University London. Nick Everett and Laurence Goldstein merit additional
appreciation, having suffered some chapters' embryonic drafts.

On more practical matters – ranging from printers to encouragement et al. – I thank Angela Joy Harvey. My thanks too to Sarah

Campbell of Continuum for inviting me to write and for sensitive handling of my delaying tactics, to Tom Crick and Joanne Murphy of Continuum for understanding and practical support, and to Gerry's Wines and Spirits, and The French House, for alcoholic support. Some indirect practical support, much appreciated, came from Phil Smith and his side-kicks Tony Seaton and Sally Mitchell – and from many others. Composers as diverse as Monteverdi and Messiaen, Britten and Philip Glass, and singers Cesaria Evora, Carolyn Sampson and Ian Bostridge, unwittingly helped, courtesy of recorded pleasures, not least through blocking the city's continually noisy, reconstructive life (see the Means/Ends Puzzle).

The staff of the British Library kindly supplied me with as many words and sentences as I required – and also coffee, extra hot – though I cannot resist adding, paradoxically, a negative acknowledgement of those library readers who lack small courtesies such as using tissues instead of sniffing swirls of merry mucus and such as silencing their laptop jingles.

I leave to last, Ardon Lyon. Apart from his fortitude and endurance in battling through meandering drafts of all chapters, Ardon over the years has provided stimulation (philosophic in nature), clarity, confusion, clarity again, humour, interest, digression, friendship, kindness, sighs, despairs, exclamations, some more confusion, sympathy, tales, provocation, encouragement, clarity yet again, more confusion, some wisdom and certainly considerable intellectual help (much needed), and many laughingly loud laughs – not necessarily in that order. This is a case where paradoxically the last should be first, without thereby switching back to last.

Peter Cave
Soho, London

1 Welcome to the rational irrational –

how to win, how to starve, and how to pump money

. . . where, after brief introductions to a depressed ass, a tortoise, a barber – and some lovers – our rationality is set spinning, courtesy of a mind-reader, some indecision and some pumping of, not muscle, but money – leading us to an imp, a silly offer and so on.

A tortoise that cannot be caught; a donkey who, unable to choose, starves to death; surprise examinations that should not surprise – simple arguments spin us into these philosophical worlds of paradox and perplexity. The paradoxes are pretty easy to grasp. What is far from easy – and leaves philosophers a-spinning – is working out quite what has gone wrong, why it has gone wrong, and what can be done to righten the wrong. After all, tortoises can be caught, indecisive donkeys do not usually starve, and surprise examinations may still surprise, as pupils sometimes know to their cost, even when informed of impending surprise. The tales may seem silly, yet, in seeking solution, deep puzzles about our reasoning, the universe and ourselves can be revealed.

This chapter focuses on some rationality paradoxes; but first, what is a philosophical paradox? The word derives from the Greek – '*para*' and '*doxa*' – 'above, beyond, belief'; but for an answer, it is better initially to offer samples rather than formal definitions. 'This sentence is false' is a paradoxical taster; for if it is true, then is it not false; and if false, is it not true?

BURIDAN'S ASS

The hungry donkey – traditionally, indeed, an ass – is confronted by two bales of hay, one to the right, one the left. He needs to decide which to eat. The bales are equally succulent, equally sized, and the same distance away; so, lacking a reason to choose one over the other, the poor ass dies, starving. How can he be so stupid, so asinine? Yet, for us to act, do we not need a reason? Paradoxically, it seems, one bale too many is the cause of his woe.

'CATCH ME IF YOU CAN!'

Achilles and a tortoise have a race. Achilles, being the fastest runner in Athens yet also a gentleman, allows the tortoise some heads' start. For Achilles to win, he must first reach the tortoise's starting position; but by the time he does, the tortoise has moved to a new position. By the time Achilles reaches that new position, the tortoise has moved a little further. Although the tortoise's extra distances ahead become smaller and smaller, it looks as if they must go on for ever. Hence, it seems, Achilles cannot reach the tortoise, let alone win the race.

Buridan's tale sets us wondering – wondering about human choices rather than asses'. If we are faced with a choice between two actions, equally appealing, would it not be highly irrational to end up being unable to choose? Yet how can we choose, if we lack reason to prefer one over the other?

The Achilles Paradox baffles us with the infinite divisibility of space. If Achilles has an endless series of distances to run, even if the distances diminish in size, how can they ever be *all* traversed? How can the endless be ended? This book deals with endlessness in various modes, but next comes a scent of further paradoxical blossoming.

BARBER

In Alcala works a barber. He shaves all and only those who do not shave themselves. So, does he shave himself? If he is someone who shaves himself, then he is not shaved by the barber, but that means he does not shave himself. If he is someone who does not shave himself, then the barber shaves him, but that means that he shaves himself. What does he do?

LOVERS

Larry loves Ludmilla – 'It's just you whom I love' – yet Larry's love must be because of Ludmilla's various characteristics. If that is so, then Larry ought to love anyone possessed of those characteristics. So, in truth, does he not love anyone like Ludmilla, rather than Ludmilla in particular?

The Barber Paradox raises a question about statements and truth, as does our title's sentence 'This sentence is false' – a version, indeed, of the Liar Paradox – but with the barber, as described, we may wonder what he does in fact do with regard to himself. The Lovers Paradox asks what you can see in someone other than their qualities. Lurking within is the question of what makes me a particular person. Further, lovers often declare their love to be eternal, yet they know that they and their lovers will change. Is it not paradoxical to make commitments to unknown futures together?

Paradoxes, reasons and rationality

Philosophical paradoxes beguile. Some topics – truth, infinity, reason, space and time – have beguiled for centuries. A sense of the fascination is gained by looking at M. C. Escher's 'impossible' drawings where, for example, a closed and continuous circular pathway of steps appears ever rising. How can that be?

The paradoxes are powerful because they involve seemingly simple and strong arguments that lead to highly counter-intuitive conclusions. 'There must be a mistake in our reasoning – or perhaps we have started off with mistaken assumptions.' If we locate the mistake, then perhaps we have a 'falsidical' paradox: the surprising conclusion is false. Perhaps, though, the conclusion is true. After all, Zeno of Elea, who gave us Achilles, concluded that motion was illusory: Zeno saw the paradox's conclusion as 'veridical', telling us the truth. Sometimes a paradox can be presented as an 'antinomy' in which two lines of similar reasoning lead to conclusions that clash, generating a dilemma. Immanuel Kant, a highly influential philosopher, despaired at some fundamental antinomies; at how, for example, our reasoning can lead us to conclude both that time must have a beginning and that it cannot.

Progress may be made in spotting where some paradoxical reasoning goes wrong, only for strengthened paradoxical versions to sidle forth. Medieval logicians spoke of insolubilia – insolubles – when analysing the Liar, 'I am lying', and variations such as 'This sentence is false.' Centuries earlier, Philetus of Cos, *c.* 300 BC, allegedly received the epitaph,

> Philetus of Cos am I,
> 'Twas the Liar who made me die,
> And the bad nights caused thereby . . .

for the Liar worried him so much that he wasted, just wasted away.

Paradoxes lead us into inconsistencies or contradictions. 'This page has fewer than 200 words' is inconsistent with the claim that it has more than 200 words. Although the claims cannot together be true, they could both be false: the page could have exactly 200 words. The two claims are 'contraries' rather than contradictory. With contradictory claims, the standard and sensible line is that they can neither both be true nor both be false. There cannot both be more than 200 words on this page and yet not more than 200 words. 'Inconsistent', then, applies both to contraries and to the contradictory.

Although we are sometimes inconsistent and contradict ourselves, we *contra* our *diction* or speak against what we say, the facts of the matter, the world – we feel – cannot be inconsistent. Should we worry about inconsistencies? Yes. If people contradict themselves, quite what do they think? Suppose friends tell you, 'This afternoon, we're travelling to Cambridge and not travelling to Cambridge', well, what *are* their travelling plans? We may iron out the contradiction. 'Ah, you mean you're not going, but we should pretend to colleagues that you are.' With no ironing explanation, we are at a loss.

Wittingly holding inconsistent beliefs is irrational – after all, it means that you believe at least one thing that is false. Irrationality, though, does not arise solely through inconsistency; well, not obviously so. Irrationality can manifest itself in what we do or fail to do. If we have a desired end in view – for example, to eat – then often it is rational to adopt appropriate means to achieve that end. The 'often' caveat is needed because other factors sometimes come into play. A desired end may provide reason to elope with the secretary, but a sense of duty could make it rational to resist. The fine feast on offer is both desired and desirable, but concern for health may rightly prevent the feasting fun.

Just because people act with reason, they are not thereby acting rationally. The reason may be poor. For that matter, what is sought may be against all reason. It would be irrational to have as your reason for going to France that you wanted to avoid French speakers and garlic. It would be irrational to have as your sole aim in life to clap your hands against your head a billion times – unless someone guaranteed you untold wealth if you so performed. Arguably, it would be irrational to wander the world completely veiled unless you had good reason to believe that it would bring ultimate joy.

With these background points in place, we turn to some paradoxical rationality: Newcomb's, originated a few decades ago, the medieval Buridan's already sketched, and then some money pumping and more. Concerning any paradox, nearly always there are different versions with different morals drawn: this book usually presents key versions.

Newcomb's Problem: how free are you?

You are a player in a strange and long-surviving television show. You face two boxes. One is open, so the contents, £10,000, can be seen. The other is a surprise box, its contents hidden. You may choose to take both boxes or the surprise box only. The surprise box is either empty or contains £1 million, its contents determined by a mind-reader's prior assessment of your character and the choice you will make. If the mind-reader judged that you will take both boxes, then nothing has been placed in the surprise box. If she judged that you will take only the surprise box, then £1 million will have been placed in the box.

The £1 million is already in the surprise box or not, so reason dictates that you take both boxes. After all, if the surprise box is empty, you should two-box so that you at least win the £10,000. If the surprise box is filled with the £1 million, you should two-box, to win the jackpot of £1 million and £10,000. But . . . well, there is often a 'but' in such scenarios. The show has run for many years, and, whenever players have selected both boxes, the surprise box has been empty – or has been empty in 99.99 per cent of cases. That latter qualification highlights that the jackpot win, of the million pounds together with the £10,000, is possible: maybe very, very occasionally the mind-reader makes a mistake; mind-reading can be tiring.

You want to secure the most money possible. What is it rational to do? You do not want to risk losing the £1 million, yet securing the £10,000 in addition to the £1 million would be worth it. Maybe it is time to have a drink – and a think . . . What would it be rational to do?

*   *   *

There are two conflicting lines of reasoning, both powerful. Given the evidence of the mind-reader's mind-reading success – who knows how she does it? – surely it is rational to select the surprise box only, for she will have correctly predicted your choice. This 'evidential' argument clashes with the 'causal' or 'already there' argument. 'Look, the money is already there or not – so you may as well take both boxes.' We are not supposing backward causation or that your choice could now cause the £1 million (if it is there) magically to vanish.

Most philosophers support the 'already there' reasoning. Were they to do so in practice, the evidence overwhelmingly suggests that they would come away from the show pretty grumpy, having secured only the £10,000: the mind-reader would have anticipated their philosophical preference in the reasoning. Participants who allow the mind-reader's past success to dominate their reasoning, who allow the evidence to dominate, thus taking the surprise box only, nearly always end up with the £1 million.

If confronted with the boxes, the reasoning can go round and round, reeling and a-reeling: silly to take both boxes as you are exceedingly likely to get only the £10,000; but whatever is in the surprise box is already there, so it is silly not to take both boxes. Yet if you do the latter, then the mind-reader will have predicted that – and so forth.

Trying to judge what another party does, if what they do depends on their judgement of what you judge and do, leads into Prisoners' Dilemma questions (see Chapter 7). Newcomb, though, raises further questions, once the mind-reader's success rates, comparative sizes of the money, and their relevance to you are varied. For example, if the open box contained just a pound, you may as well go for the surprise box only. Such frills can generate heated arguments about probabilities, leading to two basic points being overlooked.

One point questions the tale's consistency. Is the successful mind-reader possible in theory? Yes, such a reader may be successful with different player-types: some players may come over as very greedy grabbers who would grab at both boxes without reflection; other players may be timid, always inclined to take one rather than two. Another player-type may be so desperate for immediate money that no risk of losing £10,000 can be tolerated, so these players two-box. But is a successful mind-reader possible when operating with those participants whom the puzzle addresses, namely those whose decisions result solely from rationality?

Rationality – good reasoning – points, as seen, to no single answer as to what to do. So, the mind-reader, it seems, cannot consistently and successfully predict the choices of players, if the choices are based solely on rationality. Maybe Newcomb has generated a puzzle by telling a tale with impossible conditions. Whether a built-in impossibility is concealed is worth checking when tackling any puzzle. However, even if there is an impossibility, Newcomb's Problem is not worthless – for it leads to the second point.

What does determine the choices of players who think they are choosing rationally? Not rationality itself, that is for sure; after all, rationality has left us reeling. So, how are their choices made? If they are random – determined by a coin's spin – then the mind-reader's predictions must also be random, if she merely seeks correct predictions. However, if events in the brain determine the choices, then we could transform the mind-reader into a neurologist with brain-scanning equipment. This prompts a deep and more general question: how do choices and reasons relate to the causes and effects within our brains? This question is explored a little in Chapter 9. It is raised, together with Newcomb's weirdness, if we push the tale to its limit.

The first push uses the tale as given, except that the surprise box has a transparent side, so the show's audience can see its contents; but you, the player, still cannot. Those others, if keen for you to do the best, are bound to be urging you to take both boxes: they can see that what is already there is indeed already there. And you, as contestant, know that they can see; yet the evidential reasoning pointing to one-boxing should still hold as much sway as it did before.

I now suggest a second push. Suppose that you, as player, can see what is in the surprise box. In that case, rationality must surely lead you to take both boxes – there are no magical illusions in the tale. Yet this revised Newcomb tale, because it is still with a *successful* mind-reader, must be saying that most players do not take both boxes, when the surprise box's £1 million is on view. Rather, they take the surprise box alone. That is a mystery indeed, if they are seeking to maximize winnings, and able freely to choose. A story could be concocted: they do not want to appear greedy – or perhaps the sight of £1 million causes them to forget the £10,000, or perhaps despite rationally wanting to two-box, they find themselves compelled to one-box. Who knows? This brings out the mystery within the original puzzle of a successful mind-reader, allegedly successful even with players who choose on the basis of rationality. It raises questions of how rationality relates to our choice-making.

Buridan's Ass, still undecided

Whether Jean Buridan, a logician of Paris, ever owned an ass or even told the tale, is doubtful, but Buridan was certainly intrigued by logical problems. In contrast to Newcomb, the tale is a simple one. We may recognize the problem, when needing, for example, to decide between a blue toothbrush and a red, yet lacking any colour preference. How can we choose – if we have no good reason for choosing one over the other? Yet, somehow, we do choose.

Buridan's ass is faced with the two bales that, in every relevant respect, are equal. The ass lacks a reason – a discriminating reason – to choose this one over that one, or that one over this. His death results from lingering indecision. His is a tale of one bale too many – a tale of woe because of a bale of woe.

Let us rewind the tale. The ass, being rational as humans should be, assumes that he needs a reason to act – but not just that. After all, he has good reason to munch the bale to the left; it will save him from starvation, and starvation he seeks to avoid. Rationality demands that you adopt means to the ends sought, unless you have other good reasons to challenge those ends or, indeed, those means. Yet, by similar reasoning, munching the bale on the right also has a claim on him – hence the conflict under which he strains. Perhaps he should simply elect to eat of both bales, but then he must decide which merits first munch.

The poor ass – an ass indeed – reels in his reasoning, reeling potentially without end, as with Newcomb's rational players. If he focuses on the bale to the right, thinking that will be his choice, reflection on the left bale leads him away from the right; but if he is tempted to choose to eat of the left, then reflection on the right reels him back. Realizing this, he is led into no choice; but that too is no resting place, for, desiring not to starve, he is propelled back to trying to choose between the bales. Paradoxically, a potential double feeding has led to the impossibility of even a single feeding – and to his unhappy reeling. 'Bring him just one of the bundles; then all will be well. One will be nearer and hence will provide him with the required discriminating reason for choice.'

Such may seem the simple answer; but the ass would still need to choose which portion of the bale first to munch. To the observation that portions would be different – different in size, proximity and so on – he would still have to decide which features were relevant for his choosing; after all, the initial tale had bales differing in that one rested to his right, the other, his left. That right–left difference was irrelevant regarding his rational choice; and Buridan's ass is, if anything, rational.

Rationality gets us into trouble. The ass's commitment to a seeming demand of rationality has damaged his health. Maybe we – and Buridan's ass – should often resist requiring a discriminating reason for rational action. Having good reason for choosing A does not always demand having good reason for discriminating in favour of A over *all* alternatives. If we are unable to choose, perhaps we should sing-song to ourselves,

> When you just can't decide,
> let the ass be your guide;
> just recall, after all,
> that that ass nearly died.
> Stupid ass. What an ass!

In our everyday lives, we can choose one toothbrush over another, even though we have no reason for that particular choice. You have a reason to take a glass of wine, but maybe no reason for choosing the glass on the left rather than the one on the right. Of course, some brain happenings lead to your hand stretching out one way rather than the other, and picking up, say, the left-side glass.

Buridan's simple tale raises the question again of how causes relate to reasons. Having good reasons for doing something typically does not pinpoint exactly what you do. If you reach for the left-hand glass of wine, a satisfactory reason may simply be that you wanted some wine – and that would also have been a satisfactory reason for reaching for the right-hand glass. Yet what causally explains your reaching leftward is not what would have causally explained your reaching rightward. Your desire for a glass of red is your reason for taking either glass. It is also your reason for taking the particular glass on the left, even though not your reason for taking that glass *rather than* the one on the right. Rationality requires reasons, but, as Newcomb and Buridan demonstrate, it is a muddy matter how reasons work in the causal world.

Newcomb and Buridan present puzzles in our coming to prefer some actions over others. Yet, once we have our preferences, rationality also has a role: surely we should aim for consistency in our preferences – or should we?

Trading, dancing and pumping money

You want a sheep; you own a goat unwanted by you. I want a goat, yet have a sheep unwanted. If e-Bay puts us in touch, a trade may occur: we each end up with what we want and we rid ourselves of what we do not. Lives involve preferences, even if not usually of sheep and goats. We prefer some items over others. We trade, when we can –

and fortunately we can. People's preferences and circumstances differ; compromises occur. Now, people with inconsistent preferences can have money pumped from them – in principle. That is a good reason for our not having inconsistent preferences. We approach the pump gradually.

Jack and Jill are at loggerheads over holidays. Jack wants Turkey; Jill wants Tunisia. Jack prefers Turkey over Tunisia; yet Jack does not prefer being in Turkey with a sulking Jill, sulking at missing out on Tunisia. For that matter, he does not prefer being in Tunisia with an enraptured Jill, given he wants to be in Turkey. If things go well, they uncover a compromise: perhaps Transilvania suits both. If things go unwell, they may prefer holidaying apart.

We now introduce *transitivity*. If a relation holds between A and B, and between B and C, then it must hold between A and C – to be transitive. If Clarice is older than Beatrice, and Beatrice is older than Alice, then Clarice is older than Alice. 'Older than' is transitive. Many relations are intransitive, not transitive. If Clarice likes Beatrice, and Beatrice likes Alice, Clarice may yet not like Alice.

Suppose Jack prefers Turkey to Transilvania and prefers Transilvania to Tunisia, then surely he prefers Turkey to Tunisia. It would be crazy for him yet to prefer Tunisia to Turkey. Were he to prefer Tunisia to Turkey, but retain his preference for Turkey over Transilvania, and Transilvania over Tunisia, it looks as if he would prefer Turkey over Turkey. We meet a contradiction – and, were that the case, we meet a crazed and crazy Jack. The example illustrates the point that preferences, to be rational, seem to require transitivity. But now consider:

PREFERENCE

I prefer dancing with Clarice to dancing with Beatrice, yet I prefer dancing with Beatrice to dancing with Alice. This may make perfectly good sense. After all, I delight in Clarice's company, am pretty neutral about Beatrice; and when it comes to Alice, I find her so awkward that I prefer blandness with Beatrice. Hence, rationality suggests that I should prefer dancing with Clarice than with Alice. But does it? Paradox arises because, it seems, 'No' could be the correct answer.

Here are circumstances where 'No' seems correct. Alice is fragile, easily upset and feels undermined by Clarice, though not by Beatrice. Clarice is confident and sociable; so I may prefer dancing with Alice rather than causing her distress by my dancing with Clarice. There is nothing irrational, then, in preferring dancing with Alice than with Clarice – yet the earlier reasoning pointed to the irrationality of my preferring dancing with Alice to dancing with Clarice.

Perhaps the paradox errs in assuming that rational preferences are transitive. Perhaps rationality no more demands preferences to be transitive than 'likes' and 'loves' to be transitive. However, if this is so, we meander into a monetary mire. This is where money can be pumped from us. Let us continue with the dancing example – though the dancing could be replaced by other, arguably more satisfying activities.

I prefer dancing with Clarice to dancing with Beatrice, and prefer dancing with Beatrice to dancing with Alice, yet, intransitively, I prefer dancing with Alice to dancing with Clarice. These are distinguished dancers, so people buy tickets to dance with them. Suppose that I have a ticket to Alice and you hold tickets to Beatrice and Clarice. As I prefer Beatrice-dancing to Alice-dancing, I should surely trade my Alice ticket for your Beatrice ticket – and be prepared to pay you something for that trade, e.g., £100. After all, Beatrice-dancing is more valuable to me than Alice-dancing. After the trade, you have £100 and the Alice ticket. You still have the Clarice ticket. I have the Beatrice ticket. Here comes the next stage.

I prefer Clarice to Beatrice dancing, so I should be prepared to offer you the Beatrice ticket plus, say, another £100, to secure the preferred Clarice ticket. I do so, the outcome being that I now have the Clarice ticket and am down by £200. You now have the Alice and Beatrice tickets and the £200. But hold on, I prefer Alice-dancing to Clarice-dancing, so I should be prepared to trade my Clarice ticket plus, say, £100, for your Alice ticket. The outcome is that I am back to square one, holding just the Alice ticket, but am £300 down. You are happily back to holding the Beatrice and Clarice tickets, with a £300 gain. As you now have tickets I prefer, it would seem that you and I should commence trading all over again. The sky – well, my pocket and trading preparedness – is the limit concerning how much money you can pump from me.

The Money Pump shows that my preferences, being intransitive, are therefore highly irrational – unless I delight in making losses. If this demonstrates that rationality demands transitivity, then we are cast back into the Paradox of Preference. Of course, someone with the intransitive preferences, but otherwise rational, seeing where all this leads, would refuse to trade in the first place. That is true, but then we have the question of what justifies the refusal, for the preferences also appear to give good reasons for trading. In such circumstances, if the Money Pump has things correctly described, individuals may become as baffled as our asinine ass confronted by his bales of woe – I mean, hay – or as baffled when friends say both that they are returning to Cambridge and not returning.

Arguably the Preference Paradox arises because the different preferences are not fully described and ordered. Here is an explicit preference ordering:

First   Dancing with Clarice, with Alice not upset.
Second   Dancing with Beatrice, with Alice not upset.
Third   Dancing with Alice, were that the only way of not upsetting her.
Fourth   Dancing with Alice, even if she were content not dancing with me.

Whichever I do, if rational, depends on the options available; and the order is happily transitive and safe from any money-pumping. In the example, when Alice is present, I need to settle for second best, if available, and dance with Beatrice. When Alice is not around, I am safe, aiming for my first preference. The Preference Paradox arises because some significant features are slipped out of the picture.

*   *   *

Determining the conditions for rationality is far from easy – as maybe Newcomb, Buridan and Preference have shown. Economists, when constructing models for people's likely behaviour, have often concentrated on an ideal of rational individuals. For example, it may seem rational to maximize 'expected value'. This means that a 50 per cent chance of receiving £500 (the expected value being £250) should be preferred to the certainty of receiving £200. Yet many reasonable people, being risk adverse, prefer the £200 certainty. Allais' Paradox – courtesy of French economist Maurice Allais – shows that maximizing expected value is often not the most rational aim. So, economists' 'expected utility' embraces more factors. Certainty has added value; background wealth reduces the payoff of yet more wealth ('diminishing marginal utility').

What perfectly reasonable people find rational may still not coincide with the economists' rationality ideal. So much the worse for that particular ideal, we should be inclined to say. Not surprisingly, complexities also arise if infinity – endlessness – is thrown into tales of rational choice. We focus on the infinity paradoxes, of space and time, movement and more, in Chapter 4, but, for a touch of infinity's effect on choice, here is the Paradox of the Charitable Trust.

Suppose money is invested in trust to help the impoverished. Suppose that the investments' value increases more rapidly than the poverty – and the world goes on for ever. Under those unlikely suppositions, paradoxically there is no time, it is argued, when it is rational to spend the trust's money. This is because the money could always be invested longer in order to help more people. Of course, things will not go on for ever – as Keynes quipped, 'In the long run, we're all dead' – but even if we know of distant future dates when the trust must end, we may feel that it is better to do something 'good enough' *now* rather than something better in the uncertain future. This is 'satisficing', contrasting with maximizing expected utility if not suitably revised. Human that we are, we have to recognize our limited years and our circumstances. We make do.

Let me suggest a related Means/Ends Puzzle. People often deploy painful means for desired ends; they undergo disruption, noise and discomfort, causing similar to others, to improve their homes, gardens and offices; but once improvement is achieved, further painful projects are undertaken – by them or by the others. The paradoxical outcome is that the ends are rarely enjoyed, being sabotaged by new disruptive means to new desirable ends that will themselves then be disrupted by the initial disrupters or others new to the game.

Recall your aunt's china, china so fine that it must be brought out only for special occasions – and no occasion is ever special enough. Recall, too, the painting of Scotland's Forth Bridge that takes so long that the finishing time is also the time to start all over again – but that would be an unwise recall, for apparently such a painting practice is mythical. Contrast companies' road-diggings: real, repeated and peace-shattering – well, certainly in most cities.

How far we take into account troubles ahead – and anticipate others doing likewise – is nicely brought out in the Bottle Imp, a tale from Robert Louis Stevenson. The imp or genie can fulfil all your typical desires for fortune, fame, happiness and so on. He is on sale at whatever price you want to pay. The one snag is that whoever owns the imp must at some stage, to avoid eternal torment, sell him for less than he or she paid. Well, how far along the chain of tradings do you look? Nobody rational would buy the imp for the smallest amount, say one penny; so no one rational would buy for two pence – and so forth. Of course, if there were no smallest amount – if a penny could be infinitely divided – then all should be well. A practical problem, slightly similar and without the infinity possibility, arises when buying leasehold property, aware that as the length of lease declines, potential buyers are usually rarer.

Returning to infinity and rationality, Nicolaus Bernoulli proposed the St Petersburg Paradox: a fair coin will be repeatedly spun until it lands tails up, at which point the game ends. If or when tails turns up, the player receives £2 multiplied by itself the number of times that the coin has been spun. So, if tails appears after the first spin, the player receives £2; if tails does not appear until the second, £4 is received; if not until the third, £8; if not until the fourth, £16 – and so on. Of course, the probability of tails not coming up until much later reduces in the same fashion as the prize increases. A long run of just heads appearing is very unlikely, but possible. On the first spin, there is a 50 per cent chance tails and the £2; hence, that expected value is £1. There is just a 25 per cent chance of winning the £4; hence, that expected value is also £1; and just a 12.5 per cent chance of winning £8, another expected value of £1 – and so on.

The expected value of playing the game is the sum of those £1s – an infinite, endless number of them, for tails just possibly may keep on falling to turn up. Taking part in the game hence possesses the value of infinite pounds. Surely, that should lead us to be prepared to pay a very large finite sum to take part in the game. Yet that is crazy. Rationally, we may risk £5 or £10 at the game. The game's infinity aspect brings home its impracticality – and also our being unimpressed by very, very large sums, if the possibility of winning them is so very, very, very remote.

Economists increasingly seek to take into account the diverse factors affecting rationality and human behaviour – as Bernoulli did in resolving St Petersburg. We do tend to be risk adverse, but when at our wits' end, or when the potential loss is insignificant, we take part in games that on pure probability calculations are not worth playing. This may strike 'rational' individuals as the Lottery-Playing Puzzle. Lottery entrants may recognize that the total prize value is typically less than the total ticket cost, given administration expenses, profits paid and the lottery's charitable donations. Were someone able to buy all the tickets, his prizes' total value would be less than the tickets' cost. Yet, even when realizing this, people still enter. This, though, is not really puzzling and need not be irrational: some take part for the fun, others out of desperation.

*   *   *

For some thoughts on rationality in general, let us skim the waters of the Paradox of Irrationality, highlighted by a recent American philosopher, Donald Davidson.

How do we come correctly to understand someone's behaviour as irrational? It may be highly irrational for me to go to the gym, in view of my fear of exertion, strained muscles and worse, yet others may lack such fears or take them in their stride for the benefits of possessing a desirable figure – or at least the opportunity to befriend desirable others. In seeking to understand the seemingly irrational behaviour of gym-lovers, I read their behaviour as resulting from appropriate beliefs and desires. Now, suppose George hates the gym, announcing that it offers him no benefits. Suppose he has not promised anyone that he would give it a whirl – yet he keeps going. Well, we are at a loss to understand his behaviour. We may, though, keep trying; we may think that there must be some reason, some motive, maybe subconscious, that he has. That is, to understand him we need to bring his seemingly irrational behaviour into the realm of the rational – or at least into reasoned behaviour.

To understand irrationality, we seek to make it rational or at least reasoned. Touching on this is the Silly Offer Puzzle.

You are offered a million pounds to do something utterly silly – anything silly. Perhaps you decide to go silly-walking in public, wearing pink bananas on your head, clapping your ears and giving passersby items of litter, while singing 'Land of Hope and Glory'. You claim your million pounds. All will be well, unless the donor insists that your behaviour was not utterly silly: it was designed to secure the million pounds, a prize that you reasonably enough wanted, so it was not silly at all to do what you did.

We now see how the seemingly kindly offer was in fact maliciously unkindly offered – for you cannot win the million pounds. Even if you do something highly rational and unsilly, such as locking your door when leaving home, and then asking for the million pounds – after all, it is exceedingly silly to do something highly rational and unsilly in order to win a prize for silliness – the would-be donor will still refuse you. She now argues that what you did, being silly in doing something unsilly, was ultimately rational and unsilly, given its design to secure the prize. You may retort that it was thus highly irrational and silly, as it does not (it now transpires) secure the prize; hence it should secure the prize – and so on . . . Such reasoning loops us round endlessly, spiralling up in terms of the rationality of an irrational act, leading to a 'next level' irrationality, leading to a higher rationality – and so forth.

The Silly Offer was a catch and we meet more catches, including Catch-22, in Chapter 10. The Silly Offer also features the endless loopings of many paradoxes. Recall, if the first shall be last and the last shall be first, then when the switch is made, the first are now indeed last and so merit being first, but that means they should be last – and so on. We see more of the 'and so on' in the next three chapters, taking us from perspectives to truth to infinity itself.

'And so on', indeed.

2 Too clever by one-half –
or, at least, one-eighth

. . . where we encounter surprises that cannot surprise, an offer that is good and true, yet too good to be true; and we meet two Cambridge professors – oh, and also Brer Rabbit, Machiavelli and some faking.

When considering in which shares to invest, which road to take or where best to spend a good night out, bad experiences from decisions past may suggest doing the opposite of what we think. Perhaps we have noticed that, when faced with financial dilemmas, road maps, and yearnings for love, our decisions have always been wrong. Of course, what constitutes an opposition is frequently far from clear, but even when we have to choose simply between road to the right and road to the left, the clever advice of 'Do the opposite of what we think' is useless if taken as literally stated: were we thinking road right and then, as a result, switch to road left, well, now we are thinking road left, so, applying the injunction, we switch to road right. Endlessly the switching continues.

'And so on' indicates the above tale's endlessness in play. No appeal to rationality will tell us what to do; and, on the information given, no one will be able to predict, save by luck, what we shall do or rationally should do. Of course, such endless reeling in the reasoning need not threaten: an implicit assumption may well be that 'Do the opposite' should be deployed only from an *initial* thought of what is to be done. A block on, or resistance to, the reasoning is now built within the injunction, a threatening endlessness ended. The following paradoxical reasoning, though, seems resistant to block or resistance.

SURPRISE

There will be a noon examination one school-day next week, students are told; and it will be a surprise – a surprise in that, whichever day it occurs, the students will be surprised. 'Well, it can't be on the last day, Friday', think clever students, realizing that by Friday it would not then surprise, Friday being the only day left. 'With Friday ruled out, it cannot be on the Thursday; so Thursday must be ruled out.' And so the reasoning continues, the days being ruled out one after the other, working backwards. The conclusion is that a surprise examination cannot occur. Yet, of course, it can. It is given one day that week – and it surprises.

The paradox, in part, exposes some differences between what I can think and say about myself and what others can think and say about me – as we shall see.

Reasoning and a-reeling

Surprises happen and the Surprise Paradox has been delivered as surprise inspections, surprise examinations – even, surprisingly, as surprise hangings. At mundane examination level, it is not unusual for students to be told that during the forthcoming week, Monday to Friday inclusive, there will be a surprise hanging – well, all right, an examination. By 'surprise' is meant that the students will have no good reason to think or believe on the morning of the examination that the examination will occur at noon on that day. However, the students have good reason for their belief that the teacher speaks truly.

Sibyl is a clever student. She conducts the calming reasoning set out above, quickly concluding that there can be no surprise examination. Sibyl faces the week with a complacent smugness, not bothering to revise. And yet, of course, one day that week the smugness is intruded upon; an examination is given – and it surprises. Sibyl, having not revised, fails the examination, while students unable to conduct such 'clever' reasoning have revised and pass. Sibyl has been too clever by half, or at least by one-eighth. Sibyl's sibylline prophecy has let her down. What has gone wrong with the reasoning?

On encountering the paradox, people are often impressed by the days ahead in the tale, but it is difficult to see why the days and their number should matter. After all, the puzzle arises because Sibyl projects herself to the Friday morning unexamined: she understands the teacher's announcement to imply that even a Friday examination would be a surprise. Ridding ourselves of the window-dressing of the days, we move to an austere version of the paradox, where what is meant to be a surprise is soon to happen. To register that this is a revision of the traditional paradox, let us speak of the Surprise Party.

If told that there will be a surprise party this very evening, Sibyl may well be surprised at being told; but she can hardly be surprised at the party. Surprise parties, to be surprises, require secrecy, mouths to be kept shut. Of course, the surprise may be for someone else, or the announcer may be mis-speaking. 'There will be a surprise party – oops, I wasn't meant to tell you, Sibyl.' After checking out all such quibbles, Sibyl realizes that the informer, whom she believes to be truthful, is telling her that there will be a surprise party for her that very evening, a surprise because she will not expect it – she will not believe that there will be one. Perhaps the idea is that Sibyl will be hypnotized or brainwashed, her memory wiped, so then the party will come as a shock. Let us cast such possibilities away. What is Sibyl to make of what she has been told?

Before we run through Sibyl's reasoning, here is some clarification. There is a difference between your believing that there will be no party and your not knowing what to believe. In the latter case, a case of suspending belief, we can rightly say that you neither believe there will be a party nor believe there will be no party. The paradox here involves the claim that Sibyl will not know what to believe about the party and hence will not believe there will be one – and, for that matter, will not believe that there will not be one. Now, we return to Sibyl's reasoning.

She may judge that there cannot be such a surprise party: the announcer has contradicted himself. However, Sibyl, being perceptive, then reflects, 'Hold on, in my not knowing what to think about the party, I am certainly not believing that there will be one – and so, when it happens, it will be a surprise.' She now sees how the announcer was speaking the truth after all; but that flips Sibyl back into believing that the party will be given, and hence into not being surprised. As a result, Sibyl once again does not know what to think, falling again into bafflement and not believing there will be a party. Hence, she now sees, once more, how the informant was speaking the truth . . . and so the reasoning continues, potentially without end, as she switches from belief to lack of belief in an impending party. She reels as, when choosing which direction to go, we may continually reel from road left to road right and back again. There is an instability in what Sibyl thinks about the matter.

The instability is akin to Buridan's ass's, when switching repeatedly between hay-bales, and to that of box-choosing in the Newcomb game. With Newcomb, we saw how we could challenge the possibility of the successful mind-reader. Of course, we cannot sensibly challenge the possibility of teachers announcing surprise examinations and of party-givers announcing surprise parties, but we can challenge whether Sibyl has any good reason to believe their announcements to be true.

The announcements are conjunctive; they have two parts conjoined: that an event will happen and that Sibyl will lack belief about the event. The announcers may be in good positions to know whether the events will happen – after all, the teacher sets the examination; the party-giver gives the party – but can they have any good justification for their prediction about Sibyl's state of mind, namely her lack of belief?

In answer to that last question, the announcers could have good justification, if they know that Sibyl does not think much, and so, in the examination week, will have forgotten all about the examination. They could have good justification if they know Sibyl is pessimistic, so, whatever is said, she would doubt whether a party would be thrown for her. But, if the idea is that they can judge what Sibyl as a rational clever individual will believe on the basis of her reasoning, then, as she reaches no stable belief or lack of belief, they too would be unable rationally to judge what she will believe. Hence, Sibyl has no good reason to believe that their predictions about her state of mind are right.

The surprise paradoxes set conditions that are as ill-determined as the pure injunction of 'Do the opposite.' Their predictions could, though, be based on neural causes within Sibyl; then, as with New-comb, we encounter puzzles of how reasoning relates to causes, as we shall review via Chapter 9's Mary, Mary Puzzle.

Before we draw a moral or two from Surprise, let us swirl a related puzzle into the paradox pot: the Poisoned Chalice, oft known as 'Toxin'.

On when *not* to be a philosopher

First, here is a tale, unlikely, but generator of no paradox. You are a philosopher at a banquet, medieval in style, sitting beside an extremely wealthy and eccentric lady, Lady Bountiful. The time is about 11 pm. She points to the chalice – the goblet – of wine. She tells you, truthfully, 'If you drink this potion at dawn, I will give you the castle of your dreams, with servants at your beck and call, unlimited wealth for the rest of your life.'

You have no scruples: you would love such wealth, such lifestyle – such luck. There is no catch, no trick, no snag, except that, as the lady explains, the chalice is poisoned, a heady brew, an unpleasant concoction. It will leave you struggling, with intense pains for a couple of days; but then all will be well. There are no side-effects, no damage. Masochist you are not, but the pains are worth the pleasure of the reward. This is no paradox. We often choose to suffer when the suffering is the only means to a desired end. We suffer the dentist to quell the future toothache; we may suffer boring conversations to land the woman or man – or job – of our dreams.

Paradox arises when Lady Bountiful's offer is the same as described, except for one key difference.

POISONED CHALICE

You are in better luck, or so it seems. Lady Bountiful is offering you the immensely valuable estate; the only condition is that you must intend to drink the nasty potion just poured. There is no need actually to drink it; *merely intending* is enough. Let us specify: so long as at midnight you are genuinely intending to imbibe the potion at the coming dawn, you win the wealth. What's the problem?

Surely, this revised offer is so much better than the one demanding that you actually drink the nasty brew. Intending to do something is so much easier than doing it – and, in this case, intending to drink from the chalice causes no pain, in contrast to the drinking. There is the question – here, a red herring – of how Lady Bountiful can know your intentions. If the herring worries you, imagine that she has some super-duper brain scanners or mind-readers.

The paradox now surfaces. With Lady Bountiful's offer before you, you reason as follows:

> I want the wealth, so obviously I will intend to drink. Ah, but that is enough. With the intention achieved, there is nothing more I need to do, so, of course, I won't let a sip of that vile phial touch my lips. Oops! Now seeing that in fact I shall not drink the wine, I realize that I'll lack a genuine midnight intention to drink. If I intend to do something, I cannot also be set on not doing it.

But you really do want the wealth, so the reasoning may continue:

> Okay, reluctantly and sadly, I now see that I had better truly intend to drink the potion. To hell with rationality! I'll just drink it. But hold on . . . I cannot help but realize that there will be no good reason to drink it at dawn and undergo those days of poisoned agony. And I am aware of that reasoning right now; so, still I cannot place myself into the position of truly intending to drink. A poisoned chalice, yes; but also a poisoned offer!

This is no puzzle for wealth-seekers who do not reflect or who, when reflecting, fail to see relevant logical connections. They intend to drink and, indeed, they probably go ahead and do so; and, after the few days of suffering, they collect the keys to the castle. Poor philosophers, paradigms of rationality (!), have a bad time: they remain poor. The offer brings poison to reason, not solely to the chalice.

Obviously, you could utter the words at midnight, 'I intend to drink', but the wealth materializes only from a genuine intention. Whenever you envisage really intending, your rational reflection engulfs you; you are reminded that you need not then actually drink.

The reasoning reels you round and round – from despairingly deciding just to drink to realizing the sheer stupidity in then performing the drinking at dawn. Yet to step out of that reeling also leaves you lacking the intention to drink – and hence missing out on the wealth. But you want the wealth, so you are cast back into thinking that you really must just intend to drink – and so you reel again.

Lady Bountiful's offer seems as impossible an offer to the rational to take up as an offer that you must intend to drink a potion and yet not try to drink it. It seems as impossible as trying to satisfy the conditions of the Silly Offer, at the close of Chapter 1. Yet it is not the same, for it is possible sincerely to intend to do things and yet fail to do them; athletes intend to win, yet lose; students to study, yet sleep instead; and lovers to make the Earth move, yet it remains unmoved.

Poisoned Chalice makes us recognize that it can be rational to plan to do something irrational. Close your eyes to the irrationality of drinking from the chalice at dawn. Just do it! Yet it is not that easy. Consider a slight revision to Lady Bountiful's offer. The revision is that the wealth, the estate's deeds, the rights, will be signed over to you immediately after the intention has been formed and before the dawn drinking time. Once you have the wealth, having successfully formed the intention, why ever would you still go ahead and drink?

We often commit ourselves to the future when we know that, at that future time, we may regret the commitment and even fight against it. This may be the case with marriages, promises and commitments not to drink whisky alone into the night's stillness. In Greek mythology, sirens are the sensually warbling women who lure unwary sailors to their death, the sailors being overwhelmed by the sirens' ravishing sounds. Odysseus, curious to hear their song, yet reluctant to drown, bids that he be tied to the ship's mast; his crew – their ears to be blocked – ordered not to release him when, under the spell of the sirens' song, he demands release. How can Odysseus be so stupid as to place himself into a position where he will be unable to get what he then wants? Well, it is not stupidity at all. Odysseus knows that it will be in his best interests not to get what he later will want.

We may know that it is in our best interests not to have the whisky available late at night, even though we know that, as the sober night draws on, we shall genuinely want it, regretting our earlier decision not to visit the off-licence. The Poisoned Chalice, though, presents a case where it is in your interest to form the intention to drink by dawn; but you know – and know now – that it would then be stupid, so stupid, to do the drinking. After all, Lady Bountiful has not asked you to *promise* to drink. A promise, in contrast to an intention, generates a moral duty to keep it, unless more important moral factors come into play.

People can sincerely intend to perform difficult tasks. So, subtle moves may be made, generating conditions which make difficult the dawn drinking from the chalice. You could take the chalice onto the dance floor where the flinging bodies would increase chances of spillage; but your intention at midnight must be that you really do aim to drink under such circumstances – and that remains highly irrational. You could try to make yourself into an irrational individual, tying yourself to the mast of future irrationality, blocking your ears right now to what rationality tells you. That blockage could come through excess alcohol – anything which stops you from seeing at midnight the ultimate stupidity in the later drinking. Once the intention has been formed, then ideally you want full rationality to return.

'You may say that; but I . . .'

A value in paradoxes is the treasure that may be exposed when digging within. Moore's Paradox highlights a contrast lurking within both Surprise and Poisoned Chalice.

G. E. Moore – George Edward Moore – was an early twentieth-century Cambridge philosopher, highly influential. He was, so to speak, the guru of the Bloomsbury Group. He drew attention to an assertion – hereafter Moore's conjunction – of a certain form, namely '*p*, but I don't believe that *p*', where '*p*' is replaced by an appropriate declarative sentence. An example is my thinking or claiming, 'Fish swim in the oceans, but I don't believe fish swim in the oceans.' Courtesy of the anguished genius Ludwig Wittgenstein, another Cambridge philosopher, this type of absurd conjunction became known as 'Moore's Paradox'. Note that it is expressed in the first-person, present tense: 'I believe that . . .', 'I think that . . .'.

MOORE'S PARADOX

There is nothing absurd in people thinking and asserting both that
fish swim in the oceans and that Peter Cave does not believe or
think they do. Both may be true. However, when I try to express the
same facts, I collapse into absurdity. It is absurd for me to think,
believe or assert, 'Fish swim in the oceans, yet I don't believe or
think they do.'

We should enter caveats – to pop to one side. 'I've won the lottery,
but I don't believe it!' may involve an exclamation of great surprise at
the win. The mother who tells her child, 'You'll do well in the exam',
yet adds quietly to herself, 'but I don't believe it', is speaking with two
voices. We return to cases of Moore's conjunction where such excep-
tions are inapplicable.

There is nothing surprising about my being unable to express
truths that others can express. 'Peter is asleep' can be true, yet I cannot
express that truth when it is true. In a silent room, I can rightly think
that the room is silent, but I cannot express that thought out loud
and it remain true: others, outside the room, can do so. In these cases,
we can see what is going wrong. Quite what goes wrong with Moore's
conjunction?

Some suggest that 'Fish swim in the oceans, but I don't believe fish
swim in the oceans' is equivalent to saying, 'I believe fish swim in the
oceans, but I don't believe fish swim in the oceans.' We may wonder,
though, if 'Fish swim in the oceans' amounts to saying, 'I believe fish
swim in the oceans', why does not 'I don't believe fish swim in the
oceans' amount to 'I believe that I don't believe fish swim in the
oceans'? That aside, the suggested view suggests that we are typically
describing our beliefs in such cases; yet surely that is not so. Consider
the following.

When I say that fish swim in the oceans, am I not talking about
the fish and oceans rather than describing my psychological state?
When I say that I believe or think or am convinced that the Prime
Minister will attend my soirée, am I not saying something about the
Prime Minister, with some degree of hesitation or certainty? If the
Prime Minister fails to show, and other people express some irritation

at what I claimed, it would not usually be a fair riposte for me to respond, 'Well, I was only describing my psychological state.'

Uses of certain terms, in the first person, with 'I', and speaking of the present, do not describe – or do not solely do that – but perform something. When I say, in the right circumstances, 'I hereby christen this ship "Matilda"', or 'I bet you £10', I perform a christening or make a bet. I am not describing that I am christening or betting. Such examples involve 'performatives', a term from the Oxford linguistic philosopher J. L. Austin. The absurdity in announcing, for example, 'Today is Sunday, but I don't think it is', arises because it is akin to expressing, 'Today is Sunday, but [*with some hesitation*] today is not Sunday.' I express – not describe – my belief and lack of that belief concerning the day.

When I believe something, I believe it to be true. Of course, I may be wrong. There is nothing absurd in my believing something, while recognizing that I *could* be mistaken; but my current beliefs represent what I take now as the truth about the world. As Wittgenstein notes, we have no expression for 'I falsely believe that . . .' We may rightly say that someone else falsely believes that, for example, Athens is the capital of Italy, but *I* cannot sincerely announce that *I* falsely believe such a thing. Underlying Moore's Paradox is the fact that while others can describe my current beliefs and thinking as false – sometimes rightly so – I cannot, without absurdity. I cannot detach myself from my beliefs and certain other psychological states in the way that others are detached from them; and that has a bearing on Surprise Party and Chalice.

P1 There's a party tonight, yet Sibyl doesn't believe it [*said by party-giver*].

P2 There's a party tonight, yet you don't believe it [*said to Sibyl by party-giver*].

P3 There's a party tonight, yet I don't believe it [*said by Sibyl*].

These statements have the form of Moore's conjunction. They are used to express the same facts, yet P1 is not absurd, in contrast to P3. Sibyl's P3 results from the P2 announcement. What is Sibyl to make of P2? She embraces it by means of P3, saying and thinking that there will be a party, yet also suggesting there will be none. In announcing P3, she speaks against herself.

Turning to Chalice, instead of belief, we have intending as the relevant psychological state. Let us form parallel cases, with Sibyl as the person trying to formulate the intention.

C1   Sibyl intends to drink the potion, yet won't drink it [*thought by Lady B*].
C2   You intend to drink the potion, yet won't drink it [*thought by Lady B of Sibyl*].
C3   I intend to drink the potion, yet I'll not drink it [*thought by Sibyl*].

Nuances of language become involved here, but C3 is absurd, if read as Sibyl saying what she intends to do, yet also that she will not do it. Just as to say, 'I believe that *p*', is a way of expressing that *p* is true, so saying, 'I intend to do X', is to make some sort of commitment to doing X – though, of course, my belief may turn out false and I may fail to achieve what I intend.

Surprise Party, Surprise Examination and Poisoned Chalice have the puzzle of Moore's Paradox within them. Others can sensibly say both what is so yet how Peter Cave wrongly thinks things otherwise. I cannot sensibly say both what is so yet how I wrongly think things otherwise. I can take a detached 'other' perspective on my past and future beliefs, judging them in error, but not my current beliefs.

*   *   *

The contrast between what I can reasonably say or believe and what others can reasonably say or believe also occurs in the Placebo Paradox. The doctor prescribes you some pills to bring about a placebo effect. You have no idea that they are only placebos; you think they are chemically efficacious. The doctor can silently and rightly judge, 'The patient will get better only because he believes he will get better.' Paradoxically, in these circumstances, you cannot sensibly judge, 'I shall get better only because I believe that I shall get better'. The caveat about the circumstances is important. You may simply be an optimistic patient; you believe, regardless, that you will get better – and that belief may help you get better.

The paradox arises because your belief that you will get better can be used to justify the doctor's belief that you will get better; but it cannot be used to justify *your* belief that you will get better. The doctor knows the effectiveness of believing that one will get better; hence, she prescribed you the placebos to generate that belief in you. Your belief was generated by the placebos because you thought that they were chemically cure-inducing. If you discover the truth, you lose your reason for believing that you will get better – and maybe, as a result, you fail to get better.

Recognizing that first-person, present tense uses of psychological verbs are often distinctive, performing and not describing, or not solely describing – I bet; I christen; I believe – helps resolve another little paradox, the Assertion Paradox from Buridan's Fourth Sophism. Yes, Buridan reappears on the scene. The paradox has a speaker flamboyantly using the expression, 'I assert that . . .' and similar. Perhaps he shouts, 'I assert that UFOs will land tomorrow; I say that the world will end next month; I declare that man is a donkey.'

When the UFOs fail to land, the world continues, and man is shown not to be a donkey, the speaker is challenged about the truth of what he said. He replies that he spoke the truth. 'All that I said was that I asserted, said, declared those things – and it is true that I did assert, say, declare those things.'

If his get-out is legitimate, then I have an easy way of making everything true in this book – namely, simply by prefacing it all with 'I assert that . . .' However, his claim is incorrect. If I say, 'I assert that UFOs will land', I am not describing myself as asserting, but forcibly expressing the claim that UFOs will land. That differs, of course, from someone who says, 'Peter asserts that UFOs will land.'

Machiavelli, politicians and Munchausen

The paradoxes above involve informational absurdities. In telling people the truth, we may set them in a spin over what to believe, even undermining the truth that we told.

Consider Brer Rabbit who seeks to bluff Brer Fox into thinking that briars are bad for rabbits. Deception is in the air. If Brer Fox inclines towards believing Rabbit, rationally he would then reflect that it may be bluff, for he knows that captured Rabbit lacks incentive to be helpful. Perhaps briars are not bad. Yet maybe Rabbit is engaged in a double bluff and briars *are* bad. Perhaps there is triple bluff or quadruple . . . the anguishing could be relentless. So it is that an endlessness can infect informative relationships, when truth motivation is in doubt, when, as I call them, 'doubt generators' are in play and there is nothing more to go on.

Machiavelli – we deviate from the historical figure – recommends politicians to speak falsely when, though only when, such speaking promotes their glory. Take Machiavelli to be a politician. We need to determine whether he is speaking the truth; and this lands us in trouble. Consider a blatantly fictional Machiavelli. His Monday deception claim (MDC) is, 'I aim to deceive people (other than myself) as far as possible on, and only on, Mondays.' There is no problem in our informing others that this is true of Machiavelli, but could Machiavelli have informed us by saying such?

Suppose we know nothing of Machiavelli's deceptive ways, save that he makes the MDC on Monday. Well, if MDC is true, he is trying to deceive us by speaking the truth. If MDC is false, he may be asserting MDC because, perhaps, he aims to deceive more extensively, lulling us into thinking how truthful he is, by owning up to some falsehoods. Suppose the claim is made on Tuesday. He may be speaking falsely; but he may be truth-telling, intending no Tuesday deception. By raising the deception possibility, we ought to wonder whether what he says, whenever he says it, is non-deceptive – and this applies to his MDC. Of course, if he never aims to deceive, he would not make the MDC, unless knowing that it would be discounted.

The Machiavelli Puzzle is that a deceiver's declaration of his deceptive extent, however minimal the extent, is information that rational hearers ought not to accept at face value. They need more to work on. The MDC and similar are doubt generators: the announcements sabotage confidence in what is announced. This is no mere matter of psychology, but of what it is rational to infer. The matter is important, for we often have to judge the sincerity of people who explain that in certain matters they are completely honest, whereas in others they sometimes are not.

Simply telling hearers that you are truth-telling possesses an absurdity – the Truth-Telling Puzzle. Note: this is distinct from Chapter 3's Truth-Teller. If hearers already believe that you are telling the truth, then there is no informing them that you are; if they lack such belief, they have no reason to believe that you are truth-telling when you claim to be. Paradoxically – and despite popular injunctions of 'Trust me!' or heaping up the 'really truthfully's – we cannot successfully inform rational others of our own truth-telling and honesty ways.

Lives are often compartmentalized: we know that people sometimes mislead in one arena, but not in others – in affairs of the heart, but not affairs of state; or in wage negotiations, but not in print. This knowledge cannot derive solely from what they say. They may say that they are truthful in one sphere though not another; but in which sphere are they, when they tell us? Some compartmentalizations strike us as natural: from experience, we know of spheres which contain more deceit inducements than others. Money and sex spring to mind. This is, of course, of public concern, a political puzzle. If representatives lie to their spouses, are they likely to lie to the electorate?

The instability caused by doubt generators also arises in what we may call the Puzzle of Truth-Trumping. A moral philosopher tells of his crude utilitarian commitment: his commitment is that everyone should always and only aim at overall happiness, deploying all available means compatible with that aim. Happiness, it is assumed, does not necessarily involve being in touch with the truth; ignorance can sometimes be bliss. We, the audience, now have reason to believe that truth-telling and honesty are not always valued by him, if his announcement is truthfully intended – and not always valued, of course, if he intentionally speaks falsely. So, why should we believe him on the basis of what he says? Arguably, we should not.

Utilitarians who fail to value truth-telling independently of happiness are, paradoxically, in no good position to spread their gospel by words alone to rational hearers. Moralists of this ilk – namely, those who look to consequences to determine what is the right thing to do – are not alone in this paralysing puzzle. People who accept an overriding duty that we should not wittingly upset people engage similar problems with regard to spreading the word. Further, there are well-known futilities of patients and lovers telling doctors and fellow lovers respectively that they want no bad news told – and then delighting in receiving no bad news.

Of course, we usually have more evidence than the individual's claim about the conditions on his intended veracity; we have his behaviour and comments on checkable matters. Yet if, somehow, all parties know that all parties are, say, solely motivated by happiness maximization, then at an informative level we are stumped: anything someone says depends in part upon how he thinks we shall take it – as truth or falsehood – but that depends on what he thinks we think he thinks we think (and so on) regarding the likelihood of truth-telling on that particular occasion managing to secure happiness maximization.

Deception generates trouble enough, but an added twist occurs when we reduce the number of participants to one.

SELF-DECEPTION

When I successfully deceive you, I am in the know and you are not. When I successfully deceive myself I am in the know and not in the know – which seems contradictory. Yet, self-deception does exist.

The key problem within self-deception is how people, usually disturbed by some fact, jump from that disturbing springboard, because it is disturbing, to a comforting belief that is inconsistent with the fact that disturbs and which they know.

Some people may know only too well that their finances are crashing, yet persuade themselves into believing that they are financially sound. They cannot *know* that they are financially sound, if they are not; but they can believe that they are, even if they are not. When the going gets tough, some investors, who know that investments fall in value as well as rise, deceive themselves into thinking that they knew of no such risk. The opposite direction, taking people from comfort to discomfort, is also possible. A jealous nature may lead a man to reinterpret his wife's innocent behaviour – behaviour known at some level to be innocent – as indicative of her unfaithfulness.

There is no contradiction in people holding contradictory beliefs: we probably all do, but unwittingly. Perhaps Melissa holds contradictory beliefs; but *we* do not contradict ourselves in pointing out that she does, in saying that, for example, Melissa believes she will marry and also believes she will not marry. We do, though, contradict ourselves if we assert that Melissa believes that she will marry and also assert that it is not the case that she believes she will marry.

The puzzle with self-deception – really, a psychological puzzle – is how people can use one starting belief or piece of knowledge to lead them into also believing what is inconsistent with that starting position. Jean-Paul Sartre, with a novelist's skill and philosopher's reflection, described a related phenomenon in which a young woman knows full well the romantic intentions that her dining companion cherishes regarding her. She is charmed by his approach, yet deceives herself by reading his behaviour and her responses as non-flirtatious.

*   *   *

Let us end these concerns via Roy Sorensen's Munchausen Puzzle, a puzzle that involves the deceit of fakery. Someone with Munchausen's Syndrome fakes illness in order to secure the attention granted to sick people. The illnesses faked are usually typical physical illnesses that require a fair amount of medical intervention. Munchausen's Syndrome is itself an illness. Hence, we could surely encounter individuals who fake having Munchausen's Syndrome. They may even announce that they suffer from Munchausen. What are we to make of that?

If they are faking that they have Munchausen, surely they do not have Munchausen; so we ought not to believe them. Yet, they are faking an illness, so we should believe them. We may feel ourselves at sea when facing faking being faked, unless we seek to distinguish between first-level faking, that is, faking something that itself does not involve faking, and second-level faking, where the faking is of a first-level faking. 'But it is all faking!' we are tempted to respond.

And with that puzzle of whether faking can be a faking of itself, we turn to some classical paradoxes that arise because of such feedback, because of self-reference.

Bertrand Russell, colleague and friend of Moore, admirer of Moore's purity and honesty, tells of how Moore never told a lie – except that he, Russell, once cunningly asked, 'Moore, do you always speak the truth?' Moore's response was, 'No.' Assuming that Moore on all other occasions spoke truly, his response must be a lie – yet can it be? And so we have a taste of the chapter to come.

3 Lather, rinse, repeat –
'repeat' did you say?

*. . . where we encounter a seducer's silver tongue, some liars –
do they really speak truly? – and the Barber, Groucho Marx
and down-trodden secretaries – all en route to the splendid
Bertrand Russell, well, at least to his paradox.*

Question: How do you keep a blonde occupied all day? Answer: Give
her shampoo, with the instruction, 'Lather, rinse, repeat.'

This politically incorrect joke could be revised to apply to any
maligned minorities – including pedantic, pernickety and ponderous
philosophers. The joke relies on self-reference. The 'repeat' of the
instruction is understood, wrongly of course, to apply to the whole
instruction and hence to itself: repeat the repeat. The shampooing
goes on, goes on for ever – well, until the shampoo runs out: a practical end to an activity that, abstractly, is endless.

We have already suffered threatened endlessness in our reasoning
and rationality. Here we focus on some paradoxes of logic and meaning, pertaining to the truth or falsity of what is said. Here are two
sketches, without elaboration. Elaboration will come – as eventually
will Bertrand Russell's famous paradox.

SEDUCER

Seducer, silver-tongued, secures his success by asking the lucky
(or unlucky) desirable, yet reluctant lady, 'Will you give the same
answer to this question as to my next question?' His next question
is, 'Will you sleep with me?'

LIAR

Liar says, 'I am lying.' If that is all that she says, then is what she
says true or false? If what she says is true, then she is lying and so

34

what she says is not true. If what she says is false, then she is not
lying, so what she says is true; but that means that it is true that she
is lying. So, is what she says true – or is it false?

Self-reference, one way or another, occurs in both paradoxes.
Seducer's question refers to itself, asking how it is to be answered. Liar
announces something about her announcement. Self-reference need
not generate paradoxes. You can talk about yourself; I can talk about
myself; and sentences can be about themselves. 'This sentence contains more than 50 words' is simply false, not paradoxical, and 'These
words are in English' is straightforwardly true. So, when we find paradoxes featuring self-reference, we need to explain why their particular
self-references generate the paradoxical pain (if they do).

Some self-reference may mildly amuse. Printed on some pages in
management manuals is 'This page has been deliberately left blank' –
a printing practice that guarantees falsity, contrasting with the boring
but accurate, 'This page has been deliberately left blank except for
these words.' Notices apparently exist that say only, 'Do not read this
notice'. Others say, 'Mind your head' when any minding is necessi-
tated solely by the low-hanging notices themselves. These examples
indicate that 'self-reference' is a term applied more or less loosely.
After all, the sentence about the blank page speaks about the page,
not about the sentence itself; but it is the sentence itself that undermines its truth.

Silver tongues . . .

The Liar, a paradox from antiquity, has generated centuries of discussion. Disputes still rage. The Seducer, presented in such terms, is recent
and much lighter, though derives from the medieval period. It is sometimes called the 'Infallible Seducer', but that nomenclature is wildly
optimistic – and wrong. The seducer is not infallible; rather, he is silver-
tongued. Would-be Casanovas beware: he is, no doubt, a failure in the
seduction stakes. We use Seducer's silver tongue as entrée to Liar's lie.

Mr Seducer asks a question, insisting that the answer must be 'Yes'
or 'No'. He is happy that the lady of his attentions should be prudent;
so she need not decide how to answer his first question until after she

has heard his second. Seducer may even be prepared to pay her to agree to answer either 'Yes' or 'No'. That looks to be easy money: after all, she has the choice between 'Yes' and 'No', so what can be the problem? Yet she would do well to resist the Yes/No request and also the money, unless she fancies Seducer's seductive ways. Here are his questions:

S1 Will you give the same answer to this question as to the next?
S2 Will you sleep with me?

Paradoxically, whichever way she answers, she is succumbing to his slippery seduction. If she agrees that she will answer in the same way – 'Yes' to the first question – then she will have to say 'Yes' to the sleeping question. If she goes for 'No' to the first, then she cannot answer 'No' to the second, but must again answer 'Yes'. Acquiescing to the Yes/No demand leads to a 'Yes', come what may, to the Seducer's seduction.

To expose the trap, consider the lady at risk to have no intention of sleeping with Seducer – surely a possibility. Hence, her answer to the second question would be 'No', so how could the first question be answered? Suppose the questions were in reverse order, with S1, suitably modified, coming second:

S2   Will you sleep with me?
$S1^1$ Will you give the same answer to this $S1^1$ question as to the previous?

Seducer asks S2 first. Our reluctant lady answers 'No'. What can she now say in answer to $S1^1$? Neither 'Yes' nor 'No' can be said without contradicting her first answer.

The paradox relies on the mistaken presumption that it is always fair to demand Yes/No answers. It is not. If interviewers ask a Secretary of State whether he *still* squanders taxpayers' money with bank bailouts – 'Yes or No' – the Secretary cannot win, if he answers as requested. To decline the Yes/No demand may offend and lead to long arguments, but it is sometimes the right thing to do. This is no flimsy, arbitrary response expected of evasive politicians. The response is properly justified because the question falsely presupposes that the Secretary squandered some money in the first place.

Two questions are pressed into one. One question is, 'Did you squander taxpayers' money?' Answering 'Yes' or 'No' is applicable here. The second question is, 'Are you squandering taxpayers' money now?' Again, a 'Yes' or 'No' is applicable. Only if the first answer is 'Yes' is it legitimate to demand a 'Yes' or 'No' answer to 'Are you still?'

In looking at any puzzles, we need to be aware of presuppositions and what our words may suggest. Eubulides, a fourth-century BC logician of Megara, gave us the Horned Man – some have rendered it erotic – with the question, 'Have you lost your horns?' Whether you answer 'Yes' or 'No' you imply that horns were had. 'Last night, the Queen was sober.' Such a comment, although not logically implying, may misleadingly convey that the Queen is usually drunk.

. . . and liars weak

The Liar paradox derives from Epimenides, a Cretan of the sixth century BC, who announced, 'The Cretans always lie.' If some other Cretan speaks truly, then Epimenides' observation is simply false; but if all other Cretans do indeed always lie, then we have a paradox akin to the traditional 'I am lying.' A biblical reference to Epimenides occurs in the Epistle of Paul to Titus, 'One of themselves, even a prophet of their own, said, "The Cretans are always liars, evil beasts, slow bellies".' First explicit discussion of the Liar is usually credited to Eubulides just mentioned. These days, the Liar includes a family of closely related paradoxes: there are old weaker members of the family, with stronger ones developing more recently.

Talk of lying raises complexities of speakers' intentions. We may assert a falsehood without intending to, hence without lying. So, an improved Liar is, 'In saying this, I am saying something false' – a version in Buridan's Eleventh Sophism; yes, the same Buridan who has popped up a couple of times already. What is the 'this' in the Liar sentence? Well, for a few paragraphs, let us muddle through and say it is the sentence itself. Clarity will come shortly – well, maybe. Let us work with the following:

This very sentence is false,

and for ease we name the sentence above, 'L1' – Liar 1.

Suppose L1 is true, then it is true that L1 is false; that is, L1 is false. So, on the supposition that it is true, we have the conclusion that it is false. Suppose that it is false: then it is false that L1 is false, so L1 is true. We have considered both alternatives – true and false – and we have the unhappy result that the sentence in question is true if and only if it is false. That is a contradiction: it cannot possibly be true – we may reasonably think. There is, though, an heroic path along which some contradictions are accepted as both true and false. The path is followed by a few brave logicians – by dialetheists – but let us resist wandering down that garden path.

A quick and popular response to L1 is to reject the presupposition that the sentence must be either true or false – just as we rejected the seducer's Yes/No demand. A surface does not have to be red or green: it need be neither; it could be yellow. The claims, 'The surface is red' and 'The (same) surface is green', are contraries. It would be inconsistent to hold them both. They are not contradictory: one of them does not have to be true; they could both be false.

The suggested response is that, while a sentence cannot be both true and false, it can be neither. This is a third way – and it apparently rescues us from paradox. The L1 sentence, though, is constructed neither with any meaningless words nor ungrammatically; so, why is it neither true nor false? We ought not to pull a rabbit out of a hat to conjure away a paradox, without justifying the rabbit's existence independently of solving the paradox.

If someone says, 'The Queen of the USA is weeping', we may reasonably judge that to be neither true nor false, for there is something lacking – there is no such queen; well, none in the term's traditional sense. Similarly with L1, there seems to be something lacking. There is a sentence, but there is nothing that we can specify, *independently* of saying it is false, which we may then go on to assess for truth or falsity. With L1, all we can do is repeat the sentence, if asked what it is that we need to assess; but the repeat is just that, a repeat of its claimed falsity: 'This very sentence that this very sentence is false is false', 'This very sentence that this very sentence that this every sentence is false is false is false' – and so on. The problem is akin to issuing someone with the vacuous instruction 'Repeat', with nothing more to the instruction. 'Repeat what?' the instruction receiver may reasonably ask.

The above criticism of 'This sentence is false' also holds of the Truth-Teller's 'This sentence is true.' The truth-teller's sentence gives rise to no contradiction – it could consistently be true; it could consistently be false – but it seems to say nothing that is either true or false. There is nothing that could make it true – or could make it false. Vacuity is here again, as in 'Repeat' with nothing to repeat.

The above is too swift a response to the Liar, not least because it is muddled. First, the paradox can be strengthened – the 'Liar's Revenge' – for we could have the Liar say, 'I am not speaking the truth', and the Liar sentence could be, 'This very sentence is not true', where 'not true' means 'either false or neither true nor false'. Secondly, as warned, we have gone along with *sentences* being true or false, being the vehicles of truth (and falsity); but that talk is misguided. In order correctly to guide, let us distinguish between 'tokens' and 'types', a slightly curious terminology deriving from a nineteenth-century American philosopher, Charles Sanders Peirce.

How many words are in the following sentence? 'When it rains cats and dogs, cats and dogs flee for cover.' In one sense there are twelve words, in another, nine. The answer is 'nine', if we count how many different word 'types' there are. This is because 'cats', 'dogs' and 'and' are repeated: they are instances of the same type. If we focus on the instances of words – the 'tokens' – we have the answer 'twelve'. The word 'word' and the word 'sentence' sometimes has the 'type' meaning, sometimes the 'token'. With that in mind, let us see what may be said to be true or false; let us find the bearers of truth.

One and the same sentence type is often used on different occasions to refer to different things, the result being that on one occasion a truth may be uttered, on another occasion a falsehood. 'Today is Sunday', we may casually suggest, is sometimes true, sometimes false, depending upon the day of utterance – depending upon the context of the particular sentence token. 'You're my love for ever' – well, its truth depends upon who is speaking to whom and when. Suppose we gaze at the night sky and notice that the stars form the shape of the sentence token, 'Today is Sunday': it would be odd to think that the heavenly configuration was thereby saying something. This suggests that it is *what is expressed* by means of particular sentence tokens in particular circumstances that is true or false. The noisy utterances of speakers and the ink marks on paper – the tokens themselves – are not true or false.

We need a term for what a sentence token, in use, expresses. Sadly, the terminology is poorly regimented, with people switching between 'statements', 'propositions', 'assertions' and more. We have to choose. Let us use 'proposition' for what is expressed, applying 'true' and 'false', in their *primary* uses, to propositions. So, to claim that these ink marks are true is as nonsensical as saying that this pebble or wine glass is true. However, a sentence token used to express a proposition may be thought of as 'derivatively' true or false in line with the truth or falsity of the proposition expressed.

Reflecting on this chapter's introduction of self-reference, we may now see that a sentence such as 'This sentence has more than 50 words' is being used to express a proposition, a false proposition, about a sentence token. The proposition – what is being expressed – is not referring to itself, to what is expressed, but to the printed inscription.

Reflecting afresh on L1, someone uttering the sentence 'This very sentence is false' may be expressing the following proposition: these words being uttered, these noises, are false. The proposition is false, for words being uttered, noises, are not the sort of things that can be true or false. The same holds if L1 is about the sentence type.

Is L1 now paradoxical? Well, that the proposition expressed is false does not lead to its being true. The proposition is that the sentence with its words are false; the proposition is not that itself, the proposition, is false. However, there are complexities raised by the relationship between a proposition being false and the sentence used being thereby derivatively false; but even with those complexities to one side, we are not free of the Liar's paradoxical tangles. Far from it.

Return of the Liar – in strength

We are using 'not true' to cover 'either false or neither true nor false'. We now confront a version of the Strengthened Liar:

This very proposition is not true,

and let us, for ease, name the above sentence 'L2'. If the proposition expressed by use of L2 is true, then it is not true. If it is false, then, as that is one option offered of itself, it is true. And if the proposition is neither true nor false, then that is also what it says it could be; hence it is true. The Liar has returned with revenge in mind.

The Liar has indeed returned, yet we may ask: what is being said not to be true? The answer is: the proposition expressed by L2. But what is that proposition? Although concepts of truth and proposition are used when uttering L2, no proposition, no propositional content, is expressed; no proposition is independently specified which we can then assess for truth or lack of truth. L2, indeed, standing alone, is without use, save in philosophical discussions. We can truthfully say that L2 expresses no proposition and hence expresses neither a true proposition nor one that lacks truth.

Suppose we put forward another sentence, named 'L3', that says, 'L3 expresses no truth.' That sentence token fails to express a proposition, and so fails to express the proposition that it expresses no truth. Now that L3 has been introduced, we may use another token of that L3 sentence type, saying truthfully, 'L3 expresses no truth', for this is referring to the first token, L3. Different tokens of the same type – equiform tokens – are being used to do, or fail to do, different things. Conflate the differences: puzzles return. Here is how.

We saw easy examples of how tokens of the same sentence type may express different propositions with 'Today is Sunday.' Confusions arise when one and the same token is read as doing very different things: a first and only token of L3, introduced as above, is read as seeking, impossibly, to label a sentence expressing a proposition, yet may then be treated – mistreated indeed – as if it is another token, expressing something truthful about itself in the first reading.

$$*\qquad*\qquad*$$

In seeking to dissolve our Strengthened Liar, we have relied on some propositional emptiness generated by the troublesome sentence. This approach is in line with a deflationary or redundancy approach to truth, an approach whereby 'it is true that' and similar uses of 'true' are understood merely as ways of emphasis or giving authority to a claim – a flourish. Saying that it is true that the cat is on the mat is at heart to say that the cat is on the mat. Truth is pulled down a peg or two, for it is not a property or relation. Saying 'The cat is asleep is not true' can amount to a claim that the cat is not sleeping.

In using the troublesome L2 sentence, we deploy the concept of 'not true', but there is no proposition that can be pulled out independently of the 'not true' claim. Delete the 'is not true' in L2, and we have remaining 'This very proposition' which can express no proposition at all. Delete the 'is not true' from 'The cat is asleep is not true' and we have 'The cat is asleep', which can be used to express a proposition, though technical difficulties arise.

There are many variants of the Liar. 'This sentence expresses no proposition.' 'This proposition cannot be true.' Some give more trouble; some give less. There are also variants that use more than one sentence, concealing some emptiness. Here is a teeny Liar Cycle example from Buridan – his Ninth Sophism:

> Socrates says, 'What Plato is saying is false.'
> Plato says, 'What Socrates is saying is true.'

What Socrates says seems fine, until we discover that it refers to Plato's comment about Socrates' saying. Consider a calling card: side A has the sentence printed, 'The proposition expressed on the other side of this card is true', whereas the other side, side B, has 'The proposition expressed on the other side of this card, side A, is false'. Side A's proposition appears fine until we turn to side B's and hence are returned to A's.

There would be no problem for Buridan – and no cycle – were Plato saying, 'The moon is made of cheese.' Whether Socrates' words given above express a proposition hangs on contingencies, not only of their meaning, but also of what Plato happens to be saying. This sometimes surprises, yet it should not. As we saw earlier, what is expressed often depends on speaker, time and place – on context.

Puzzles continue with self-referential creations, ones not obviously of a Liar ilk. A century ago, Bertrand Russell introduced Berry's Paradox. '"The least integer not nameable in fewer than nineteen syllables" is itself a name consisting of eighteen syllables; hence the least integer not nameable in fewer than nineteen syllables can be named in eighteen syllables, which is a contradiction.' In recent decades, Willard van Orman Quine – a name to be savoured – suggested:

> Q 'Does not yield a truth when appended to its own quotation' does not yield a truth when appended to its own quotation.

If Q is true, then it yields a truth as set out, yet says that it does not – and vice versa. The expression in quotation marks is a noun as subject term, standing for the string of words; and the sentence is used to tell us that that string when appended to its quotation in a particular sentence fails to express a truth – yet, in so doing, a truth is expressed. What grounds have we for saying that Q fails to make a proposition – or for saying that there is something illegitimate about Berry's naming of numbers?

Such problems, such continuing problems, lead some to despair of natural languages such as English. The eminent Polish logician Alfred Tarski, for example, spoke of the English language as inconsistent. Well, that terminology is somewhat odd – for it is not at all obvious what it means to say that a natural language is inconsistent, though – of course – inconsistent and contradictory thoughts can be expressed in natural languages. Tarski spoke of sentences rather than propositions and, believing that every indicative sentence should be either true or false, was unhappy with sentences that entail their negation – for example, 'This sentence is false', which apparently is true if and only if it is not true.

An obvious response, ridding inconsistency, is to delete the aberrant sentences from the language. We could reduce English to kosher English, so to speak. The response lacks appeal, not least because the questionable sentences seem grammatically and semantically in order. In fact, any sentences that involve 'true' or 'false' in the right circumstances could give rise to Liar-type paradoxes. Hence, the search began for another way of sieving out the paradoxical sentences. We have promoted one way above, namely, charging that there is nothing to make such sentences true or false. Other heroic attempts, from Russell to Tarski to Quine, have been in terms of levels, either as a way of modifying English or as a claim that this is what English really involves, or as a proposal for working with artificial languages that avoid inconsistencies. Here is a very, very brief outline.

Think of sentences that lack terms such as 'true' and 'false' as all at level one; they belong to what is called the 'object language'. Sentences which directly apply such terms as 'true' and 'false' to those sentences of level one are sentences of level two, constituting a meta-language, one that can contain sentences about the object language. Sentences that apply such terms to sentences of level two are of level three – and so on. This hierarchy operates according to the rule that it is only legitimate for a sentence to apply (say) 'true' and 'false' to another sentence if that other sentence is at a lower level. Thus – somewhat artificially – the errant sentences that seem to involve self-reference are ruled out by fiat.

Barber, Groucho and Liberating Secretaries

The Liar family generated contradictions through some self-referential or seemingly self-referential assertions. We find more self-referential problems, as we journey further, heading for Russell's Paradox. We revisit the Barber first.

BARBER

Barber is a barber in Alcala. He shaves all and only those who do not shave themselves. So, does Barber shave himself? If he is some-one who shaves himself, then he does not shave himself. If he is someone who does not shave himself, then he does shave himself. What does he do?

To demand that it must be either true or false that Barber shaves him-self is to ignore the third possibility that it is neither true nor false. Why should it be neither true nor false? Well, it presupposes that there can be such a barber; but, there cannot. The situation described is contradictory.

There would be no problem were the Barber of Alcala to shave all and only those in the next village, say, Balcala; but the paradox arises because his shaving interests – to shave or not to shave – cover a group of individuals which includes himself; he himself, it seems, being a possible shavee in Alcala. There need be no puzzle if the barber shaves all and only those *men* who do not shave themselves – for Barber could be a woman. We may minimize the tale so that Barber is the sole inhabitant of Alcala and he shaves all and only those who do not shave themselves. That is, he shaves himself if, and only if, he does not shave himself.

The Barber Paradox passes off as a tale about a flesh-and-blood individual. Were we casually to talk of such a barber in a properly populated Alcala, the natural way to understand his description is as someone who shaves all and only those others, other than himself, who do not shave themselves, thus engaging no contradiction. The condition originally given is taken to specify the barber, and if the barber is specified solely in that way, then no barber is specified. If, however, we have a barber in mind, all that we can conclude is that the paradoxical description fails to apply: the barber is, so to speak, not all that he is cracked up to be.

We now step closer to Russell's Paradox. Russell's Paradox involves sets or classes, but clubs can be more accessible.

Groucho Marx quipped that he would not want to join a club that would have him as member. Let us add that he would want to join any club that would not have him. In summary, Groucho wants club membership if and only if the club does not want him. So far, there is no contradiction; but now let us add that the club wants Groucho if and only if he wants the club. With such supplementation, it is a tale of frustration for both Groucho and club, frustration brought about by perverse human nature. They will never get together.

Suppose Groucho, not yet knowing whether the club will have him, wants club membership. Once the club hears of his want, they want him and tell him. This ensures that he does not want the club; and this in turn means that the club now does not want him – which means he now wants the club – and so forth. There need be no contradiction, just ever-changing wants, depending on what the club and Groucho learn of each other and when. But with perfect knowledge of each other's wants, contradictions arise; for example, the contradiction involved in Groucho both wanting membership and not wanting membership.

LIB SECS

Some clubs have membership rules that ensure their secretaries are ineligible. We restrict the example to full-time secretaries, working therefore for just one club at a time. The secretaries of such clubs, aggrieved, form their own club, Liberated Secretaries. Eligibility for Lib Secs' membership is solely that an individual must be a full-time secretary of a club that prohibits membership by their secretaries. All is well, until one day Lib Secs employs a full-time secretary. Is this secretary eligible to join Lib Secs?

There need be no contradiction in rules that prevent secretaries of clubs from club membership. Further, there is nothing impossible about secretaries of such status-conscious clubs, feeling unappreciated and slighted, forming their own liberating secretaries' club, Lib Secs. As we see, though, trouble brews.

Trouble brews with Ms Secretary's arrival, employed as the Lib Secs' secretary. Ms Secretary asks to join Lib Secs as a member. If she is ineligible, then she is working for a club which does not permit her membership – and so she is eligible. If she is eligible, then she is permitted to join a club for which she is secretary – and so she is ineligible. The membership rules mean that Ms Secretary is eligible if and only if she is ineligible. There seems to be no third way.

With Barber, we concluded that he could not exist, if to exist he must satisfy exactly the conditions specified. With Groucho, we sought logical harmony by allowing the disharmony of changing wants. Typically, people conclude that Lib Secs cannot exist, but that conclusion needs careful handling.

There can exist clubs – no doubt they do exist – with contradictory rules of membership, rules that cannot be applied in all possible circumstance without contradiction. Barbers can exist who have been misdescribed. There exist many individuals who hold contradictory beliefs: they can get through life pretty well – and sometimes well just because they do contradict themselves. Mathematical reasoning, textbooks, laws of the land, even this book – these exist, yet may contain contradictions.

Lib Secs could claim that its rule determines for all possible individuals, including any secretary who works for the club, whether the individual in question is eligible for membership. If Lib Secs' very existence hangs on its rule having such application, without contradiction, then the club cannot exist. Of course, a 'real live' club's existence does not hang on whether its rule book avoids contradictions.

Barber, Groucho and Lib Secs concern items of a type that we encounter in the everyday empirical world. Their paradoxes arise because a relation that holds of some individuals leads to contradiction, when conditions are clarified. An item is postulated that stands in the relation to all and only those who do not stand in that relation to themselves – and the 'all and only those' covers the item postulated. Thus, we end up with: the postulated item stands in the relation to itself if and only if it does not stand in that relation to itself. The barber shaves himself if and only if he does not shave himself. Lib Secs permits Ms Secretary club membership if and only if it does not permit her club membership.

Russell's Paradox now enters the fray. It presents similar problems to those of Lib Secs, save Russell's deals with an abstract world and – because abstract – the problems may seem of greater depth. Indeed, Frank Plumpton Ramsey, much admired for his brilliance, but who died when young, viewed Russell's Paradox as having logical depth, in contrast to, say, the Liar that results from faulty ideas about thought and language.

Russell's Paradox – and more

You are a reader of this book; so you belong to the set of, the class of – even the club of – individuals who are readers of this book. Sets can be distinguished from classes; but here it is unnecessary.

The set of readers of this book may be large, in that it has a large number of members; but more likely – and sadly – it is small. You can read and you have many other attributes, being biological, with a certain spatial and temporal position; but the *set* of readers – the set itself – cannot read or be read. The set is not to be thought of as a weird physical, flesh and blood, combination of readers, with, for example, a weight made up of all its members. It is abstract – as are numbers.

We identify the set of readers by pointing to a feature that items must have to be members of the set. Any feature of individuals – any predicate expression or description we employ – can determine a set, or so it seems. The predicate expression 'is a sheep' determines a set consisting of individual members which are sheep. Also, 'is sheepish' determines a set, but maybe the members are just some people feeling shyness and guilt, with no members being typical sheep. (Can sheep be sheepish?) The set of sheep and the set of the sheepish are not themselves sheep or sheepish. That is, every sheep is a member of the set of sheep, but the set of sheep is not itself a member of the set of sheep. Thus we have the concept of 'being a set that is not a member of itself'.

Individual sets that possess the feature of not being members of themselves can be assembled, it seems, into a set; namely the set of those sets that are not members of themselves.

Many sets are not members of themselves, yet presumably some sets are members of themselves. Consider the set of items that are not tea-drinkers: it includes some people, lots of other creatures, also computers, trees and numbers – and also itself. The set of non-tea-drinkers is itself a non-tea-drinker; so the set of non-tea-drinkers includes itself – or so it seems. Of course, if we think of sets as containers, then we would doubt that a set can ever be a member of itself. However, a set is not a container but an abstraction – an abstraction determined by a feature common to its members.

Now we meet the set highlighted by Russell. The predicate which determines the Russell Set – the condition for membership of the Russell Set – is that the member be a set that is not a member of itself. As we have seen, this consists of most sets we would normally think of; in fact they have sometimes been called 'normal' sets. The Russell Set thus contains the set of animals, the set of tin cans, and the set of builders: these sets are not themselves animals, tin cans or builders. The Russell Set would not contain the set of non-tea-drinkers, for that set is a member of itself. Now – and here comes the inevitable question – what of the Russell Set itself? Is it a member of itself?

Let us hypothesize that the Russell Set is a member of itself: well, then it belongs to the set of items that are not members of themselves; so it is not a member of itself. Let us hypothesize that it is not a member of itself: well, then it qualifies to be a member of the set of items that are not members of themselves; so it is a member of itself. The Russell Set seems impossible because contradictory.

When Russell discovered the contradiction, he perceived it as a major set-back for logicism, the project of deriving mathematics from logic. It also showed a flaw in Gottlob Frege's system. Russell thought it best not to keep the bad news to himself: he quickly wrote to Frege. It is to Frege's credit that he valued the discovery, despite the hole that it made in the project. Frege's work on logic, by the way, is now recognized as being of immense significance.

A quick and obvious retort to Russell's Paradox is: let us follow the procedures with the Barber and Lib Secs. We described conditions such that the proposed Barber and Lib Secs could not exist; they were as impossible characters as round squares are impossible figures. Let us simply conclude that the Russell Set cannot exist. Many, though, are reluctant to see matters as simple as that. After all, the predicate 'is not a member of itself' seems to make clear sense in giving a condition that can determine a set. Further, reference to such sets occurs in various valuable mathematical proofs.

To tame the paradox, Russell and others developed a hierarchy of levels or types, the Theory of Types, with objects being type zero, sets or classes of objects being type one; sets of such sets being type two – and so on. The idea is that it is illegitimate to mix up types – just as we saw Tarski arguing, later on, when dealing with the Liar.

This is no place in which to examine the mathematical and logical complexities of set theory – I let readers assess why – but it is a place in which to step back and muse upon quite what is meant when there is talk of a set existing or not. It is a special case of whether an abstract entity exists; but abstractions, of course, do not exist as flesh-and-blood items. Presumably arguments about whether abstractions exist hang on whether they contain or lead to contradictions. Russell's Paradox troubles because a very basic understanding of conditions for forming sets can lead to contradiction – and once contradictions are allowed into a system, there is the danger that anything goes.

We cannot squeeze in all other self-referential paradoxes that relate to these matters. Let us, though, mention two contrasting directions for self-referential hunting.

In one direction, we move back explicitly into language. Grelling's

Paradox, for example, starts off innocently enough. Consider the words 'short' and 'long'. The word 'short' is indeed short; but the word 'long' is not long. An expression is autological if and only if it applies to itself. An expression is heterological if and only if it does not apply to itself. There is no problem in applying these terms to a whole range of words. The puzzle is whether – as can now be anticipated – 'heterological' is itself heterological? The familiar structure comes into view: 'heterological' is heterological if and only if it is not heterological – a paradox courtesy of Kurt Grelling and Leonard Nelson.

One way out, a crazy and *ad hoc* way, is again to construct rules concerning levels, so that to speak of the word 'short' as short is illegitimate. A far more acceptable approach is to argue that the proposition that 'heterological' is (or is not) heterological is empty – and so is neither true nor false. Why? Well, there is no way of telling – and no fact of the matter – just as there is no determination of whether 'This sentence expresses a truth' is true or not.

Another direction for self-referential hunting is mathematics, heading further within set theory. The nineteenth-century mathematician Georg Cantor, the discoverer – or creator? – of transfinite mathematics, mathematics of infinity, exposed various puzzles. Cantor's Paradox concerns the *set of all sets*. That should be the biggest set whose members are sets. However, Cantor showed that every set, even infinite ones, has more subsets than it has members. So, the set of those subsets – the 'power set' – is a bigger set than the so-called biggest set; and the power set of that 'bigger set' is bigger still – and so on, without end. Hence, we have contradiction at the heart of the set of *all* sets.

*   *   *

We meet various paradoxes – accessible paradoxes – that engage with infinity 'in the world' in the next chapter. To finish off here, let us return to the Liar – and introduce Infinite Liars, Yablo's Paradox, designed to challenge self-reference as the Liar's heart. It does this by supposing an infinitely long sequence of sentence tokens or utterances of the same type – that is a sequence without end, written or spoken out across the universe, so to speak. Imagine, for example, an endless queue of individuals, each individual aiming to refer to all the utterances being made by the endless others ahead in the queue.

Each token being uttered is 'All the succeeding utterances are untrue.' Each token refers to the remaining infinite number of other similar tokens inscribed further down the page, across the universe, or about to be uttered in the queue. The sequence – paradoxically, it is said – permits no consistent non-arbitrary assignment of 'true' or 'untrue' to what is expressed by the tokens thus used. Yet, the paradox challenges, are not the utterances expressing meaningful propositions? This may seem even more plausible if we try the variant sequence consisting of the utterances, 'Regarding each succeeding utterance, if a proposition is thus expressed, then it is untrue.'

Difficulties with infinity – illustrated in the next chapter – should make us cautious of the scenario proposed, namely, one of an actual infinity of meaningful tokens. The 'and so on' is casually said. It should not surprise that we are at sea when asked whether the tokens are true or not true or express a proposition or not – just as we would be seaward bound concerning which drinks to order, if Andy requests the same as Bertie, Bertie the same as Clarence, 'and so on', without any alphabetical or other end. The Drinks Order Challenge should make us cautious of casual 'buck-passing' with regard to truth or meaning, where infinite series are concerned.

Even if sense can be made of the infinity talk here in Yablo's paradoxical land, we ought still to be unsurprised at the tokens' lack of truth value or failure to express propositions. Similar problems arise with the Liar Cycle, as seen above with Plato referring to Socrates who refers to Plato 'and so on'. Indeed, the Liar itself can be viewed as the limiting case of such cycles. Andy will have the same as Bertie, and Bertie will have the same as Andy, but if nothing more is said or done, we loop from Bertie to Andy and from Andy to Bertie endlessly, with no idea about which drinks therefore to order – and also no idea of which drinks to order if Andy says that he will have the same as what he himself will have.

'The truth that this sentence expresses is the truth that this sentence expresses' expresses no truth. Or does it?

4 Infinity: without end, without beginning –

yet with a flea, a fly and a bandit

. . . in which we encounter a tortoise, courtesy of Zeno's paradoxes, a flea taking up an infinite challenge – but also a Trojan fly, a mysterious hotel, Tristram Shandy – oh, and a utility man, lots of gods and the mystery of when a killing takes place.

'Infinite' applies when there is no end. We have already encountered paradoxes involving reasoning without end. Not surprisingly, difficulties engulf us when what we reason *about* also appears bereft of end.

Start counting, 1, 2, 3, 4 – and continue. We can readily see how there is no last number, though there will be a last moment of counting, when we become distracted, bored or expire. The natural number series is infinite, as are many other series – an infinite number of them. Take the series, half, then a quarter, then an eighth, then a sixteenth, and so on. That is an infinite series. To say that a series is infinite is simply shorthand for saying that it does not end.

If we think that lengths can be divided infinitely so – for example, half, then a quarter, then an eighth – we are likely to strike trouble; and we do. Zeno of Elea, the fifth-century BC Greek already briefly met, is most famously associated with the trouble. What remains trouble for us was, for Zeno, an entry into understanding reality, realizing that movement and plurality are sheer illusion.

DICHOTOMY

In order to journey from A to B, we must first arrive at the halfway point H_1; but to journey on from H_1 to B, we must first arrive at the halfway point between H_1 and B, namely H_2. We must then reach the halfway point between H_2 and B, namely H_3 – and so on. This halving never reaches an end, so we can never reach our journey's end.

ACHILLES AND THE TORTOISE

Achilles has a race with a much slower participant, the tortoise, given a many-heads start, as Chapter 1 sketched. Before Achilles can overtake the tortoise, he must reach the place where the tortoise is currently placed, by which time the tortoise will have moved a little further, prize-ward bound. By the time Achilles reaches that later position of the tortoise, the tortoise will have moved on yet a little further – and so on. This is philosophy for the downtrodden: happy is the tortoise, for, it seems, Achilles cannot catch him.

There is nothing magical about the tortoise's particular smaller distances ahead or the Dichotomy's halving. Before you can reach the wall opposite, you need to move through, for example, a third of the distance, then a third of the remaining distance, then a third of what then remains – and so on. Carving up space, or indeed time, into smaller and smaller parts, with the carving continuing infinitely, leads to many seeming impossibilities.

How to apply the concept of infinity to the world is puzzling, and how to apply other concepts also puzzles. Yet mathematicians and scientists do make successful use of infinity in their theories, aiding correct predictions and successful technological developments, from machines to electronics to drugs. Mind you, sometimes applications lead to unforeseen outcomes, such as financial chaos, ozone layer depletion and some species' destruction.

In the Dichotomy and Achilles, the ever-decreasing moves – let us stay with the example of half, quarter, eighth and so on – form the elements of an infinite series. To reach a proposed end following the rule of 'first move one-half of the distance of whatever distance now remains' ensures that the end is unreached, an endless number of moves always remaining. A similar endlessness infects Achilles' attempt to reach the tortoise.

Both paradoxes presuppose that distances are traversed; but, of course, with regard to any of the distances, we could raise the same puzzles – and Zeno does, concluding that one cannot get started, let alone be finished. In fact the Dichotomy is sometimes understood as Zeno arguing that, starting from A, before reaching B any distance away, we must get halfway to B, and before reaching that halfway, we must get to halfway of that halfway – and so on. Hence, we can never set off. Some infinity paradoxes, then, focus on starting, some on ending – and they apply to any part of any length. Some paradoxes concern infinity itself. By the way, if Zeno is right and all motion is illusory, he needs to explain how the illusions contain movement – or, at least, appear so to do – and seem to undergo change themselves.

Puzzles arise even when items are not moving. For the pebble to exist over the coming minute, it must exist for one half-minute, then an additional quarter, then a further eighth and so forth. These paradoxes are puzzles of how any extensions – be they spatial lengths or durations of time – can be traversed or endured. Let us group them as Zeno's Traversal Challenge, a challenge that seeks to show that both motion and lack of motion are impossible, if all extensions and durations are divisible. The puzzles arise because of two assumptions in combination. Taking movement as an example, the assumptions are, first, if anything moves, it is engaged in infinitely many smaller movements or tasks; and secondly, nothing can perform infinitely many anything. Performing an infinite number of tasks would be to perform a 'super-task'.

'Theft over honest toil' – and the fleeing flea

A temptation is to float mathematical ignorance as the force of the Traversal Challenge. Here is the temptation, applied to the Achilles Paradox presented in terms similar to the Dichotomy.

From experience, we find that Achilles does draw level with the tortoise at a certain point – the tortoise point. To reach that point Achilles must, let us say, traverse half the distance to the creature, then a further quarter, then a further eighth – and so on. Halfway is quite a way from the point, but half plus a quarter is nearer, and half plus a quarter plus an eighth is nearer still – and so on. These partial sums *approach* the tortoise point – in fact, these 'converge' to one – but never get there.

The 'sum' of a convergent arithmetical infinite series is *defined* as the limit to which the sequence of partial sums converges. The limit in our example is the tortoise point that Achilles in practice reaches. Such defining, though, fails to explain how the point can be reached by following an *endless* series. To converge is not to reach. To speak of Achilles gradually closing in until he reaches the end – the tortoise point – is to have eyes closed to the difficulty. Let us not weaken under Bertrand Russell's tongue that any difficulty here is but a sham, a sham because some infinite series have ends. True, a convergent series has a limit defined as the series' sum, but – to repeat – that does not show how Achilles can perform the super-task of traversing an infinite number of distances, even though they become teenier and teenier.

Defining oneself out of puzzles merits the condemnation of preferring 'theft over honest toil' – a complaint Russell once quipped of others. If such definings were permitted, philosophers should soon be queuing up for their redundancy notices and subsequent flights to retirement lands, ideally (from their perspective) where extraditions are refused for business unfinished.

When asked how it is that the fleet-footed Achilles reaches the limit, the tortoise point, some explain that, solely in following the series completely, he can never be short of the tortoise point nor yet further than it. If he is anywhere – as he surely is – he must be at the point. He cannot be beyond the point, since the series does not go beyond the point: the point is the limit to which the series converges. He cannot be short of the point because he would then still have infinitely many traversals to make, for any distance can be divided again and again, infinitely. The Traversal Challenge, though, stubbornly remains of how he gets to the point, given his means apparently involves the impossibility of completing a series of traversals without end.

To make the puzzle more vivid, I offer the Flea Challenge. Suppose, as far as we can, stretching throughout the universe at one-inch intervals, inscriptions solely of the fractions of the mentioned series of the partial sums: inscriptions for one-half, three-quarters, seven-eighths, fifteen-sixteenths, and so forth. Suppose, too, an immortal flea, for some reason eager to flee, or perhaps mistakenly thinking she could win a prize, who hops along from the inscribed half to the inscribed three-quarters to the seven-eighths and so on. No one could rightly argue that the flea, however speedily she fled, would reach an inscription of the number 1: an inscription of that number does not exist in the endless series inscribed.

There is nothing magical about the tale being of a flea and the distances being small. A gazelle could be pictured gliding across the inscriptions separated by feet (or hooves) rather than inches. The gazelle too would never glide upon any inscription of the number 1.

The question of whether all the items of a series can be run through, be they inscriptions or abstract, is distinct from the question of whether all the items can be summed. Some infinite series, for example, 1, 0, 0, 0 . . . , where only 0 is thereafter repeated endlessly, can be easily summed, even though no flea could hop upon all the series' inscriptions.

Some argue that what is required is that *all* the moves be made of the infinite series, but not that there be an end to the moves in the sense of a 'last move'. Muse again upon our flea hopping from one inscribed fraction to the next. Her hop-a-longs would indeed continue without end, so it remains unclear how *all* could be hopped upon. Suppose she happened to miss one early on: there is no way she could first finish all the others and then return to that earlier omission. Trying to complete all of an endless series is as difficult as reaching the series' last member – when there is no last member.

What can be said – though, as Aristotle saw, puzzles remain – is that, assuming constant velocity, the times taken for Achilles to traverse the distances to reach the tortoise shorten in line with the distances' own shortenings. There is an endless series of ever-decreasing temporal sequences that matches the endless sequence of ever-decreasing spatial distances. We may therefore picture the endlessness of the temporal sequences being divided through, so to speak, by the endlessness of the spatial distances. We ought, though, to retain logical queasiness at an endless number of anything being completed, be it distances traversed or times for traversing. Return to the flea, hopping from one inscribed fraction to the next. Suppose the inscriptions are now becoming appropriately closer or her speed regularly increasing after each hop. The hopping time-spans therefore proportionately diminish; but there is still no inscription of the number 1 at an end upon which to hop.

Thomson's Lamp – a reading lamp – has its On/Off button repeatedly pressed, switching the lamp on and off, the intervals between the pressings decreasing. For example, the button is pressed precisely at the end of a 30 seconds interval; then fifteen seconds later, at the end of a total interval since start of now 45 seconds; then seven and half seconds later, at the end of a total interval of now 52½ seconds – and so on. Even if sense can be made of the amazing finger activity appropriately accelerating – and even though the series converges to the one-minute limit – the description given says nothing about whether the switch is on or off, and hence whether the light is on or off, at the one-minute limit when the super-task is said to be complete.

Where will it end?

To meet Zeno's Traversal Challenge, allow me to present a similar challenge in what I term the 'Proportion Puzzle'.

Someone argues that there can be no determinate third of an amount because the fraction one-third is the decimal 0.333 recurring endlessly, the '3's continuing 'and so on'. There is, of course, the question of what is physical exactitude, given objects are composed of moving subatomic particles. Let us, though, suppose – as surely we can – that three lengths are the same in length, and hence that one of those lengths is one-third of the totality of the three. As one-third, expressed as a decimal, is 0.333 recurring endlessly, the length lacks a determinate end and so cannot exist. This is paradoxical for, of course, the length is also exactly the fraction one-third, even though it is exactly neither 0.33 nor 0.333 nor 0.3333 etc. As any length can be conceived to be one-third of a longer length, all lengths have contradictory properties being both determinate and indeterminate. The puzzle does not rest solely with lengths – but applies to all measurable quantities.

We could, of course, have represented things differently so that one third had a clear and determinate decimal-type formation, though it would not belong to a decimal system based on ten, but, say, a 'nonimal' system based on nine. Other fractions would then give rise to the Proportion Puzzle, being represented as recurring nonimals rather than decimals.

The Traversal Challenge and Proportion Puzzle may be brought under a general challenge concerning extension, determinateness and measurement: the No End Challenge. An example from the ancient Greeks is the Pythagorean distress at the discovery of irrational numbers, numbers such as the decimal expansion for π: they cannot be represented as fractions. The underlying assumption is that whether it be movement or unmoved extension, be it in space or in time, it needs to be determinate; that is, with determinate boundaries.

The No End Challenge twins a No Beginning Challenge – for whatever is suggested as the first stage or step or segment would also suffer from the same indeterminateness as that of an end. The challenges can also be related to the Puzzle of Difference. Suppose a belt, red from one end to the midline; and purple from the midline to the other end. What is its colour at the common midline? It would be contradictory to insist that it was both red and not red. Yet there exists no uncoloured line in the band's middle; and there exists no gap. Paradoxically, it seems as if the line must be coloured either red or purple, yet cannot be coloured either.

These puzzles of proportions and differences should leave us untroubled. Consider proportion. That the decimal expression of one-third involves an endless series and that decimals can be used in measuring should not lead us to think that a one-third length has no determinate end or involves in some way a contradiction – even if it happens to be true that tables and chairs, trees and butterflies, lack determinate ends. Further, we should not think that to reach the end of a length we need to complete an endless series or that the length must be composed of an endless number of smaller distances. Yes, measuring a third can involve the approximation of 0.33; measuring a circle's radius may involve π as roughly 3.142 – but that is that. There is nothing in the physical world such that the flea could be set hopping on the equivalent of an infinite number of inscribed '3's of the decimal for one-third. Things would be different, were we to seek to construct a one-third length by adding to three-tenths, three-hundredths, then three-thousandths and so on. Such activities, because endless, could not be completed.

The paradoxes arise because what holds of abstract entities – numbers, series, lines without breadth, points without size – is being imposed on the physical world. In the Puzzle of Difference, the midline that is said to be common to both segments of the belt is an abstract geometrical entity. In the physical world, if we dig down, we shall encounter molecules, atoms, electrons, photons – maybe even Higgs bosons – but not abstract lines. Indeed, without much digging, were the belt knitted, we could see where one colour ended and another began.

The previous paragraph is not meant to imply that all is clear. Although we gain considerable understanding of the world through mathematical applications, how and why applications work remains puzzling. The best we can do here is to bring ourselves down to earth – 'let us be human' – and that is what we try next regarding the particular Zeno paradoxes falling within the No End Challenge.

*   *   *

When we sip the wine, taste the brie and meander home, we engage in actions that take time and occur in space, yet these actions cannot take ever-decreasing times, or occur over ever-decreasing spatial extensions, and still be actions of those types. To sip, taste and meander requires sufficient time and space. Analogously, when we gaze at the wine-stained skirt, admire her coquettish walk and delight in the voice's foreign lilt, there is no temptation to insist that therefore we gaze, admire and delight at all the parts that make up, respectively, the stain, the walk and talk. Some parts, of course, do possess the properties of the wholes – a long meander can consist of smaller meanders – and even when parts lack the properties of the wholes, the wholes may yet correctly be understood as having parts. A sip involves some movements of the lips that themselves, taken separately, are not sips, yet compose the sips.

Now, tasks, runs and restings can sometimes be composed of tasks, runs and restings of smaller spatial or temporal extensions; but no sense can be made of tasks, runs and restings of teeny extensions, such as one billionth of an inch or minute. Zeno's paradoxes, though, need not hinge on the mistaken belief that there can be ever-decreasing activities of those types. The challenge is that such activities require extension in space or time, and, whatever the extension, it is endlessly divisible. If Achilles runs to town, he must surely traverse the distances making up that distance to town. If the tortoise sleeps for a day, he must surely sleep for the hours that make up that day and the minutes that make up the hours and so forth. If we accept such divisibility at the level of easily perceivable extensions, we ought to accept that such divisibility can continue infinitely so – yet then we have paradox.

What is the resolution? Perhaps the following is a useful background point. That an extension is divisible no more implies that it is divided than that the wine is drinkable implies that it is drunk. Just because an extension *can* be divided without end, it does not follow that it *is* divided. Actual runs and tasks must cope with actual divisions, not potentially infinite ones. Perhaps the Traversal Challenge assumes that anything extended must actually be composed of, or consist of, an infinite number of smaller extensions. But what leads us to believe that?

True, it is difficult to make sense of extensions consisting solely of a finite number of indivisible discrete distances. What would be the size of those smallest distances? Well, are we talking of distances that we can see – with good vision, on a clear day, without telescopes or microscopes? If so, ophthalmologists could probably tell us. Are we speaking of particles postulated by physicists and the distances between them? If so, we may reasonably turn to physicists for answers. One thing of which we can be sure is that an infinite number of parts will not be stumbled upon in any empirical investigation.

The simple point distinguishing between the actual and the potential or conceivable – perhaps it is Aristotle's – may yet be thought to miss the point. The feeling may persist that we can at least *conceive* of lines endlessly dividing a surface – and the paradoxes concern how such endless conceived divisions can be traversed. Yet what are these lines? They must be lines that we cannot experience, being lengths lacking thickness; and, even if we can conceive of abstract lines dividing actual surfaces, we may question the relevance for understanding how Achilles, or the tortoise or a fleeing flea, manages to move from A to B.

'And so on' bedazzles. It is akin to a magical incantation. In general, the paradoxes arise, it seems, through mistakenly transforming abstract fractions generated endlessly by mathematical rules into physical spatio-temporal divisions. If traversals required such rules to be followed, then indeed no end would be reached – as our hopping flea reminds us – but traversals do not require that following. In Chapter 3, misunderstanding the instruction's 'repeat' in 'Lather, rinse, repeat' generated an abstract shampooing without end; but there can be no real shampooing without end. What can be conceived in the abstract is not thereby applicable to the empirical world.

Where did it begin?

Zeno is such a fertile and provocative purveyor of space–time paradoxes that some more merit mention. Consider a line. If we take it to be infinitely divisible, what is the size of the parts into which it can be infinitely divided? If the parts are of no size, then obviously they fail to account for the line's length. If they have some length, then – however small – given that there is an infinite number of them, the line must be infinitely long.

The above Paradox of Plurality once again engages the problem of how mathematical concepts apply to the world. With regard to physical lines drawn in ink on paper, or by fingers in the sand, we may understand them in terms of the latest physical theories – or, more practically, not the latest – but not as composed of abstract mathematical entities. With regard to the abstract lines of geometricians, well, over to the mathematicians to explain in what sense abstract points may or may not be said to compose abstract lines.

Regarding motion, we have met the Dichotomy and Achilles. Zeno also presents the Stadium (see Notes) and the Arrow. The Arrow relies on the thought that at a particular instant an arrow is in a particular position. In that instant, it has no time to be moving – and it exactly fills the space it is within. Assuming time is a sequence of instances, if the arrow is moving at no instant of its flight, then it seems that there can be no flight.

A quick response is that it is not moving *during* an instant, but *at* an instant; a flying arrow has an instantaneous velocity which distinguishes it from an arrow unmoving. We may wonder about the quick dismissal. Russell, for example, saw the paradox as important in our understanding of change: at any particular point, there exists no distinction between being at rest and being in motion. Motion is, so to speak, composed of immobilities. The distinction, at a particular instant, between a moving and a resting arrow rests – oops! – on the position of the arrow at other instants

Let us now move to some puzzles of how things get started. Here are some recent paradoxes, Zeno-inspired.

TROJAN FLY

Achilles, somehow, has drawn level with the tortoise, where there is also a fly. Immediately, as Achilles moves ahead of the tortoise, the fly flies between them, continually, back and forth, as our two runners race to the finishing line. If we know the participants' speeds and relevant distances, is it possible to calculate the fly's position and which way she faces when Achilles reaches the finish?

The Trojan tale was originally told of a boy and girl, with a dog; it was then applied to Achilles – and once had a fly flying between trains. A typical thought is that, if we know the speed of the fly's flight, how long she flew, and pretend she can change direction instantaneously, we could surely answer the question. And yet . . .

Paradoxically, the fly could be anywhere, facing either direction. Place the fly anywhere, so to speak, between Achilles and the tortoise, just when Achilles reaches the finishing line. Now imagine the race being rewound – as if playing a DVD backwards. As we watch the rewind, Achilles moves backwards, nearer and nearer to the tortoise, as the tortoise moves backwards more slowly, the fly's to-ing and fro-ing therefore becoming of shorter and shorter distances. She is bound to end up level with Achilles and the tortoise when they are level.

The fly must, of course, travel faster than Achilles, given that she manages to fly, to and fro, between him and the tortoise. So, at the beginning point, when the three participants are level, it is impossible for her to be *immediately* flying *between* them; her speed would put her ahead of both. The puzzle arises because that 'between' impossibility is hidden from view; no first distance for her to fly is specified. We find more hiding in the following 'starting' paradoxes.

GODS

Sam plans to walk to Memphis, starting from Nashville. Yet, as is not unusual (well, in paradoxical lands), an infinite number of gods intend to stop his walk, albeit they are ignorant of each other's intentions. One god will raise a barrier immediately in front of Sam, if he reaches the halfway point to Memphis; a second god will do similarly, if he reaches a quarter way to Memphis; a third god will have stopped him, if he even reached as far as one-eighth – and so on. The conclusion is that Sam cannot get started, for, if he had done so, then a god would already have erected a barrier preventing him. Sam is stuck in Nashville, even though paradoxically no barrier goes up.

CABLE GUY

This individual – in Britain, a utility or TV employee – will arrive today any time after 8 am up to and including 4 pm, the times being equally likely. Let us assume that is true – however implausibly. So, it is equally probable that he turns up from 8 am up to and including midday as from midday up to and including 4 pm. We should bet, up to 8 am, that morning and afternoon are equally likely arrival periods. Yet however short a time after 8 am it is, we should then think his arrival more likely (very slightly initially) in the afternoon than the morning. After all, some morning has gone. Paradoxically, it was irrational to bet on morning and afternoon being equally likely.

With the tale of the gods, we may be immediately suspicious of the scenario's coherence. If a barrier has not yet been imposed, then that means that Sam has made no move. If a barrier has been imposed, then it means that Sam has travelled some distance, however small; but an 'earlier' god should by then already have blocked him. The possible actions of the gods need to be such that a barrier is raised if and only if Sam gets to somewhere. Yet if Sam gets to somewhere, then a god has failed in his barrier-raising – and had that god not failed, then another god would have failed, and so on. The Gods Paradox concludes that Sam cannot get anywhere. This conclusion arises because the scenario contains, it seems, an impossible condition: namely, that the gods can fulfil their intentions to block Sam if and only if an infinite number of them fail to fulfil their intentions.

The Cable Guy is a more realistic tale. The tale excludes a precise 8 am arrival, but any time immediately afterwards is possible, as set out. If the guy arrives exactly at noon, that belongs to the morning; if he arrives exactly at 4 pm, that belongs to the afternoon. There is parity in the durations. As there is no 'first moment' after 8 am, we know that whenever he appears, even seconds after 8 am, there are times between 8 am and his arrival when it would have been rational to have bet on the afternoon appearance as more likely. So, why think at the beginning that morning and afternoon are equally likely?

What it is rational to bet on at one time may differ from what it is rational to bet on at another. There are likely to be times after 8 am when it would be rational to change our bets in favour of the afternoon. Maybe dissolution of the paradox is by resisting the casual abstract division of time – as we earlier sought to resist casual abstract division of space when dealing with Zeno. Bets and thinking take time. The cable guy could appear so soon after 8 am that there would be no time for us to revise our initial betting or thinking. Hence, there is nothing irrational in betting beforehand on morning and afternoon being equally likely.

Troubling infinity

We knew there would be trouble with infinity. Are there as many odd numbers as even and odd numbers together? Surely not – the number of odd numbers necessarily fails to include the even ones. Yet, consider the two lines opposite: we can match each odd number with all the whole numbers.

$$1, \quad 2, \quad 3, \quad 4, \quad 5 \quad \ldots$$
$$\Updownarrow \quad \Updownarrow \quad \Updownarrow \quad \Updownarrow \quad \Updownarrow$$
$$1, \quad 3, \quad 5, \quad 7, \quad 9 \quad \ldots$$

Paradoxically, there seem to be just as many odd numbers as even and odd numbers, despite the fact that the odd numbers are not all the whole numbers. Indeed, similarly, there would seem to be as many squares of the whole numbers as whole numbers – Galileo's Paradox. Galileo could not quite believe this, and thought questions of whether collections of numbers are equal or unequal in number could be properly raised only for finite collections.

When we wonder whether we have the same number of cups as saucers, we try to pair all of them off. If we succeed, then we have the same number. Sets of numbers, where the numbers are infinite, are now defined as 'equinumerous' when there is *at least* one way of doing the pairing – as there is above. Paradoxically, the set of whole numbers is therefore equinumerous with the set of even numbers. An infinite set whose members can be paired off one-to-one with the positive integers is labelled 'denumerable'. Not surprisingly, puzzles arise.

TRISTRAM SHANDY

In Laurence Stern's 'autobiography', Tristram Shandy takes two years to relate his first two days of life. If he carried on at the same speed, he could never finish his life's story. Yet, were he immortal, paradoxically he could – for each successive couple of days could be matched with each successive couple of years. Mind you, he would need an amazing memory.

The puzzle matches the members of one infinite series with just some of the members of the same series, albeit still infinite in number – and of the same size, being equinumerous. 'The same size'? – well, Cantor showed not only that some infinite sets are the same size, given the understanding of 'equinumerous', but also that some infinite sets must be bigger than others. Having secured an intellectual grip on many infinities, Cantor, a religious man, seemed drawn to the inconsistent totalities which came into view – for example, the contradictory set of all sets, mentioned in Chapter 3 – as elusive and 'truly infinite'.

A similar puzzle to Tristram is Heaven and Hell, which has Goody eternally in heaven and Baddy eternally in hell, save that God kindly allows Baddy one day per year in heaven. The number of heavenly days for Baddy, being infinite in this way, is the same number as Goody's heavenly days. Baddy's single heavenly days (one a year) can be placed into a one-to-one correspondence with, can be paired with, Goody's days. True, it takes 365 years for Baddy to cover Goody's first year of heaven, but Baddy has infinite years ahead, each with one heavenly day available to match Goody's infinite number. Weirdly, Baddy's heavenly days and hellish days are also equinumerous.

A related paradox is that of the Numbered Balls, an infinite number, labelled from 1 upwards. At the start, one minute to noon, balls numbered 1 and 2 are thrown into the red room, with ball 1 immediately thrown out. Thirty seconds later, balls 3 and 4 are thrown in, with 2 immediately thrown out. Fifteen seconds later, balls 5 and 6 are thrown in, with 3 immediately thrown back. And so the process continues, with ever-decreasing time spans – infinitely. What is in the red room at noon?

We could argue that the room must be empty: all the balls must have been thrown back. We could equally well argue that there is an infinite number of balls in the room, for, although an infinite number would have been thrown back, there is an ever-increasing number – an infinite number – building up in the red room. As with Thomson's Lamp, the description of what is happening regarding an infinite series fails to specify what happens at so-called completions of the series.

Suppose a spaceship travels continuously in a straight line. The spaceship amazingly and regularly doubles its speed, akin to Thomson's lamp-button pressings. So, the speed doubles at the half-minute point, then doubles again at the next quarter-minute point, then doubles again at the next one eighth-minute point – and so on. Where is the ship at the one minute point? The correct answer to this Spaceship Puzzle cannot specify any finite position on its line of travel for it would reach any position suggested before the minute is up; yet it cannot be infinitely far away – for that is no place at all.

Once again, we are applying an *endless* operation – doubling, then doubling, and so on – so, it is hardly surprising we meet puzzlement about the end of the endlessness.

Probably the most used example of such infinity puzzles is Hilbert's Hotel, named after the great German mathematical logician David Hilbert.

HILBERT'S HOTEL

This hotel has an infinite number of rooms. Every room is occupied. Suppose a traveller comes. He can still be accommodated. How? Well, the Room 1 occupant is moved to Room 2, Room 2 occupant to Room 3 – and so on. Room 1 is now available for the new guest. Suppose an infinite number of travellers arrive. Accommodation is still no problem. The occupant of 1 moves to 2, occupant of 2 to 4, occupant of 3 to 6, and so on – leaving the infinite number of odd-numbered rooms free for the new guests.

Hilbert's Hotel is often described without batting an eyelid – yet we should surely recognize the need for some batting. After all, 'all' rooms being occupied is in tension with the thought that one can be made empty for a new guest. Further, suppose all odd-numbered room are freed as suggested: if the infinite new guests are numbered, then all those rooms could take the odd-numbered guests, the even-numbered now left room-less.

In the context of the infinite, 'all' needs to be understood differently from our normal use. An infinite collection is not like a normal finite collection, save bigger. Performing an activity an infinite number of times, a super-task – pressing on/off buttons, throwing in balls, hopping on inscriptions, releasing hotel rooms – is not just a very difficult performance, maybe with medical dangers, compared with performing an activity a finite number of times.

We can imagine meeting some individuals, exhausted by a charity event that required their counting the numbers down from one million – and they are now gasping out the last few numbers: 3, 2, 1. That makes sense. But we could make no sense, were the tale that the individuals had been counting backwards *all* the positive whole numbers – and now were reaching the weary end, 3, 2, 1.

Wittgenstein supposes the knight's move, in games of chess, being carried out by two movements, one straight and one oblique. When the comment is made that in chess there are no half knight's moves, this is not something amazing. The relationship of half a knight's move to a whole knight's move differs from that of half a bread roll to a whole bread roll. A knight's moves, in chess, cross the chessboard's squares, yet are not such that there is any place for halves or quarters. Similarly, physical space may elude the abstract, the infinite.

To insist that, because there are *moves* in chess, there must therefore be *part* chess moves, is to misunderstand the nature of chess moves. What is and is not possible with regard to chess moves does not carry over to what is and is not possible regarding wooden pieces being moved, be they shaped as chess pieces or not. So, too, what is and is not possible with regard to abstract mathematical series does not carry over to what is and is not possible in the world of wood, of individuals running, resting and counting. Of course, in various ways mathematical models can be properly applied to what Achilles does in the empirical world – to movements, to durations. For that matter, computer simulations can model weather changes and be applied to the weather. The models may involve flashing colours and graphs, but the weather is not similarly coloured – and the simulation and the computer, when modelling rainfall, usually remain dry.

Application of our concepts needs sensitive handling, as we shall shortly see with ships and rivers and heaps. To establish this point simply, consider a puzzle concerning jurisdiction:

BANDIT

When at a remote ranch, Bandit shoots Sheriff. Sheriff dies from the shooting a few days later, having returned home to Little Rock. Bandit, however, is also dead by then, having been lynched by a mob who found him in his hideaway. Bandit killed Sheriff. But when? When he shot him at the remote ranch? But Sheriff was not dead then. When Sheriff died in Little Rock? But Bandit was already dead himself by then. Similar puzzles arise in answering the question of the location of the killing.

Abstruse questions of infinity strike many people as not mattering. Here, there is clear mattering. When and where killings take place has consequences concerning which laws apply.

The Bandit Puzzle tries to force us into thinking that there should be greater spatio-temporal specificity to a killing than there often is. If you kill the rat, you cause its death; but the cause and the death may be some time apart: the killing maintains temporal spread. To insist that, because there is a fairly specific time and place where and when the bullet struck Sheriff, there should be a fairly specific time and place of the killing, is to misunderstand killings. The law, of course, may need to deem when and where a killing took place, so that just one jurisdiction is involved, if bringing a killer to trial.

The time of death could be deemed the time of the killing (were a time required). In this case, Bandit would have killed Sheriff when he, Bandit, was already deceased. This should not generate queasiness. Someone who has deliberately taken a slow-acting poison only becomes a successful suicide when dead, not when imbibing. A woman in Jerusalem may become a grandmother because of events in New York. The changes to the woman in becoming a grandmother, and to deceased Bandit in becoming a killer, are instances of 'Cambridge' changes – changes that do not have to involve anything physical or psychological occurring in the items undergoing the change.

When wondering about the correct application of our concepts, let us remember: in chess there are no half knight's moves. Let us, though, also remember that what may be seen as a nonsense at one time may later take on significance. A tribe new to the telephone once described telephone messages as 'messages on poles'. Later, when they encountered the wireless, wireless messages were referred to as 'messages on poles without the poles'.

How to apply 'infinity' to the world can generate serpent windings through an endless labyrinth of puzzles and muddles. Yet, if we step back, we may view matters more calmly, seeing them in a new light.

To worry over how we can perform infinite numbers of tasks is akin to worrying how the knight can move when there are no half moves, and maybe to how there can be messages relayed on poles without the poles.

5   Heaps and haze, colours and clocks –

and 1,001 cats

. . . where we encounter a famous ship or two of Theseus, Sir John Cutler's stockings, some rivers, heaps and pigeons – to say nothing of too many cats, some clock-watching, a Frenchman and a few cross-dressings.

We live much of life courtesy of the rough and ready; and the rough and ready is all that we often need. We want the volume turned down, yet the precise number of decibels is unimportant; and when ordering a goose big enough to feed six, a few ounces either way are irrelevant. One decibel makes no difference to the perceived loudness of the music; one ounce, no difference to the culinary success or failure. Yet sufficient of those 'making no difference' decibels – and we have quiet. More than a few of those ounces in either direction – and the diners suffer from eating too little, or too much. Zeno of Elea argued that as a large number of millet seeds makes a sound when poured, then so should just one seed or one teeny seed portion.

Lest these seem trivial examples, Susanne, a 30-year-old woman, is an adult, a person. One second removed from a life does not change an adult, a person, into a non-adult, a non-person. Susanne, one second younger, was still an adult, a person. Reflecting again that one second removed does not convert an adult, a person, into a non-adult, a non-person, Susanne, two seconds younger, was still an adult, a person. Yet if we carry on, subtracting the seconds, we conclude that a teenager, a child, a baby, a foetus are all adults, grown-ups and persons. This is bizarre.

The above Sorites Paradox or Paradox of the Heap – the Greek '*soros*' means heap – is attributed to Eubulides, the Ancient Greek logician already honoured as paradox spinner. The paradox prompts many questions, one of which is what makes an object one and the same object over time. Let us set our stage with Theseus' Ship, derived from Plutarch, albeit with, first, just stage one.

THESEUS' SHIP, I

Theseus, an Athenian hero, had his ship repaired over the years.
Old planks, ropes and sails were replaced by new planks, ropes and
sails. Eventually, Theseus' ship consisted totally of new parts. Was it
the same ship?

This paradox and also the Sorites may lead a quest for dividing lines.
When, so to speak, does Theseus' ship cease to be the same ship?
Acorns become oak trees, tadpoles become frogs and, glancing along
a colour spectrum, red transforms into orange. But when? Sorites
often concerns small changes, even unnoticeable ones. We notice first
the easily noticed.

Axe: the identity of entity

A woodcutter, pointing to his axe, boasts of how it has served his
family well – an impressive buy. It has been in his family for generations, passed from father to son, as axe-worthy as ever. You listen, very
impressed, yet soon realize that you were too readily impressed, for he
casually remarks, 'Mind you, the axe's blade has needed to be replaced
quite a few times. For that matter, the handle wears out quickly; we've
had a few new handles over the centuries.'

'But the axe consists only of its handle and blade', you sigh. 'So, it's
not really the same axe passed down the generations.'

The woodcutter responds that, in each generation, the father
passed on the axe, identified it as the same axe, and used it to axe. The
'it's in the previous sentence apply to one and the same item.

All items that we encounter – including ourselves – undergo
change, if only because electrons spin off. An item needs, in some
respect, to be the same item in order to undergo change. The shirt,
after dyeing, is numerically the same shirt, yet qualitatively different,
being of a new hue. Further, an item may be numerically the same,
yet – to some extent – compositionally different. The shirt is the same
shirt as when first bought, even with some buttons now missing. 'The
same', it has been quipped, quipped by J. L. Austin, does not always
mean 'the same'.

The seventeenth-century Sir John Cutler, goes the story, was so fond of his worsted stockings that, instead of throwing them out as holes developed, he had them darned with fine silken thread – so much so that eventually they were composed solely of silken threads. Yet they were still his much beloved stockings. This is an extreme example of how an item can persist as the same item, despite compositional change. It is also an extreme example of one man's affection for his stockings.

The Axe Puzzle also presents an extreme, one of simplicity. The axe has only two parts – and they both are repeatedly replaced. The question is: what is the criterion for an object being numerically the same? The answer depends on the item's type. The axe possesses a continuity: a new blade is added to an existing handle, which itself has been added to an existing blade. Blade and handle were not discarded at the same time, with a new axe being bought. We should rest content with the thought that in some respects the axe is the same, in other respects not. Let us resist the Yes/No demand for answering the question, 'Is it the same axe?'

Theseus' Ship, first stage, presents similar problems to those of the Axe Puzzle. The ship underwent many changes, its material composition eventually being completely different from when it first set sail. Use of 'it', 'the same ship', is perhaps justified by the continuity through space and time. There was no moment when the ship was in dock, yet, within a second, 'it' was miles out at sea. A ship, though, has more to it than an axe – and so does the Paradox of Theseus' Ship.

THESEUS' SHIP, II

Theseus' ship – well, it seems to be his ship – consists totally of new parts. However, scavengers hoarded the old discarded materials and eventually re-combined them into the original ship, albeit battered and unseaworthy. Which ship is Theseus' ship?

Two ships, now, compete for the accolade as 'Theseus' ship'. Yet, if the ship that Theseus now owns, with all the new parts, counted as the same ship as the original when the old discarded parts were not re-combined, why should this sameness be undermined when the old parts are re-combined?

There is a clash of criteria. In our everyday experiences, we identify something as numerically the same item over time if (a) its parts are largely the same and (b) it possesses some appropriate continuity in space and time – and typically if more conditions are satisfied, for example, retaining the same form, and not being permanently broken into parts. With Theseus' tale, these criteria point in different directions. The scavengers' ship has (a) the compositional sameness, whereas the ship that Theseus currently sails satisfies (b). The paradox dissolves, some say, if we simply accept the need for linguistic decision. Recall how legal decisions about jurisdiction over 'drawn out' killings might have been required concerning Chapter 4's Bandit.

If true that decisions are needed, matters are not thereby trivial. Suppose the two ships are as outlined. Suppose Theseus, in a will drawn up years earlier, bequeaths his ship to his eldest daughter: she may be incensed if courts take his ship to be the old unseaworthy one. Of course, if the old unseaworthy one is then historically more valuable, she may argue in its favour: the possibility of valuable inheritances can have remarkable effects on how we see things. What matters is clarity, from the very beginning, over which of the criteria should be applied.

What also matters is the awareness that the mantra 'we need to decide' may blind us to the fact that sameness can be a matter of degree. Suppose only half of Theseus' ship's components are replaced; and suppose the scavengers combine the discarded components with some new material to make a 'half-new' ship. We should surely recognize that here we have two ships that *to some degree* are the same as the original.

Degrees and decisions apply in Axe and Theseus, but the paradoxes touch on two deeper puzzles, one particular, one general – to be discussed in the final two chapters. First, what makes me the same 'me' over time? Answers suggestive of my persisting only to some degree, or that it is a matter of linguistic decision, lack the ring of truth, in contrast to similar answers for Axe and Theseus. Secondly and generally, to what extent do our decisions and language determine the way the world is carved into items? After all, we cannot just decide that Theseus' ship could be the same as this book or these words.

For another sameness puzzle, we turn to Heraclitus, the fifth-century BC Greek philosopher of Ephesus, who would speak in riddles.

RIVER

Heraclitus observed that you cannot step into the same river twice, for the waters are ever flowing. From that teeny fragment, we may ponder thus. The river we step into today is the same as this water, yet tomorrow the river is the same as a different volume of water. So, paradoxically it cannot be the same river.

Heraclitus may be reminding us, albeit obscurely, that change is essential, certainly to most objects. Water would not be water if it did not bubble and boil at high temperatures, assuming normal pressures. For that matter, a cocktail is not much of a cocktail if the ingredients are not suitably stirred. Let us approach Heraclitus with a little logic in which identity is seen as all or nothing.

The river (R) into which I stepped on Sunday (s) is surely identical with a certain moving mass of water (W) on Sunday. We write this as: $Rs = Ws$. When I step into the river the next day, Monday (m), I step into different moving water, Monday water, so: $Rm = Wm$. But the river is the same river; so, $Rs = Rm$. Therefore, we should conclude that $Ws = Wm$. Yet Ws is not identical with Wm. The waters on Sunday have flowed away and the Monday waters are new. Hence, we have the paradox.

Some resolve the paradox by insisting that the river is a four-dimensional object, with different parts in time as well as space. Just as a part of the Nile is in Egypt and a part in the Sudan, so the Nile has parts or stages in Sunday and in Monday. My river steppings are into different temporal stages of the river: the Sunday stage, then the Monday stage. Zeno's Arrow Paradox from the previous chapter suggested that a moving arrow should be understood as a sequence of immobile parts. A river is here understood as a four-dimensional collection of unchanging parts and stages. Paradoxically, change seems to be lost. This leads some to reject such a four-dimensional view (see Chapter 10).

A different approach argues that the river is not identical with its waters: rather it is composed of waters and composed of different waters over time. Were it not composed of different waters, it would be a long, thin lake, not a river. The mistake is to think that, because the river is composed of these Sunday waters today, it is identical with these waters – and so, everything true of these waters must be true of the river. All these Sunday waters, though, end up in the oceans, no longer in the river. True, the river ends at an ocean and, we say, 'flows into the ocean', but the river as a whole is not in the ocean. All of the river, so to speak, is both more and less, in different respects, than the moving waters present on Sunday.

Sorites: a heap of arguments

The above paradoxes make us wonder what makes an item the same item. Sorites highlights a sequence of small changes such that, by plausible steps, we move from obvious truths to obvious falsehoods. Wang's Paradox uses a soritic argument related to numbers and size. Zero is a small number. Add one to any small number, and a small number remains. The number one is small; but, therefore, so are two, three, four – and so on, to millions and trillions. In mathematics and logic, this type of argument can be set out as a 'mathematical induction' (see Notes), not to be confused with the inductive reasoning of Chapter 6. We return, though, to everyday things.

SORITES

A heap of grains – say it is a million seeds – remains a heap even with one grain removed. One grain does not make the difference between a heap and just a few grains. From the heap, remove one. We retain a heap. Removing another should, therefore, still leave us with a heap – and it does. And so we continue the process – yet, of course, we end up without a heap. We end up heapless. What has gone wrong?

The Baldman Paradox uses similar reasoning, taking us from the truth that a man has a head of hair to the falsehood that a bald man has a head of hair. We can construct soritic reasoning with lots of concepts – wealthy, generous, painful – yet not with pregnant, prime number, and winner.

The reasoning typically takes the form of *modus ponendo ponens*, the mood of affirming by affirming: if so and so, then such and such; so and so: therefore such and such. If it is raining, then the roads are wet; it is raining: therefore the roads are wet. If Emilie has another drink, she will be lap-dancing; Emilie is having another drink: therefore she will be lap-dancing. We affirm the lap-dancing by having affirmed the drinking. This form of argument is undoubtedly valid – if the premises are true, it must follow that the conclusion is true – but it may not always be rational to believe the conclusion, even though rationally believing the premises (see Notes).

Here is the simple 'Heap', assuming that the grains are suitably piled.

Starting Point	A million grains form a heap.
Sorites Principle	However many grains: if they form a heap, then with one grain fewer they form a heap.
Conclusion 1	A million grains, with one fewer, form a heap.

We may, of course, apply the principle to Conclusion 1, thus reaching

Conclusion 2   A million grains, with two fewer, form a heap.

Continuing down the numbers, building up our own argument heap, we could reach

Conclusion 999,999   One grain forms a heap.

We could even conclude that, when we have no grains, we may yet have a heap.

The expressions, 'heap', 'bald', 'adult' and so on, it may be suggested, are ambiguous: ambiguity accounts for the paradox. That, though, is a mistake. 'Entrance' and 'polish', as written, have more than one meaning. An ambiguity occurs with 'rains' and 'reins' when spoken – and 'bank' is ambiguous in both modes. Yet soritic reasoning does not lead us from banks as financial institutions to the conclusion that they are riversides – nor from polishing to the Central European nation of Poland.

Whether someone is tall, large or heavy is relative to others – to an average, a measure. Perhaps the paradox results from the *relative* nature of the problematical terms. Yet this also is mistaken. Being heavier than the average weight of philosophers is a relative matter, yet does not (on the surface) create a soritic puzzle. Suppose the average weight is twelve stone. If Erskin is eighteen stone, then he is heavier than the average. One stone fewer makes no difference over that; but it is not true that, whatever the weight, one stone fewer would make no difference to whether Erskin outweighed the average. No general principle works here that is akin to the Sorites Principle.

What is distinctive about soritic terms is that they are vague – well, so it is said. This is curious terminology because there are many, many cases where we have no problem in applying these 'vague' terms. There often is no disagreement about whether someone is tall – or something is a heap, or someone an adult. The vagueness only arises in certain cases, where we hesitate, disagree, worry about what to say. These are the so-called borderline cases, yet this too is curious terminology, for it suggests a line; but, with soritic terms, it is questionable whether there is a line at all. The terms possess both clear and hazy applications. They are hazily edged – so hazy, in fact, that they lack edge. The haze can arise whether or not we have discrete distinctive jumps – one grain after another – or whether there is a continuous flow, for example, the gradual change of the colour red into orange.

Of course, it is not unusual that lots of a little should lead to a lot – a 'lottle'. One apple may not tip the balance, and adding another may not tip, yet the fifth apple added, although also only one apple, tips. Each individual apple lacks the relevant tipping feature, yet the five combined possess that feature. To be worried by the apple phenomenon, it is said, is to be bedazzled by the fallacy of composition. Maybe that fallacy seeps into Sorites.

The fallacy is to think that what is true of the parts must be true of what is composed of the parts. The parts of a machine may be small, but the machine is large. If tobacco company A stops advertising, its sales will fall. That would also hold of tobacco companies B, C and D separately. However, if all tobacco companies ceased advertising, there may be no fall in overall cigarette sales. Any particular company's sales would fall because the other companies' advertising would pick up extra sales. Overall sales remain constant – and constancy, indeed, may be retained, even if all tobacco companies ceased advertising and even if some companies' sales fall.

In our Sorites as given, heaps are decomposing into non-heaps – though we could easily construct soritic arguments running in the opposite, uplifting 'composing' direction. Is Sorites guilty of the fallacy of composition or decomposition – depending on which way we run the argument?

Well, if some such fallacy is involved, we need to explain where things go wrong. Yet soritic arguments are so simple that our options for attacking them are severely limited, despite an explosion of words on the topic.

One path is to attack the Sorites Principle. 'Heap' has some haze. Removing a grain from a heap will often leave a heap, but sometimes things are hazy over what should be said. Hence, some philosophers speak of propositions, such as 'This is a heap', often being only roughly true. This can lead to talk of degrees of truth, with numerical measures given to the degrees. For example, it is totally true that one million grains are a heap and indeed that 999,999 grains are, but far less true that 50 grains are a heap. A teeny bit of reduced truth, compared to the 50 example, is the proposition that 49 grains are a heap.

'If 100 grains is a heap, then 99 grains is a heap' moves us a little towards less truth and greater falsity – hardly a recommendation for acceptance. Sorites fails because the second premiss, the general principle of the Sorites as set out, is not true, but at best partially true.

The 'degrees of truth' approach has the high artificiality of assigning numerical values to the extent of truth. How does one tell which numbers to give? Further, is it really the case that some simple propositions are, for example, 0.7 true? Rather than ascribing degrees of truth to propositions, it would be more reasonable to think of items being heaps to a greater or lesser degree. Claims such as 'This is more of a heap than that' would simply be true or simply false. Sorites has its paradoxical source in terms such as 'heap' rather than 'truth'.

Even with a 'degree' approach, the Sorites' puzzles persist, for when should we start moving from 'heap' to 'less than a heap' or from 'true' to a lower degree of truth? The approach seems to require boundaries between heaps 'proper', such that they are fully heaps, or such that it is fully true that they are heaps, and borderline heaps or partial truths about heaps. The requirement, though, raises the soritic puzzle again. There is no stage at which a granular removal transforms a fully-fledged heap into a borderline hazy heap or makes it less true that it is a heap. How could a grain make such a difference? At which point?

Some argue that some claims about items being heaps, adults or whatever, are 'super-true' or 'super-false', these terms applying only when no one standardly would disagree about the items' heap status, adult status or whatever. There would, of course, be many cases which are neither super-true nor super-false. Shirts sometimes come in sizes small, medium and large. Because of various factors, manufacturers may decide differently on the line between small and medium – but all may agree that a 26-inch chest would be small and a 36 medium. The problem remains, though, of how a small inch change could justify a move from a super-true claim to one not super.

Haze (even purple)

Soritic terms have haze. For example, 'purple' has haze. There are some clear cases of purple, and many hazy cases. Further, there is no fixed line where we agree that haziness begins: we hesitate – and hesitate at different points.

How do we learn to use words such as 'purple', 'bald', 'tall' and 'heap'? The answer is: from others who also sometimes use them hazily. On some occasions, we picked up that 'purple' definitely applied; on others that it definitely did not apply – and, with regard to some instances, either the matter was not mentioned or hesitations set in. Those hesitations would occur at different points at different times, depending on contexts and people involved.

A slogan, inspired by Wittgenstein, is 'meaning is use'. Undoubtedly our grasp of the meaning of terms involves our using them appropriately. Sorites brings out that our use, in certain circumstances, involves hesitations, disagreements – and sometimes a refusal to commit. Such disagreements and hesitations are to be expected. To hesitate about who is the United States President manifests some ignorance; but to hesitate, in many contexts, whether to call something purple or someone tall manifests no ignorance at all. For indeterminate ranges of cases, the right thing to do is also to hesitate whether to apply the Sorites Principle, the soritic general premiss. Applying the principle universally is to unhaze the haze. The principle should not be accepted as it stands.

If we refuse assent to the Sorites Principle in its universality, are we saying that sometimes one grain does make the difference between a heap and a non-heap? Again, maybe we should resist answering 'Yes' or 'No'. To grant a 'Yes' or 'No' is to commit to a specification which is absent in these cases. What is true is that people will, with varying degrees, hesitate about what to say at a variety of points.

Many philosophers are dissatisfied at things left in this state. Some make the curious claim that there really are sharp boundaries between heaps and non-heaps, the tall and non-tall, the purple and non-purple, and so on. It is just that we – human that we are – cannot find them. We have, so to speak, poor eyesight or intellect-sight. On this view, a god-like figure could presumably tell us where the boundaries – the borderlines, the haze, the edges – reside.

The above view – the 'epistemic view', because it relates to our knowledge or, more accurately, ignorance – is curious indeed. Its stance is that we users of the language with soritic terms are ignorant of key features of their proper use and hence their meaning. Suppose God told us where red became orange, where a heap ceased to be a heap – and so on. What could we make of it? We could hear it as a divine stipulation about how now to use the terms; but could we make sense of God telling us the correct use or meaning of our terms – when our use clearly displays haze?

Reflect on our deliberate use of hazy expressions – 'about midnight', 'reasonably attractive', 'roughly ten stone' – or, indeed, our deliberate introduction of new terms stipulated as hazy. How is the epistemic view to respond? If the view fails to apply to such terms, then we still have the Sorites' puzzles applying to those terms. If the view applies to such terms, then it is ruling that there really are boundaries to their correct use, and that, when we stipulate absence of boundaries, we are, in some way, contradicting ourselves. This latter alternative is most odd, not least because if we simply make up an expression, deliberately hazily edged as far as we can tell, then, according to that alternative, somehow we have really managed to place a determinate carving on the world. Sorites' reasoning is puzzling, but the epistemic view is even more so.

Cats and pigeons

Some philosophers feel distressed by the haziness in our language – by hesitations over what to say. They crave greater accuracy than approximations, than the rough and the ready; yet greater accuracy is often unnecessary, even a nuisance: witness Shylock's sticky moment in *The Merchant of Venice*. With Portia's demanding precision – a pound of flesh exactly to be extracted – Shylock is thwarted. Yes, greater accuracies are often conceivable, even available, but for much of day-to-day living they capture no truths intrinsically superior to the rough and ready. It is all right, at times, to treat France as hexagonal. A bread knife, when sliced bread is needed, is more valuable than the sharpest of razor blades.

Sometimes definiteness is valuable. An arbitrary line may be chosen, for example an eighteenth birthday, to fix when a minor in law becomes adult in law. It puts a stop to some legal squabbles. A speed limit is fixed at 30, when 31 or 29 would do equally well. Having some definite limit around that speed is sensible. If we think a little further, even what appears precise is not usually intended to be that precise. Having arranged to meet at 7 pm, Sadie would be weirdly sadistic if berating her lover for arriving at 7.01 or, indeed, 6.59. Many of our so-called precise terms hover with hazy horizons.

This has a bearing on the Chaos Paradox, the paradoxical claim that, even if the world is deterministic, it is in principle unpredictable. The paradox seems to arise because teeny changes, such as the famous butterfly flapping its wings in Australia, are magnified into vast changes; and, the story goes, it is impossible for us ever accurately to measure the teeny changes. Perhaps the paradox rests on an empirical hypothesis that the precision needed for prediction is greater than the precision available to us. Crudely, for example, the prediction needs, so to speak, measurement to 99 places of decimals, but we can manage only 69.

Whatever we make of this chaotic speculation, many scientifically minded philosophers who think that vague terms should be regimented into precision – discipline brought to their use – assume that vagueness belongs to language, not the world. Yet there are puzzles about the vagueness or otherwise of objects. Ask for a third of the cake, and according to one way of thinking – recall Chapter 4 – you will not receive exactly one-third or 0.33 recurring; yet 'exact', paradoxically, need not be that exact: it is, as already implied, a term with haze. When we take exact measurements, there remains much haziness over which we slide: recall the electrons spinning at edges. So, it is appropriate here to touch a paradox for those bounded to boundaries.

1,001 CATS

Professor Geach's Tibbles is a regular cat, the only cat, it seems, sitting on the mat. Tibbles has, let us say, a thousand hairs. Were she to have any one of those hairs missing, she would still be a cat on the mat. So, on the mat are one thousand cats, each lacking a different hair – and, of course, also Tibbles.

The curious paradox – also known as the Paradox of the Many – has Tibbles sitting on the mat. The thousand other cats each have a different collection of 999 hairs, though happening to have a different extra hair attached. Look at Tibbles and picture that cat in front of you, but with a single hair missing. There are a thousand such cats. Surely they are all cats. We may reflect that, were one hair plucked from Tibbles, then we should still have Tibbles, the cat on the mat.

If we identify an item, Tibless, on the mat as the item having all the bits of Tibbles except for one particular hair, then Tibless is part of Tibbles; but, we may argue, not thereby another cat. Tibbles does not contain cats as parts – well, not usually. Are we not, though, being arbitrary in deeming Tibbles a cat, but not Tibless? After all, why should plucking out one hair from Tibbles transform Tibless into a cat? We undoubtedly would still have a cat, even if one hair is lost.

The puzzle derives from the Stoic philosopher Chrysippus, third century BC, who put forward the Dion and Theon Paradox. Present is Dion, a complete man. Present also is all that is Dion except for his left foot: call that individual Theon. Now, suppose that Dion has his left foot amputated. Do we have two men or one – and if one, which? Dion or Theon?

These puzzles can lead to the thought that objects 'out there' are vague, be they clouds, mountains or cats – even to the thought that composite objects such as clouds, mountains and cats cannot exist. More central soritic arguments, though, rest on our perceptions, on what we notice and our resulting judgements.

We may feed the pigeons, seeing that there are a lot. One pigeon absent from a lot is not noticed by us: we still see a lot. So, even with another pigeon absent, we still see a lot – and so on. Yet, not 'and so on', for we eventually notice that there are no longer a lot. When delighting in and using intriguing collective terms – a 'murmuration' of starlings, an 'unkindness' of ravens, or just the common 'flock' of sheep – we usually can tell when a murmuration, an unkindness or a flock is present, without being able to specify the number of creatures needed to form such collections.

Suppose there are 50 pigeons in front of us – and consider what we can tell just by looking from some distance. We cannot usually tell whether there are exactly 51 or 50 or 49 – but we may be able to tell that there are *about* 50. We can certainly tell that there are not as many as 1,000 pigeons; yet we cannot spot the difference between 1,000 and 999 pigeons present just by looking; so, we can surely tell that there are not as many as 999 pigeons. But we cannot spot the difference between 999 and 998 pigeons present; so, surely we can tell that there are not 998 pigeons. And off we go down the line of numbers, the reasoning seemingly leading us to conclude that there are not 52, 51, 50, 49, 48 pigeons present – and so on. Yet, being unable to judge the exact number was not meant to imply that there exists no exact number around the 50 mark. Ruling out many exact pigeon numbers has paradoxically led us to rule out even those that we know the pigeons may well number.

The 'About' Puzzle arises because we cannot tell the difference in pigeon numbers, if a few more or a few less, when large numbers are involved – and we slip into mistakenly maintaining that remains true even without the caveat of 'when large numbers'. We ought, though, at times to hesitate over what to say about the principle concerning what we can notice, given that we sometimes rightly hesitate in the application of 'large'. The paradox defender is demanding that our 'about' perceptions be determinately dressed by 'exact'. Now, our 'about' perceptions can be crossed-dressed in some 'exact' clothing – if there are about 50 pigeons, there are not exactly 100 – but not comprehensively so, not such that every 'exact' case has a place in the 'about' space.

The logic of 'about' and 'exact' differ. Here is a simple example of the point. If the pigeons number exactly 50, then they do not number exactly 51; but if the pigeons number *about* 50, then they may number about, or exactly, 51 or 52 or maybe a few more, or a few less, but not thereby about or exactly all further numbers, increasing or decreasing by one. To ask for determinate boundary lines, where 'about 50' ends, is to seek finer grains in the coarse-grained 'about' – but, at exact boundaries, ne'er will meet the grains of exactitude and those of 'about'.

Clocks, colours and cross-dressings

We often lack the ability to see the exact number in a large group; but paradox also arises when our experiences are suddenly of clear alterations.

CLOCK WATCHING

You spy that it is one minute to five. You focus on that minute-hand, eager to leave work. From second to second you spy no movement: one second makes no difference to what you can see. At some stage though, an extra second makes the difference. You can now see that the hand is virtually vertically at the twelve.

COLOUR SPOTTING

There is a long array of fashion dresses, all the same save for slight differences in the shade of purple. They are ranged so that the purples gradually move from a pinkish to a blue. Let us pretend they are numbered from 1 to 100. Looking at any two adjacent dresses, you can spot no colour difference at all. Number 3's appearance is the same as number 4's; number 4's the same as 5's; 5's the same as 6's . . . Yet compare 3 to, say, 19 and there is a noticeable difference in colour.

Perhaps these changes in how things – the minute-hand locations, the dresses' colours – appear to us demand merely empirical explanations. Perhaps shades 3, 4 and 5 register differently on our central nervous systems, yet trigger no awareness of difference. The neural differences generate experiential differences, changes in awareness, only when they are, in some way, at least as great as those between the ones caused by Dresses 3 and 19.

In the Puzzle of the Self-Torturer, volunteers accept teeny pain increases in return for monetary rewards at each increase. Each pain increase on its own is sufficiently tiny not to be noticed. So, it seems rational to accept each increase for the money. Yet, at some point, the increased pain level is noticed and may well lead to sacrifice of the monetary gain. The Mañana Puzzle, noting that putting off seeing the dentist by one day makes no relevant difference, asks, 'Why not put it off until tomorrow, then the morrow of that tomorrow – and so forth?' There are numerous similar examples. One extra whisky makes no noticeable behavioural difference, yet at some point an extra whisky makes a huge difference. A slight increase in bath water temperature goes unnoticed, but, as the increases accumulate, we begin to notice and may even leap out.

Contrast the plight of the frog whose sensory apparatus seems unmoved not just by slight temperature increases but also by the gradual accumulation of such increases. Frogs leap when hit with immediate big changes, but apparently sit complacently unleaping, as the cook brings them slowly to the boil. Changes in our environment impinge on us, often without our noticing; yet the changes build up, giving rise, in ways unknown, to our awareness of change. A puzzle is how small neural changes, each of which leaves no conscious mark, eventually cause conscious awareness.

We perform many complex actions, respond to many changes, yet are unaware of quite what we do or why we respond. Think of your unlocking a door, hitting a tennis ball, or responding to a greeting. Some people possess 'blind sight'. They are not conscious of seeing anything beyond certain edges, yet provide many correct descriptions of what lies beyond those edges – and not just by luck. All they have to go on is, so to speak, what they cannot see.

*   *   *

Sorites' puzzles have us judging that A and B are the same, B and C are the same, perhaps that C and D are the same, yet insisting that A and D are different. How can that be? If Osbert and Oscar are the same person, and if Oscar and Oswald are the same person, then Osbert must surely be the same person as Oswald. Sorites, puzzlingly, has us offending such transivity of sameness. When we encountered a similar puzzle with Heraclitus' River, we bounded free by understanding the river to be *composed* of today's water rather than being the same as today's water. What can be done with the Sorites' perceptual puzzles?

The mistake perhaps is in over-simplification, a mistake leading to the seeming intransitivity displayed in Chapter 1's Preference Paradox. In Colour Spotting, the argument runs thus:

Dress 3's colour as experienced is pink-ish purple.
Dress 3's colour as experienced is the same as Dress 4's.
Therefore, Dress 4's colour as experienced is pink-ish purple.

Arguments similarly structured lead to the paradoxical conclusion that Dress 3's colour as experienced is the same as 19's – paradoxical because we see a clear difference in colour between Dresses 3 and 19.

The over-simplification of the above is to ignore context. We experience Dresses 3 and 4 as the same colour when adjacent; we experience Dresses 4 and 5 as the same colour when adjacent, and so on. But it is a different experience when Dresses 3 and 19 are adjacent or when we are reflecting afresh on Dress 19's colour. After all, you can probably recognize your father in everyday wear, but not when in fancy dress. If you have only wild erotic encounters with lovers always in the dark, you may recognize them in unlit beds and shadowy intimacies, but never in daylight public environments. What you see as being the same colour depends, in part, on surroundings in time and space. Perhaps that accounts for why the Perceptual Sorites' reasoning goes wrong.

We have dealt with a 'forced march' Sorites where we march our eyes from Dress 1 to Dress 2 and so on; but there are also 'random' versions. When the dresses are shown randomly, perhaps separately, it may transpire, for example, that we end up describing Dresses 4 and

5 as possessing slightly different colours, yet when 4 and 5 are adjacent, we spot no difference. Again, perhaps some neurological explanation could be forthcoming based on the effects of context and of previous colour samples seen and remembered.

*   *   *

One and the same item may be seen in different ways, in different contexts; and what we believe about one and the same item can be contradictory, unless some distinctions are deployed. Here is Eubulides again, now with the Masked Man Paradox.

You know who your father is. Your father is identical with the man in the mask. Therefore you know who the masked man is. Yet you do not. This is the Identity Paradox or Hesperus Paradox (see below).

The reasoning has obviously gone wrong, for knowing who your father is does not mean being able to recognize him under all circumstances. Consider, now, the following.

You greatly admire your father, and hugely despise the leading city wheeler-dealer. Unbeknown to you, they are one and the same person. Do you not hold inconsistent attitudes and contradictory beliefs, believing of the same person that he is to be despised yet also admired? We may rightly describe you as unwittingly admiring the dealer and unwittingly despising your father; that is not, of course, how things strike you. You admire the man with the fatherly features; you despise the man with the wheeler-dealer ways. You maintain two distinct dossiers in your mind, so to speak, not realizing that they are of one and the same person. Were you to realize, then you would adjust some of your beliefs; you may merge the dossiers.

With psychological states, 'referential opacity' comes into play. If opacity is present, then terms that denote one and the same object cannot always be substituted for each other in a given sentence such that the proposition expressed remains true (or remains false). A famous example derives from Frege, the great logician, already encountered, whom Russell troubled with his paradox.

You may want to know whether the heavenly body Hesperus is identical with the heavenly body Phosphorus. In understanding your want, we cannot sensibly substitute the name 'Hesperus' for

'Phosphorus', even though Hesperus *is* Phosphorus, the planet Venus possessing both names. If we could substitute, then the claim would be the false one of your wanting to know whether Hesperus is identical with Hesperus. Russell tells of George IV wishing to know whether Scott was the author of *Waverley*, 'yet an interest in the law of identity can hardly be attributed to the first gentleman of Europe'. George IV did not wish to know whether Scott was Scott.

Solutions are by way of claiming that different 'senses' – the Fregean term is 'Sinn' – or dossiers or clusters of descriptions are associated with the names, making the 'name' substitution in sentences ascribing psychological states misleading. We may, though, raise the puzzle again, through the Paradox of Analysis.

'A brother is a male sibling.' If this offers the correct analysis of what it is to be a brother, then presumably 'brother' and 'male sibling' have the same meaning. Perhaps they therefore have the same sense. If so, then paradoxically the analysis amounts to no more – and no less – than 'A brother is a brother' or 'A male sibling is a male sibling.' Yet, surely, such analyses can be informative. Maybe this suggests that senses need to be distinguished from meanings; but quite what are they – and how do they stand in relation to meanings?

Identity matters matter – and continue to generate paradoxes, even with awareness of the relevance of referential opacity.

KRIPKE'S PIERRE

Parisian Pierre learns a lot about London solely from photographs and teachers. He concludes, 'Londres est jolie,' manifesting his belief that London is beautiful. Later, he finds himself in a city called 'London'. He has no reason to think that London is the same city as Londres. He is living alone in a run-down part of the city and sincerely says, 'London n'est pas jolie.' Does Pierre believe London is pretty?

There is a tendency to demand the 'Yes' or the 'No' – a danger encountered in earlier chapters. 'Surely, his belief must be one or the other.' Pierre is a rational logical chap in the tradition of Descartes. As far as he is concerned, he is clear that Londres is pretty and London is not. He may consciously and explicitly contrast the two.

Does Pierre believe London is pretty? Perhaps the correct answer is: in a way, yes; in a way, no. He has two distinct dossiers of beliefs, a different one for each name, which he takes to be of different cities. Were he to learn that they applied to the same city, he would revise some beliefs. He may refine some, realizing that some beliefs should be held of some parts of the city, some of other parts. He had been too hasty in his aesthetic evaluations of the city.

The Pierre Puzzle directly concerns psychological matters; another identity puzzle may initially appear distinct from the psychological.

The puzzle was recently presented by Jennifer Saul in terms of Clark Kent entering a phone-booth and, a few minutes later, Superman emerging. Yet, Clark Kent *is* Superman. So, what happened is just as much a case of Superman entering and Superman emerging, or Superman entering and Clark Kent emerging. Yet these alternatives seem false. The paradox, thus far, involves no psychology, but psychology soon puts in an appearance. Why do we resist the alternative descriptions, even when we know that Superman is Clark Kent? Well, we picture the event in a certain dressing. In fact, let us use a Cross-Dressing version that requires no Superman magic or mystery.

CROSS-DRESSING

David delights in dressing up, playing different roles. In womanly mode, he is the highly desirable, elegant and cool Lady Davinia, stilettos so sharp. In masculine mode, he is rough and tough, the leather-clad Dave, mean machine to the ready. Some girls fancy Dave – who knows why? – yet are unmoved by Davinia. They think Dave and Davinia are distinct people. The girls kiss Dave, not Davinia. Yet how can one and the same person be both kissed and not kissed at the same time?

Many, many things, it seems, are true of Dave, yet not true of Davinia. Men, for example, buy champagne for Davinia, but never for Dave. Assuming restriction to heterosexual girls who fancy Dave, an example of the puzzle is set out in the following.

Girls kiss Dave.
Dave is Davinia.
Therefore, girls kiss Davinia.

Girls do kiss Dave, and Dave is Davinia, yet we – even we in the know – may well resist agreeing that the conclusion is true. Thus it is that we are pushed into the contradiction that Dave is kissed by girls, and Dave (being Davinia) is not kissed by girls.

Unwittingly, the girls hold, so to speak, two different files on David – one associated with Dave, one with Davinia. Thus it is that we can explain their different beliefs about Dave and Davinia and their kissing desires. The puzzle, though, addresses *us*. We know about the identity of Dave and Davinia; so, why do *we* resist the conclusion that girls kiss Davina? Well, we also have different dossiers, pictures and stories associated with the different names – dossiers that we keep apart, given the radically different roles that David plays.

'Do girls kiss Davinia? – yes or no?' We should resist being bullied into compliance. Let the answer be, 'It is not as simple as that; the girls kiss Davinia, thinking (s)he is Dave.'

'Can you play chess without the queen?'

That question from Wittgenstein should lead to hesitation and explanation, not to a quick one-word answer.

Suppose Miss Jones weds and becomes Mrs Smith. When did she first meet her husband? Before they were married? But he was not then her husband. After they were married? You mean, she married a complete stranger? Really?

Thus it is that we may anguish pointlessly with the Husband Puzzle. Thus it is that we should beware the insistent demand for the unqualified 'Yes' or 'No'.

6 Ravens, lotteries, medical matters –

and a gruesome tale or two

. . . in which we discover how, by staying in bed, we can yet conduct fieldwork and research of an ornithological kind; how some gruesome tales may make us baffled in our expectations; and how those medical results may not be as bad as they seem.

Down on the farm, we may be surprised to find philosophical debate. However, on McDonald's farm, there are intelligent partridges – though not intelligent enough – reflecting on what a wonderful world their world is: day after day they receive fine food from Farmer McDonald. They ignore the Cassandra among them – a scraggy old pigeon – who warns against such philosophical contentment. And so, the fine and feathered regularly feed and expect, and regularly expect and feed, until one day when snows snow, sleighs sleigh and the bells jingle, McDonald's morning footsteps bring forth no sunrise delights, just hands in unexpected wringing motion – and a knife. The fine and feathered in due course find themselves, were they able to find themselves at all, at the yuletide feast – while the Cassandra pigeon reflects on the value of being scraggy and unfine, small and unplump.

This is Bertrand Russell's tale of a chicken, inflated to partridge for today's table, with the thrill and frill of Cassandra's warnings. McDonald has cooked the partridges' goose. Partridges should realize that past farmer performance is no good guide to farmer's future performance. Yet we all do form expectations on the basis of past evidence – what else have we to go on? – and Cassandra may have justified her wails of woe by previous Decembers' footfalls.

Inferring how things will be in the future from how they have been in the past is an example of inductive reasoning, not to be confused with mathematical induction, mentioned in the Sorites' context of the previous chapter.

Water freezes at approximately 0 degrees centigrade – well, the water observed so far has – hence, we infer that all water, in typical circumstances, freezes around that temperature. Perhaps we have observed numerous ravens, noticing that they are black. We may inductively infer that all ravens are black. Induction is, indeed, usually characterized as moving us from *some* instances to *all*, from the particular to the universal – though it may move us from observed particulars to unobserved particulars. All ravens to date have been black; so, I infer that the next raven lined up for me is black.

RAVENS

Encountering some ravens that are black constitutes some evidence that all ravens are black – let us assume. However, if all ravens are black, then anything that is not black is not a raven. 'All ravens are black' amounts to 'All non-black items are non-ravens'. A purple pillow is a non-black non-raven, so that ought to provide some small evidence in favour of 'All non-black items are non-ravens' and hence, mysteriously, the same small evidence for 'All ravens are black'. This is ornithology from the bedroom. The orange alarm clock, the yellow wallpaper, the red duvet – the list goes on – all contribute helpful support for the claim that all ravens are black.

A certain German philosopher of the 1940s, C. G. Hempel, set the ravens swooping within the philosophical community. Let us muse on some background.

Just because things have regularly happened in the past, or over here, we cannot logically deduce that they will carry on happening in the future, or over there. Even if all observed ravens are black, it logically follows not at all that currently unobserved and future ravens are black. Even if observed regularities have themselves regularly continued, we still have the problem of why that regularity of regularities will continue.

David Hume, most associated with the basic problem of induction, settled for habit. We do just form habits and expectations from repeated experiences. After seeing numerous ravens that are black, we find ourselves expecting future ravens to be black. The expectation, as Hume saw, is no justification, no justification at all.

We do, though, consider some inductive arguments bad, some good. To generalize from one cat's obesity to all cats being fat is crazy or lazy – and from the fact that all your male friends are trustworthy, it would be a bad move to conclude that all males are trustworthy. Yet, past regularities seem rightly to lead us to expect rain when certain clouds form, planes to fly and not turn to olive oil, and ten glasses of wine to lead to slurred garrulity in some and slumber in others. These are surely good inductive moves, though without any logical guarantee of success: freak weather conditions occur; some people seem able to hold their drink – and, while planes do not liquefy (well, not yet), they occasionally fall from the skies.

We all form expectations on the basis of noticed regularities, yet which regularities is it wise to notice? There has been the regularity for each one of us that, since birth, we have breathed. Should we conclude that for all days in the future we shall breathe? The partridges hit unlucky on which regularities they chose. We all hit unlucky eventually – though whether death is a misfortune is for Chapter 9. Hempel's Ravens Paradox prompts our thinking about evidence. Let us mull things over.

Bedroom research – ravens and grue

Encountering ravens, and noting that they are always black, contributes in a teeny way to evidence in favour of the universal generalization, all ravens are black. Well, let us assume the acceptability of that inductive enumeration. A black raven is said to *confirm* the generalization: this sounds as if it could mean 'make certain'; but this is not intended. We speak, instead, of instances *supporting* a generalization: the support may be teeny. The pink teddy bear supports the generalization 'All non-black things are non-ravens.' This latter generalization, as already implied, is logically equivalent to 'All ravens are black'; they amount to the same thing. So the evidence that supports one should equally support the other. Yet, it is paradoxical that a pink teddy bear supports a scientific hypothesis about ravens. What has gone wrong – if anything?

Is there something amiss with the logical equivalence between 'All ravens are black' and 'All non-black items are non-ravens', the latter being the 'contrapositive' of the former? In some intuitive sense, the two propositions do say the same thing; so it appears reasonable that whatever is good evidence for one is good evidence for the other.

The paradox, of course, assumes that a generalization is supported to some extent by its instances. That is not implausible. Yet, a conclusion reached – that Penelope's pink teddy bear is support in favour of the raven generalization – is paradoxical. Perhaps we should bite the bullet and accept the paradoxical conclusion as true.

Hempel bites. The pink teddy bear, purple pillow and so on, all offer support for the raven generalization – and the same degree of support as for 'All non-black items are non-ravens.' How should we respond?

Well, we should note that these items – the pink teddy bear, purple pillow – offer support equally well for 'All ravens are blue', 'All ravens are pepper pots' and so forth. It seems pretty negligible support for the black raven generalization, in view of its support for these opposing generalizations. A further reflection is that the support that the pink teddy bear provides for 'All non-black items are non-ravens' is exceptionally slender. Perhaps we need to take into account the vast number of non-black things compared with the number of ravens. With non-black things radically outnumbering ravens, we should do better to support the 'All non-black things are non-ravens' by concentrating on ravens, to see if any are not black.

The best way to support a generalization need not be by searching for instances that directly satisfy its descriptive terms. The best way to proceed depends on context. For example, suppose you are at a bird sanctuary, the numerous ravens being pointed out. They are all black so far, but then you notice something pink in the trees. It would be useful to find out more about it – for example, discovering it to be a teddy bear and no raven.

Instances of a generalization paradoxically can offer support for the generalization's contrary. 'All pigeons fly outside London's W1 postal district.' Well, we encounter numerous instances of pigeon flight outside, but – unless more information is available – the sight of pigeons in adjoining postal districts would be evidence for their flight in W1, not its absence. After all, pigeons are no respecters of postal districts. Resolution of Hempel's Ravens, then, needs attention to context in determining when instances of a generalization are supportive. 'Non-black' fails to describe items with much relevant similarity concerning future behaviour. 'Flight outside of W1', 'non-black items', 'non-ravens' are not typical ways in which we classify things. Nor is 'grue'.

Grue? The gruesome tale of 'grue' has been embellished over the years, since Nelson Goodman's introduction. Grue makes us wonder why we favour some classifications over others.

GRUE

All emeralds examined to date are green: that allegedly offers support for the claim that all emeralds are green. Now, here is 'grue'. Items are grue if they have been examined before a future date, say before the year 2025, and are green, otherwise are blue. So, all the evidence to date also points to all emeralds being grue, hence being, from and including 2025, blue. Paradoxically, the same evidence supports inconsistent claims. One line of reasoning leads us to expect emeralds to be green in 2025; another line leads us to expect blue.

Although the definition of 'grue' first invoked 'examined', others dropped it without, it seems, any Goodmanian protest. Yet others have taken Grue – the New Riddle of Induction – way beyond induction, into a radical scepticism alluded to by Wittgenstein. We defer that gem until Chapter 10, staying here with Goodman's examined gem. Goodman, sometime lover of formal symbols, spoke of a future time t; we popped in an arbitrary date for clarity.

The current evidence is such that all observed emeralds are green and all observed emeralds are grue. So, the very same evidence – depending on the term – points to generalizations that cannot both be true. Let us also introduce 'bleen' with the same conditions as 'grue', save that the descriptions within the definition are reversed: items are bleen if they have been examined before the year 2025 and are blue, otherwise are green. When we consider predictions, perhaps we should think of the sky as bleen rather than blue.

Of course, the puzzle does not just engage colours and years. We could move into other properties and even items – even emeroses – whose definitions involve reference to any future times, however close or distant. The intolerable result is that any instances seem to support virtually any generalization concerning those instances. Something has gone wrong – or inductive reasoning is completely without justification.

Something has gone wrong, but what? Some criticize the term 'grue' as deviant and artificial, but it is clearly defined. Scientists do introduce new terms. Some attack the time element, claiming that 'grue' changes; yet the definition does not change, though to tell whether something is grue, we do need to consult the calendar. It can be argued, in response, that 'green' and 'blue' also contain time elements. After all, 'green' applies to those things examined before 2025 and are grue, otherwise to bleen things. Which terms contain temporal elements perhaps depends on where we start.

What justifies our preference for 'green' over 'grue'? True, we have theories of light waves and photons that explain differences in our regular colours, but we could doubtless reconstruct such theories so that they contained inspired grue-like deviancy in their concepts to match 'grue' and 'bleen'.

If we turn to the biographies of the terms 'green' and 'grue', we see that 'green' is entrenched: we have used it and synonyms and translations for centuries. Our use perhaps shows that it has survival value for us – though only to date, of course. However, using 'grue' would also have reaped the same value for us. It would presumably have reaped benefits for a gruesome tribe that partially categorized the world in terms of grue and bleen – and would continue to do so, at least until 2025.

With the 'examining' to the fore in the 'grue' definition, let us note that examining can affect what is discovered. Shining a light, to see how dark it is, is not typically the wisest of moves. Consider refrigerators whose lights come on when and only when their doors are opened. All observed interiors of fridges are lit. This supports the generalization that all fridge interiors are lit. Yet, given what we know, it would be better to read the evidence as all observed fridge interiors are *lit when doors are open*.

Scientists seek to take account of their effects on what they observe. Indeed, this has led to increasing awareness that, given that we exist, the universe's properties obviously include those necessary for our existence. The awareness has, by the way, brought forth a muddle of anthropic principles. We do not, though, usually think that being observed is essential to the items observed. We do not argue that all *observed* emeralds are observed; so this is evidence for the generalization that all emeralds are observed.

We could add a temporal element to the refrigerator example. Maybe from 2025, to save energy, fridges must no longer have interior lights: so, we could sensibly form the generalization 'All fridges are lit internally when doors open and before time 2025, otherwise unlit.' Perhaps we would introduce a grue-type term for items that possess the feature of interior lights until the energy-saving regulations are operative. Here we have an explanation of what is going on in using such a new term. Defenders of the 'grue' use, though, lack explanations of why examination makes a difference and only until 2025. With refrigerators, had they not been inspected for interior lighting, they would not then have been lit. In contrast, with the emeralds, we believe that, had they not been examined, they would still have been green – and hence not grue – but we may still ask, what good evidence do we have for our belief?

The Grue Riddle has us questioning whether observed samples are representative samples; yet the understanding of 'grue' ensures that we cannot secure a representative sample – for all the instances we have to go on are examined and before 2025. The hypothesis that all observed emeralds are grue, if true, rules out our discovering whether there are any blue emeralds before 2025, for 'grue' applies to any blue items before 2025 only if unexamined. Hence, we may as well bring the time location in 'grue' down to right now. Then, any future observed emerald, on the 'grue' hypothesis, is expected to be blue, even though observed. The only good reason we can have for that blue expectation is that our observed emeralds to date fail to constitute a representative emerald sample.

Let us take matters further. Suppose we have observed all emeralds that exist to date – and the 'grue' definition has 'now' or today's time and date replacing the '2025'. The grue generalization raises the question. how do we know that past and present emeralds constitute a representative sample of all emeralds, including therefore those formed in the future? If emeralds forming afresh is too long term, consider daffodils. All daffodils to date, when blooming, have been, say, yellow. Equally, then, they have all been yellue (yellow until now, then blue). The daffodil season is over. Let us pretend that currently no daffodil blooms. We 'yellue' speakers, with the hypothesis that all daffodils are yellue, should expect the next season's daffodils to be blue.

The Grue Riddle is now collapsing into the standard problem of induction, save that it also encourages us to wonder whether what *we* count as regularities may be seen by others as irregular. Our expectations are based on regularities, but, as Goodman writes, 'Regularities are where you find them, and you can find them anywhere.' That thought leads into a meaning paradox, to be entertained in the last chapter. What makes a future use the *same* as a past?

If I doubt . . .

Induction is one source of scepticism, of doubting whether we know things. If we are not justified in our beliefs about the future, how can we possibly know anything about the future? – yet paradoxically we act *as if* we do. And we do. You know full well that in the next few minutes, the print before your eyes will not leap off the page, transforming into a walrus that proceeds to dust. People sceptical of knowledge of the future are often relaxed about the past and present; yet if what undermines knowledge of the future is the possibility of error, then we should also be sceptical of knowledge concerning the past and present, for, of course, we may be mistaken about them – and sometimes we are.

EVIL GENIUS

If I know something, then I cannot be mistaken about the matter. But concerning the vast majority of things that I claim to know, I can be mistaken. After all, I do not know that there is not an all-powerful evil genius out to deceive me. Hence, I do not know most things that I think I know.

Scepticism about the future is a scepticism confined to a particular locality: the future. Localities about which some people are strongly sceptical today include religion, ethics and aesthetics – and perhaps we should add economics and, most recently, banking. Maybe knowledge is unlikely or impossible, if addressing the realms of God, moral values, or beauty – or some banking activities – but not impossible, if addressing those of mathematics and physics.

In the seventeenth century, Descartes sought to offer a global scepticism, trying to doubt everything that he could, and then trying to overcome that scepticism. With regard to our beliefs and what we take to be knowledge, could we not be mistaken? We can surely doubt whether there are seas and skies and birds and bees and banks and stock-markets and even this book before us. We could be dreaming or be but brains in vats – or there could be the evil demon creating an unreal world, a virtual world. This is paradoxical. We started off with some sensible beliefs and recognition of our fallibility – and ended up with an extreme global scepticism.

Descartes' escape route from scepticism involved, first, uncovering something that he could not doubt, secondly, working out that God existed, and thirdly, realizing that God would not deceive us if we used our reason aright. Thus it was that Descartes reached the light of knowledge. Well, that is an exceptionally brief outline.

'However much I am being deceived or making mistakes, I must surely exist. In thinking about these matters, I exist.'

That is Descartes' line, yet if doubting is a matter of what one psychologically can do, then Descartes is even mistaken about this. Ply him with sufficient wine and he may crazily doubt whether he exists, even though he would, of course, still be existing. Yet, whatever we may or may not psychologically achieve, are there not some beliefs that are so guarded or minimal that they are true, maybe even making themselves true? There certainly are self-refuting beliefs. For example, if I think that I do not exist, in thinking I at least am existing – so the thought is self-refuting. In contrast, we can have practical self-fulfilment: recall the Placebo Paradox, where the belief that I shall get better makes me better, though without guarantee.

The Paradox of Self-Fulfilling Belief comes about by seeking the most minimal belief that can guarantee its truth, a belief even more minimal than the self-fulfilling 'I exist'. A seemingly reasonable thought is that if I merely believe that I am believing, then my belief makes itself true. Now, if I believe that I believe men and women are equal, I could be mistaken: I may come to realize that I did not really believe such equality, though it would be true that I was believing. If, though, the content of my belief is solely that I hold the belief – my belief is solely about itself – surely my belief is immune from error. Or is it? Let us see. 'I believe this very belief.' What is being believed? The answer is the belief that I believe this very belief. But what is that belief? – and so we could question and answer, without end. There is nothing which provides a content to the belief. A belief with no content is no belief at all. Recall how the self-referential 'This very proposition is true' expresses, it seems, no proposition at all.

The Puzzle of Empty Knowing could be added to this group of self-referential paradoxes. Consider 'I know that this proposition is true', where 'this proposition' refers to 'I know that this proposition is true.' There is nothing there to know. We appear also to have vacuities, though also additional complexities, with the Knower's 'I know this very proposition is false', and the Believer's 'I believe this very proposition is false.' Further, if we read the following as self-referential, then 'I hope that this very hope is fulfilled' expresses no hope; 'I know what I know in knowing this' expresses no knowledge; and 'Obey this very order to obey' gives no order.

Returning to Descartes' labours on these matters, his thoughts typically possessed content, in contrast to the emptiness of the thoughts just mentioned above. At least it seems to him *as if* there is a fire blazing before him, *as if* he is wearing a cloak – and so forth. Descartes thought that he had shown that thinking – being conscious, having experiences – was essential to him. That is, that he could not exist without consciousness. There is no sleep, it seems, without dreaming experiences, according to Descartes; presumably, we must then be pretty forgetful. Of course, whenever Descartes thought about these matters, he would indeed be thinking; he might well notice that fact. However, that does not support Descartes' implausible conclusion, namely that he could not exist without thinking.

Descartes' error might have resulted from the fact that whenever he existed without thinking, he would not be thinking and hence would not be noticing his absence of thought. The error may remind us of the refrigerator's interior being lit when the door is open. Noticing the light on, when looking inside the fridge, does not establish the state of the interior lighting when the door is closed and there is no noticing.

If Descartes' escape route from the evil genius fails, is the right conclusion that we know nothing? That conclusion would also suggest that we do not know whether the argument itself is any good. Perhaps the conclusion should be that all is doubtful, including that conclusion. If we held to that general conclusion, we should have to reinvent our everyday old distinctions. If all is doubtful, we should still need to distinguish within the so-called 'doubtful' matters, distinguishing between, on the one hand, the existence of a book here right now, water's eventually boiling when heated, and the existence of trees and treacle, ditches and dew; and, on the other hand, the prediction that the filly Lady Jane will win the Kentucky Derby and your unreliable belief that you remembered to put the cat out. Scepticism can, so to speak, push things to such extremes that nothing is achieved; no wheels are turned.

At an initial stage, Descartes thought that he could not know a whole range of things because he could be misled about them. If we know anything, then we are not mistaken. Knowledge possession, though, neither requires infallibility in the sense that we must lack the capacity to make mistakes, nor that what we know could not have been otherwise. We know that the planet Venus orbits the Sun, but we might have thought otherwise, or it might not have done. Either way – or both ways – we might then have possessed a false belief and not knowledge. There are, though, more puzzles lurking. Here is one.

HARMAN'S PARADOX

If I know that a proposition is true, then I know that any evidence against that proposition must be misleading. Such evidence ought to be ignored. Yet, even though I know many things, surely I ought not automatically to ignore contrary evidence.

We could add that, if we know something, we must already have sufficient evidence. Thus, once we have knowledge, we can stay in bed and do no more researches, delighting in the Lazy Puzzle.

The lazy life with regard to our knowledge is paradoxical even if desirable, and the laziness should be resisted. Possibly Harman's Paradox overlooks that, if we know something, we may not know that we know. Even when we are confident that we know something, any new evidence needs assessment – and the result could be a justified change of mind, making us realize that, after all, we failed to know what we thought we knew. Claiming to know ought to be no mere whim; but it ought also not to set what is claimed in stone, with no preparedness for revision. In any revision we need, of course, to avoid contradictions; we should surely seek consistency. Or should we?

Medical matters, humility and lotteries

Your doctor may have good evidence for believing a range of medical claims. She announces them, one after the other, as her sincere and firm beliefs, all well grounded. You respond that it is likely that she has a few wrong: after all, it is rational to believe that doctors make mistakes – there is good evidence for that.

The scenario sketched is not odd, though possibly touches on tactlessness. Let us not, by the way, engage the complexities that, in practice, some beliefs are likely to be firmly held, and others held with less conviction. If your belief that she has made some mistakes is true, then at least one of her beliefs is false. If all of her beliefs are true, then your belief is false. That's life.

The doctor may, though, be aware that doctors – all of us – sometimes get things wrong. We are fallible creatures. Human as she is – and in humility – she believes that a few of her medical beliefs are mistaken. This is a rational position to hold. So, it is rational for the doctor to believe both that each claim on her list of medical beliefs is true and that it is not the case that all the claims on the list are true. She is wittingly holding some contradictory beliefs – a tribute to, yet also a puzzle of, medical humility.

To make the Medical Humility Puzzle vivid, suppose her medical list is short, containing solely propositions P, Q and R. Given her refreshing humility, we also suppose that she has the further belief: that is, she believes that it is not the case that P and Q and R are *all* true. So, of one of those medical beliefs – she does not know which – she both believes it true and believes it not true. She holds contradictory beliefs – yet rationally so, or so it seems. The example could generate a self-referential Liar-type problem, were her further belief to be included as one of her medical beliefs. This is because if P, Q and R are all true, then her further belief is made true by its not being true, and made not true by its being true. Recall Russell on Moore's honesty at the end of Chapter 2.

In our simplified example of just three medical beliefs, she may easily review the three, be reassured of their truth, and so no longer believe one to be false. However, with 33 medical beliefs, or 303, or, if we turn to authors, all the statements sincerely made in their books . . . ? Well, where large numbers of our beliefs are involved, it appears rational to believe that some are false.

Holding in combination a belief and also the belief that you are mistaken in that belief – '*p*, but I am mistaken over *p*' – is absurd and may remind us of Moore's Paradox. Holding a vast number of beliefs, yet also believing that you are mistaken about some, seems, though, far from absurd. The medical humility example is but a version of the Preface Paradox. A sincere author, committed to the claims in her book, asserts in the Preface that there are bound to be mistakes. Spreading beyond books and doctors, we have the more general Paradox of Fallibility. We all hold vast numbers of beliefs, yet we recognize that we make mistakes, so surely we believe – or ought to believe – that not all the beliefs are true.

Perhaps these paradoxes should remind us that, even when we hold a set of well-justified beliefs, we ought often also to believe that we *may* be mistaken about some. That is not inconsistent – well, seemingly not – and, further, it is a far cry from someone consciously assenting to a seeming belief of the form *p* and not-*p*, such as Vesuvius will erupt tomorrow and Vesuvius will not erupt tomorrow.

Continuing the medical theme, you learn that your blood test was positive, though your doctor points out that statistically one in 10,000 such tests yields a false result. Despite the small chance of error, you are surely rational in believing that your blood test is accurate. There is nothing special, though, about your blood test; so, concerning each of 10,000 tests, randomly taken, you would be right to believe that it is accurate. Yet you also believe that a teeny percentage is inaccurate. Here, again, you cling to a set of inconsistent beliefs: you believe this test and that one and the other – and so on – are each accurate, yet you believe that not all the tests are accurate. This inconsistency is often presented via a lottery.

LOTTERY

You buy a lottery ticket. Your chances of winning are one in a million. If you knew that your ticket would lose, it would be a pretty silly purchase. However, the odds are so stacked against you that you are surely justified in *believing* that your ticket will lose. There is, though, nothing special about your ticket. With regard to each ticket, you are justified in believing that it is a loser. Yet, one ticket will win; so, added to those justified beliefs is the further justified belief (indeed, knowledge) that not *all* the tickets are losers. Yet can it really be rational to hold inconsistent beliefs?

Given sufficient time and will, you could run through all your justified beliefs about the lottery matter: Ticket 1 will lose; Ticket 2 will lose; Ticket 3 will lose – and so on. Yet, inconsistently, you also believe that one of them will not lose.

This conclusion of inconsistency is avoided, if you ought not to believe of any given ticket that it will lose: perhaps good justification needs to guarantee the truth of a belief – and your ticket's losing is not guaranteed. But that demand on good justification is highly implausible, making all well-justified beliefs, if properly well justified, into knowledge. Yet we are surely justified in believing a whole range of matters on the basis of good but inconclusive evidence – evidence such that our beliefs may turn out false and, hence, certainly not constituting knowledge. In view of the evidence, you may be well justified in believing the trains to be running this evening, but cancellations can occur – and perhaps they will. We may rightly believe the lectures will be given, but there could be unexpected timetable changes. The known high probability of an event – such as your ticket losing – makes it rational to believe in that losing event occurring, even though the belief may, just may, turn out mistaken, as you hope.

If the teeny possibility of my ticket winning prevents me from rationally believing that it is a loser, then we can flounder again in seas of global scepticism, for it is teenily possible that you may be dreaming or deceived by an evil genius. Even if these outlandish possibilities can be ruled out, everyday possibilities cannot. Suppose on average one in 10,000 people are mugged in your girlfriend's neighbourhood each day: ought you – because of the teeny possibility of mugging – conclude that you are not justified in believing that your girlfriend has had an un-mugged day? Ought you to conclude that you are unjustified in expecting to see your girlfriend undamaged this evening?

The mugging example differs from the lottery. The lottery is purely random, whereas there is a variety of factors relevant to your girlfriend and possible mugging – where she is likely to shop, the strength of her glare, and the black karate belt she so delicately displays. Nonetheless, if the minuscule possibility of your lottery ticket's winning rules out your being justified in believing the ticket a loser, then, it seems, the minuscule possibility of your girlfriend being mugged, being a 'muggee', rules out your being justified in believing your planned candle-lit dinner will be with your un-mugged loved one.

Perhaps we should accept that it is rational wittingly to hold two contradictory beliefs, as in the lottery; but that opens a can of worms, one worm being whether it even makes sense to say that one wittingly and consciously can believe both p and not-p together. Would it then be belief?

Arguably, though, we need to be more sensitive to cases, circumstances and what is involved in believing. Maybe it cannot be rational to believe – perhaps it is not even possible to believe – a claim of the form p and not-p, where the alleged believing involves conscious assent at the time. Try to imagine sincerely and consciously believing, say, both that today is Sunday and today is not Sunday. But denying the rationality, even sense, of believing p and not-p is not the same as saying that it cannot be rational to believe p and also be rational to believe not-p, when these are distinct belief states not brought together in consciousness with their contents fully exposed.

Diagnosis: good or bad?

Resolution of the above paradoxes continues to generate controversy: this contrasts with some 'paradoxes' in the rationality woods of probability calculations. The conclusions strike people as paradoxical because they are so counter-intuitive – because, indeed, most of us are pretty bad at probability assessments. There may be evolutionary explanations for this: roughly, in times of danger, it is better to play safe than achieve accuracy. Even if only a few snakes are poisonous, it could be wiser to avoid any snake and anything that looks like a snake than to stay and muse upon the probability of its being poisonous.

Recall the blood test in which you tested positive – perhaps for some nasty condition C. Let us change the figures, making them more manageable. C on average occurs in one in 100 tested people with your symptoms. The test is 90 per cent accurate. Woe and despair. You probably think you almost certainly have C. After all, of 100 people tested, the test gives the correct result in 90 cases, and an incorrect result in ten cases, saying negative when positive or positive when negative, either way equally likely, we unrealistically assume for simplicity. The woe and despair is, though, irrational – despite that 90 per cent accuracy rate. This False Positives Puzzle ought not to puzzle, once the reasoning is set out.

Suppose 1,000 people with your symptoms are tested: there are likely to be ten with C and 990 without C. The test errs in 10 per cent of the cases: so it is likely to be wrong in 100 of the 1,000 cases. That means, in all likelihood, that nine of the ten people with C will be correctly told they are positive. However 10 per cent of the negatives – namely, 99 people – will be wrongly told they are positive. So, of the 108 positives, only nine are correct. That means that your chance of having C is less than 10 per cent – radically different from the feared 90 per cent.

Depressingly, various surveys of medical practitioners suggest that they are almost as bad as the general public in assessing such probabilities – well, maybe. Another depression is the current tendency to aggregate statistics, providing an overall view of comparative performances of, for example, hospitals, police authorities and schools. Here is an example, to justify the depression.

When comparing hospital survival rates, successful crime detections and school examination passes, Hospital Happy, Police Force Forceful and School Successful bathe in much better overall performance rates than Hospital Humble, Police Force Feeble and School Slothful – as they became popularly known. Yet, if we dig into the figures, we could find that Humble, Feeble and Slothful do much better than Happy, Forceful and Successful. Paradoxically, they may do much better both in, say, difficult operations and in easy operations, in major crimes and in minor, and with pupils from poor home backgrounds and those from good. How can this be?

The answer to this paradox – Simpson's Paradox – is that the overall aggregate figures can utterly mislead: they can mislead because the so-called successful institutions deal with very few of the difficult cases, handling mainly easy operations, minor crimes and pupils with good backgrounds. Even though the allegedly successful institutions are worse performers with both the difficult cases and the easy cases, their high proportion of easy cases means that their performances in the easy cases swamp the other figures. Of course, in all the cases differences in successful outcomes could well result largely from factors outside the control of the relevant institutions – factors such as smoking, leisure facilities and genetic make-up.

'Lies, damned lies and statistics!' – yet it is a mistake to think that statistics can be used to prove anything, just anything. Caution is, though, always required. After all, as the number of birds far exceeds the number of elephants, it is true that most creatures that are birds or elephants cannot trample us to death. Yet, when we encounter an elephant, we ought not to conclude that it is unlikely to be able to do some trampling.

Being a bird or an elephant – a birphant – is a poor way of classifying creatures, when concerned about trampling dangers; performing well at operations overall is paradoxically a poor way of classifying hospitals when concerned about the likelihood of our surviving – and to think otherwise leads to puzzles of a gruesome kind in more ways than one.

7   Morality and politics –
blackmail, buck-passing and voting

> *. . . where we encounter some dubious and guilty characters, from blackmailers to investors to murderers – or are they really innocent? – and we puzzle over democracy, prisoners' dilemmas and our altruism – or are we really selfish?*

'When I'm good, I'm very, very good; but when I'm bad, I'm better.'

This splendid quip, courtesy of Mae West, sounds paradoxical, yet simply trades on ambiguities and various readings. When we speak of what is good or bad, we are not always raising matters of morality. A good knife is not a moral knife. 'Her looks are good, but her singing bad' may recommend silent romance, but nothing moral. Even when romantic ventures are morally bad, the sexual dalliances could well be better than very, very good. Of course 'good' and 'bad' often do place morality on the agenda, as does talk of virtues such as courage, honesty and modesty, and feelings such as admiration, remorse and shame.

Morality concerns what we ought or ought not to do. It may often conflict – or at least seem to conflict – with what we want or want not to do. We really ought to resist the tempting delicious infidelity, even though we prefer no resistance. As with 'good's and 'bad's, there are, though, non-moral or amoral 'ought's: they tell us what to do, *if* we want to secure ends of a certain sort. 'If you want to kill him, you ought to aim at the heart' deploys no moral 'ought', but tells of appropriate means, given an end. Moral 'ought's address questions of which ends are permissible as well as which means. Morally you ought not to harm others, full stop – well, at least a significant pause until some greater benefit perhaps can justify an exception. Arguably, you ought not to steal someone's organs to save lives, even though the end is morally desirable in that many people would benefit.

Morality has not been much to the fore when deploying 'paradox' labels. We do not expect contradictions in logic and reason; so, when we meet them they hit us as paradoxical, surprising and challenging. In morality, conflicts and differences are so familiar that we see 'problems' rather than paradoxes. We do not expect the rigours of logic, though we ought to – arguably a moral 'ought'.

Many people casually accept a relativism in what is morally right and wrong. Now, that can generate a Relativism Puzzle. The alleged relativity of morality leads some people to conclude that cultures ought not to interfere in each other's moral practices: we ought to be tolerant. Those 'ought's though are moral. They are not relative. So, contrary to the starting point, there are some non-relative moral values. Many preachers of relativism would dislike lining up with defenders of the moral permissibility of slavery, female genital mutilation, and the killing of non-believers.

Rejection of relativism is not a denial of genuine moral dilemmas. It is not surprising that there are many such dilemmas, given that morality requires weighing up competing demands, from welfare to rights to mercy to fairness to freedoms to virtues – and so on. Indeed, there is, here, the Puzzle of Weighing, for do we know what weight freedoms possess compared with security, or arts funding compared with medical research and aiding the starving? There are clear cases – lying in order to save many lives is surely right – but imprisonment without trial because of possible terrorism? Road traffic despite the many injuries? In practice, governments, families, individuals muddle through, while sometimes pretending a firm basis exists for their fine judgements.

Let us focus first on some moral problems with the 'paradox' label openly worn. Puzzles of weighing lurk within.

BLACKMAIL

Informing Senator Saintly that you intend to tell the press of his promiscuous ways is not immoral. Asking Senator Saintly for money – perhaps you fancy a world cruise – is not immoral. Yet, put them together, letting him know that if he fails to hand over the cash, you will go public, and we have blackmail, considered highly immoral. Why?

DIVESTITURE

I own shares in a company that, as I now realize, is engaged in morally dubious activities. I ought to sell the shares to keep my hands clean; but I am thereby involving buyers in those dubious activities. If it is morally wrong for me to hold the shares, then it is morally wrong for them. Religious groups divest themselves of immoral investments, wittingly sullying the hands of others.

Both paradoxes are presented here as moral, but they also raise matters for political authorities – for example, the relationship between companies and shareholders, and whether a state should have laws prohibiting blackmail. This is not to suggest that what is lawful and what is moral maintain the same spread or ought to do so. There are many actions that seem immoral – for example, lying – yet that are often legal; and there are many morally worthy actions – such as certain civil disobediences – that may be illegal.

With legality in the air, we may notice, in passing, the Paradox of Perfect Punishment. The perfect punishment would surely deter people from committing crimes, while causing the least possible harms. Suppose you want to stop illegal parking. Make the punishment horrendous – torture or the loss of limbs – so horrendous that no one would risk the punishment. In such circumstances, there would be no illegal parking – and also no exercise of the punishment. Maybe, just possibly, we have missed out some relevant factors in the scenario – but we move on.

Blackmail, casting couches and supermarkets

Blackmail has a bad press – and so do the blackmailers' victims, if they fail to meet the demands. Blackmailers often threaten public exposure of discreditable behaviour. Most people evaluate blackmail as morally wrong: in many countries it is illegal. The paradox has two stages: the first generates, at best, something mildly paradoxical; the second has more bite. Let us consider the first – first.

If Senator Saintly is indeed a philanderer, cheating on his wife, perhaps involved with numerous call-girls, many people would find it morally permissible for someone in the know to inform his wife and the press. Suppose that I have uncovered his shenanigans. It is, of course, permissible for me to tell Saintly of my intentions to expose him. It is also morally permissible for me to ask a senator for money, even if he does not want to give any. However, if I combine the two, asking Saintly for money, letting him know that if he pays me, my lips shall be sealed about his peccadilloes, then that is blackmail. It is blackmail – even if he accepts the exposure, deciding against paying. How can two permissible activities combine to make for the impermissible?

A moment's reflection suggests that this is no deep paradox. It relies upon the fallacy that if what is true of A is also true of B, then it should hold true of A and B combined. As we mooted when discussing lottery paradoxes, you may hold contradictory beliefs P and Q – but they are never to the fore of your mind in combination. Were they to become so and the light dawns, you would either not know what to believe or find yourself rejecting one. Drawing nearer to action, right now we may yearn for champagne and also for chocolate, but not thereby yearn for champagne and chocolate combined. Working in the opposite direction, you fancy a gin and tonic, yet have no fancy for a tonic separate from the gin. Returning to permissibles in combination, it is permissible for Jack and Jill to engage in sexual delights and also permissible for Jack and Jill to be in church, but it is not permissible for sexual activity to take place in church, even if it sometimes happens – and even if claimed to be to the glory of God and not merely to the flesh.

The assumption that the combination of two permissible activities is itself permissible manifests a fallacy of composition, a fallacy met in Chapter 5. An explanation, though, should be available of why combinations lack features of their parts, when they do. Champagne does not taste well with chocolate; tonic lacks the bite if lacking the gin – and holy surroundings demand a certain reverence, a reverence that is usually understood as incompatible with bodily entanglements. What is it about blackmail combinations that make them morally impermissible, yet their parts permissible?

Blackmailers typically blackmail to benefit themselves – usually with money. Blackmail has a monetary request given teeth by the exposure threat; but why should that dental link make the combination of request and threat morally different from its parts? True, the request now hits home. Failure to comply means that Saintly is harmed by the unwanted exposure; and compliance means that he is harmed by the financial loss. However, because of the blackmail, Saintly receives an option that would otherwise be missing – namely, not to be exposed – an option which he may eagerly embrace, given the alternative.

The paradox – first stage – demonstrates nothing more than what sometimes happens, so to speak, on a casting couch. There is nothing wrong in film directors asking actresses to sleep with them; there is nothing wrong in directors casting actresses in their films. It strikes people, though, as morally wrong for directors to cast actresses only if they will undergo the sleeping. The Casting Couch Puzzle is easily solved. Casting should be based on actors' role suitability, not their bed suitability and willingness (unless it is that kind of film). Whether I expose Saintly's behaviour should be determined by whether it morally merits exposure, not whether I am the happy recipient of blackmail money. 'Horses for courses.'

At one extreme, when the activities in question morally ought to be exposed, the blackmailer is manifesting a character defect, being prepared to buy himself off from his duty to release the information. The information may be about fraud or politicians' hypocrisy or company directors' dubious dealings: the threatened exposure may be not merely morally permissible, but morally desirable. The blackmailer and the blackmailed may end up conspiring to block a morally desirable outcome.

At the other extreme the threat is to expose something that really ought to remain private – perhaps pertaining to the victims' sexual hang-ups or their charitable donations. There are, of course, many cases in between the extremes, cases that would generate discussion and could tip either way, re-engaging us with the Weighing Puzzle.

The Blackmail Paradox prompts the puzzle of which demands are morally permissible or required, and which not. An injured man, crumpled on our pavement, deserves our help – yet those others injured, crumpled, thousands of miles away? Should geographical location be morally relevant?

Another example is the medical assistance available – and most people feel rightly so – for couples with fertility problems. Morally we should help people secure flourishing lives, and, for many, having children is a major component. Yet, so is having sexual partners and pleasures – hence, ought not the attractive and desirable be helping the unattractive and undesired with regard to, what we may term, 'sexual healing'? Puzzlingly, such healing services rarely receive state support.

When grading essays, supervisors should not be influenced by students' wealth, yet when deciding whom to date? We may be sexist, racist, blonde-ist and wealth-ist, in our coupling practices – and, arguably, sexist in our religious practices – but not in our teaching, employment and political practices.

When one set of practices is permissible but another set not, and when discriminations are acceptable in some contexts but not others, we need to uncover the justification – and this leads to Blackmail Stage Two.

*   *   *

Blackmail Stage One concentrates on how permissible activities, when combined, become impermissible. Stage Two compares permissible combinations with other similar combinations that constitute impermissible blackmail – and finds no justification for the difference in permissibility assessments.

We frequently need to assess whether differences between two activities justify differences in their moral or legal treatment. If there is no justification, then we may be guilty of simple prejudice, of an 'ism' such as sexism or racism. When the cotton industry used slaves, the solution was to prohibit the slavery, not the demand for and supply of cotton; so, we may wonder why some argue that, because many prostitutes have been coerced into the profession, the demand for paid sex should be prohibited. Reason would suggest that the coercion should be outlawed, not the service – not least because many permissible sexual relations, including marriage, involve monetary transactions and understandings, or at least expensive dinners, jewellery or cruises. There is here a 'sexual-relations-ism'.

Many permissible activities present some similarity to blackmail. Unless wages are increased, city bonuses paid and taxes reduced, employees may strike, executives walk out and companies relocate in offshore tax havens – with resultant damage to business, colleagues and country. Within the current Western ethos, threats of such action are rarely treated as morally equivalent to blackmail. Are there relevant differences?

The individuals are exercising their right to trade freely, and financial returns are relevant factors in trading, though when the demands, in some no doubt obscure way, are viewed as excessive, then the 'blackmail' label may be informally bandied. Ignoring the problem of excess, are not many activities in the trading world akin to blackmail? Consider the following.

Researchers uncover Saintly's wayward ways; newspapers offer to buy the information. Many people today consider such deals perfectly acceptable. The researchers, though, feel sorry for Saintly – but not that sorry. They offer to keep quiet and not sell, if he pays them instead. That is now blackmail and wrong. Why? Or suppose the researchers have not yet discovered anything untoward, but suspect that they would, were they to dig; so, they offer to decline a newspaper's 'digging' contract, if Saintly reimburses them. This latter muddiness may raise the thought, 'If we don't do this, someone else will.' Before turning to that thought, let us spin one additional example.

There is nothing illegal – and arguably nothing immoral – about a large supermarket corporation planning to open a new store near, say, 50 small shops, even though the shopkeepers would quickly be undercut and go out of business. The supermarket offers to cancel its plans, if the shopkeepers, pooling resources, make significant monthly compensatory payments. The latter is akin to blackmail – yet is the only objection that the free market of price-cutting is endangered?

Perhaps the law takes a wider view than that of personal morality. Legislators are often concerned to promote society's overall benefits. Permitting the harms resulting from the free movement of labour and capital, with free markets, competition, and little state intervention, leads to flourishing capitalist economies, it is claimed, with overall benefits – though, with the recent banking crisis, the claim now receives significant caveats even from many ardent free enterprise lovers.

Now, what overall benefits would result if typical cases of blackmail were made legal, with blackmail open to free competition? Presumably companies specializing in blackmail would be set up, vying for trade: a Blackmail plc's slogan could be 'We cover your uncover'. That would lead to increased surveillance and intrusions into private lives, yet maybe, paradoxically, a considerable increase in cover-ups, as the wealthy pay up. That may well not benefit society. Of course, we may also doubt whether the workings of free markets are as beneficial as often claimed, even ignoring the banking disaster. On the small scale, a company may deliberately undercut its local competitors, driving them out of business, knowing that it will then be able to increase its prices. On the big scale, directors of investment houses may know they can make substantial short-term profits – and be safely away, with bonuses and golden goodbyes, before the later disasters hit.

When dealings are morally suspect, consciences are often soothed by the mentioned 'Someone else will, if I do not', an attempted justification used by arms-dealers, international bribe-givers, and investors in dubious companies. Investors, indeed, give rise to a distinctive paradox, the Divestiture Paradox, when they seek to wash their hands of morally unacceptable companies by selling their shares.

Suppose some investors have seen the moral light or have only just now been enlightened about the companies' activities. In selling their shareholdings, they pass the immoral buck to the buyers. There would be nothing wrong in such buck passing if they were selling because of personal peccadilloes, but suppose their view is that the company is beyond the moral pale. They surely ought not to pass on that wrong, even to buyers who lack qualms.

The sellers' defence ought not to be that they are merely selling; others are doing the buying. Selling necessarily involves buying. No doubt, the buyers are acting freely, but the sellers are still involving them in doing what they ought not to do.

As shareholders we jointly own the companies – whether we like it or not. Perhaps the paradox points out that if we truly believe a company morally bad, we should cease to benefit: we could re-direct dividends to charities, though that raises problems about their benefiting from the dubious. Indeed, by people not buying shares in morally undesirable companies, they allow existing shareholders to retain dirty hands.

There are further factors. On the one hand, we could seek to justify the shares' sale by arguing that, in a teeny way, it helps to reduce the companies' values. On the other hand, perhaps we should stay invested, arguing against the companies' activities at shareholders' meetings. In either case, the effects are likely to be negligible.

Divestiture is one small example of problems about collective decisions, one's involvement in them and the thought, 'What if everyone . . . ?'

'I make no difference': from murder to voting

Moral responsibility differs from causal responsibility. I may be causally responsible, but not morally responsible, for Orford's death – I have fallen from the ladder and crushed him – but the fall was not my fault. To be morally responsible, I should surely have intended to harm or kill him, or have been negligent in my ladder skills. Is having just the intention to kill as morally disreputable as killing? Well, if I fail in my intention, I can hardly be a murderer. For complexities, consider how Orford's death may occur as a result of my intention, yet not as intended. Perhaps my intention to kill poor Orford tomorrow causes my nervousness today, leading to my fall and Orford's demise today. These things happen – well, in philosophical thought experiments. Moral Luck, in Chapter 9, reveals the problems.

When we seek to excuse ourselves from moral responsibility, we sometimes play the card that really our actions were causally irrelevant to the outcome being assessed.

INNOCENT MURDERERS

Poppy and Lena – for reasons that need not concern us here – are independently intent on killing Barrington, when all three are crossing the desert. Poppy and Lena are unaware of each other's plans. First, Barrington's water flask is contaminated with a lethal poison by Poppy. Secondly, Lena, unaware of the contamination, punctures the flask, and the water trickles into the sands. In due

course, Barrington dies of thirst. Lena denies murder. 'I drained
away poisoned water that would have killed Barrington had he
imbibed,' she pleads. Poppy denies murder. 'The poisoned water
was untouched by Barrington' is her defence.

'SOMEONE ELSE WILL'

Lowes considers the arms industry morally disreputable; he feels
that he ought not to take a job promoting the industry. Yet if he
does not, someone else will; so, either way, he makes no difference
to the outcome. He concludes that he may as well do what he
ought not to do.

In the murder puzzle, the death was due to lack of drinkable water.
Who caused that? Well, Lena the Leaker. Yet Lena may respond that
she 'made no difference': had she not acted, Barrington would still
have died due to lack of drinkable water.

We respond that Lena caused the dehydration that led to Barrington's death: had Lena not acted, then Barrington would have died of
poisoning. Lena replies further (if true), 'Ah, but the poison caused a
horrible tell-tale smell. Barrington would not have sipped a drop; so,
he would still have died of dehydration.' We could make the assignment of causal responsibility even more difficult, for suppose Poppy's
poison was a solidifier: had Lena not drained the water, then after a
few more minutes the poison and water would have cemented, leading to Barrington's death by dehydration.

The puzzle is primarily about causal responsibility. As both women
intended Barrington's death, they would seem equally morally repre-
hensible. In our arms industry example, though, Lowes is a serious,
morally concerned young man. Even though what he does may make
no difference to progress in the arms industry, we may un-puzzle any
puzzlement by pointing out that what he does makes a difference *to
him*. If he takes the job, he is involved. He may simply not want to
'dirty his hands' – and perhaps he ought not to dirty his hands. My
knowledge that a gunman is intent on killing his victim does not make
defensible *my* killing that victim instead. Killer, I would still have been.

Naturally, other factors may enter the moral assessment. If Lowes
accepts the job, he may be able to whistle-blow and expose some

wrongful activities. Perhaps he desperately needs the job because he has children to support. These factors could justify his dirtying his hands: more accurately, they may help cleanse the hands. Perhaps, indeed, he becomes aware that sustaining his 'moral purity' in not engaging with the job is a luxury and something of a selfish act.

The cleansing of dirty hands may occur when a wider picture is in view. A government, turning a blind eye to some international fraud, may be justified by the long-term benefits for society that outweigh the fraud's disvalue. A morally concerned company, assuming the expression is no oxymoron, may help improve labour conditions in the long term for workers abroad, if, for the present, it accepts products involving child labour, poorly paid. It may ultimately benefit people more than the company which, concerned about its image, or even moral 'purity', completely washes its hands of any involvement.

Shuffling moral responsibilities is not unusual. A committee – a cabinet, a board of directors – make collective decisions. The members accept that they are jointly responsible, yet each may reject personal responsibility. The members wear different hats. 'As a doctor – *qua* doctor – I present the argument for banning smoking; as a smoker, I present the argument against the ban.'

'As government officer, I implement the closure of offices; as local congressman, I demonstrate against.'

We have different roles – my duties as teacher differ from my duties as citizen – and the roles can lead to tensions. They may also lead to a belief paradox: the *Qua* Puzzle. 'As a doctor, I believe in the cigarette ban; as a smoker, I do not.' Yet, although that type of comment is made, beliefs cannot usually depend on the hat worn and audience in view. The typical government minister who speaks the government line, yet personally disagrees with it, does not also, *qua* loyal minister, somehow *believe* the government line.

Beliefs, unlike duties, cannot usually be held relative to role. It is, though, possible for a person to lead two so very different lives that, in a sense, he no longer is one person, but is fragmented. In that exceptional way, it may be possible to see his conflicting beliefs as beliefs *qua* different roles or lives. Even then, his beliefs are not straightforwardly under his control, to switch between at will. Pascal's Wager, which argues that it is prudent to believe in God, does not thereby make you believe. You may have good reason – that is, the end may be desirable – to believe that all will be well, yet you may lack good reason – that is, you lack evidence – for believing all will be well. 'Having good reason to believe' is ambiguous.

Conflicts arise between our beliefs and preferences. Various paradoxes have been highlighted in this area. Here is one.

DEMOCRACY

A democrat, Dee, believes that the majority decision ought to prevail, yet the majority vote goes against what she thinks morally ought to be done. For example, Dee votes for higher taxes, yet the democratic machinery delivers a majority vote for tax reduction. *Qua* democrat – she insists – she supports the reduction; *qua* social reformer, she does not.

The paradox, presented in this way, possesses the unhappy feature of the individual's beliefs depending on her hat – *qua* democrat or *qua* morally concerned individual. We may, though, understand what is going on far more straightforwardly – and without puzzlement.

The resolution resists the implied simplicity of each belief. 'Does Dee want taxes raised? Yes or no!' Well, she possesses an ordered set of preferences: first is increased taxes, implemented democratically; second is reduced taxes, implemented democratically; third is increased taxes, implemented undemocratically; and fourth is reduced taxes, implemented undemocratically. The world is such that she finds that her first preference is unavailable, but at least she has her second preference satisfied. Conflicting preferences of this order are not confined to democracies. Someone who lived in a dictatorship and approved its political system could have her first preference as a tax increase by diktat, her second being tax decrease by diktat.

The Democracy Paradox would be more disturbing, were it to show that Dee both believes that, whatever the democratic vote is, it is right – and believes that lowering taxes is wrong. In this case, when the majority do vote against lowering taxes, her beliefs are contradictory, though, even if she realizes that, she may still feel a pull towards holding both beliefs. Recall the Medical Humility Puzzle.

These matters may remind us of some troubling conflicts in a liberal society. Ought the tolerant to tolerate the intolerant? What is to be done if the democratic vote is for tyranny, suspension of democracy, and persecution of minorities? These may raise the puzzle of whether a democracy has the power to overturn itself. A divine version of that puzzle is whether an all-powerful God could make himself not all-powerful. There are troubles of a self-referential kind here.

With some kinship to Chapter 3's Liar, there is the Self-Amendment Paradox, where a constitution refers to itself with regard to how it may be amended. Now, there is no problem with a constitution's clause authorizing the amendment of other clauses, but can it authorize amendment of itself? In contrast to the Liar, though, such a self-referring clause would seem to have content. For example, to amend the clause 'that any amendment needs at least a two-thirds majority', we need at least a two-thirds majority. If at least two-thirds vote to change the clause, the clause is satisfied and the change may then take place. Thus it is that law can self-revise.

Democratic decisions: no hands – and hands

People often disagree about what should be done – about taxes, freedoms, citizen rights and duties – yet something has to be done. Individuals usually want some say; they become part of the collective decision-making process. There can be a small puzzle here, the Puzzle of No Hands. We may hide in the crowd.

'The committee made the decision. True, I cast my vote in favour of that decision – but it is the committee's responsibility, not mine.'

Although we are part of the whole, we – each and every one of us – may resist the responsibility of the whole and of the decision. Somehow a decision was made, yet none takes responsibility – a decision with no one deciding. Further, a voter, feeling guilty at voting for a racist party that achieves power, may assuage his guilt by reflecting that his vote made no difference to the result regarding who won.

In democracies, it is our duty to vote – or so it is said. The elected politicians speak of winning a popular mandate, of people having expressed their will, of wanting manifesto promises to be effected. The politicians conveniently forget that they have usually been elected by a minority of votes even of those who voted, on packages of policies poorly understood, of which only one or two may be popular – and their win may be attributable to smart, shrewd and expensive publicity campaigns. We may see why E. M. Forster gave only two cheers, not three, for democracy – and perhaps was being generous.

VOTING

In many, many cases, an individual voter knows that his vote in an election will make no difference. Elections are rarely won or lost by a single vote. Yet, individuals, well aware of this, still feel that they ought to vote or are encouraged to vote. Surely, this is paradoxical.

The Voting Paradox arises because one vote more, one vote fewer, in the vast majority of cases makes no difference at all to who wins. If I clap with others, applauding the singers' performance, my clap may go unnoticed, yet I make a teeny difference to the total volume. If a candidate wins an election by a margin of 2,567 votes, my single vote in that 2,567 does not make the candidate become 'more elected'. Winning is a black or white matter.

My voting is highly unlikely to influence many others with regard to their voting. Sadly, I am not an alluring supermodel, a role model.

'But what if everyone were not to vote?'

My answer is: that will not arise, unless vast numbers read this book and catch on to the idea – but that, also sadly, will not happen; so why is it relevant?

With the opera's applause, I may want to join in – and I may just want to join in the voting, showing my commitment. That is fine, but fails to explain the feeling that citizens have a *duty* to vote. It is a curious duty, for it is typically a duty to do something pointless. Instead of voting, an activity more worthy – with greater point – could be undertaken, be it feeding the cat, visiting the lonely or, for that matter, having a nap.

If I decide not to vote, I may rest content that others will still vote, though – note – they do not have to vote any 'harder' to make up for my absence. I am wanting others to do what I am not going to do. I do not want them to follow suit. In the arms industry dilemma above, Lowes, though, wants his ideal, namely that of others following his desire – of not working in the industry.

*   *   *

A curiosity of morality is its frequent appeal to 'What if everyone?' – an appeal closely associated with the austere Immanuel Kant. You ought not to break a promise. Why? Well, Kant saw contradiction looming in promise-breaking, but more simply, were everyone to break promises, then the whole valuable institution would break down. My decision to give up eating *foie gras* has no noticeable impact on the relevant French farming fetish; but maybe I still ought not to buy the pâté. Why? Well, were everyone not to buy, there would be far less mistreatment of geese. Moral duties are thus being held, paradoxically, partially to depend on factors that will not occur. People will be influenced neither by Lowes resisting the arms industry job, nor by my food purchases and avoidance of polling stations.

We have different preferences, preferences that often conflict, be they about the arms industry, *foie gras* or, for that matter, voluntary euthanasia, taxation levels and welfare benefits. How should society reach decisions, given the different preferences?

COLLECTIVE CHOICE

People have different orders of preferences; so there needs to be a rule for combining them to produce consistent outcomes. Yet, on reasonable principles, there is none.

Collective decisions are made in various ways – sometimes by mob and frenzy. In November 1938, Kristallnacht, the Night of Broken Glass, occurred, named thus because Nazi mobs smashed windows and set fire to Jewish homes, shops and synagogues, murdering and terrorizing – leading to the Holocaust. Far more recently, stirred by raving ignorance, small groups have apparently attacked paediatricians, thinking them paedophiles.

In our much-beloved democracies, we usually reach decisions by majority votes. We raise hands. Yet we sink into confusion, when the majority of hands is for what is wrong. The majority vote is often revered, but it deserves to be brought down a peg or three. The majority could vote for me to do everyone's ironing or for a minority to be enslaved. That everyone's preferences should count equally fails to guard against such injustice. Yet even with such cases satisfactorily handled, with some rights protected – votes being supplemented by vetoes – majority votes remain too casually approved. This is because of collective choice puzzles, notably the Cyclical Majorities or Voters Paradox or Condorcet Cycle. It concerns how to put together individual preferences to reach majority preferences.

'The order of a society's preferences should be determined by the order of the individuals' preferences.' That is the reasonable assumption. We may be concerned about how those individual preferences are reached – misleading advertising? – but, leaving that question hanging, what do we do when citizens lack unanimity over proposed changes? We could decide to make no change; but that, of course, gives excessive weight to tradition.

Economists seek a social welfare function, a collective choice rule that specifies orderings for a society. Innocent looking conditions, needing to be satisfied, have been proposed. An example of innocence is, if everyone prefers X to Y, then the collective choice should be for X over Y. Other examples are that no one individual be dictatorial, and the function work for any possible orderings. Despite the conditions being seemingly so innocuous and acceptable, inconsistencies result. In 1785 Condorcet drew attention, for example, to intransitivities in majority voting. Here is an example.

> Phil prefers improved medical facilities to tax reduction and prefers tax reduction to increased defences. Sally prefers tax reduction to increased defences and increased defences to improved medical facilities. Tony prefers increased defences to improved medical facilities and improved medical facilities to tax reduction.

If we count up the preferences, we see that improved medical facilities defeats tax reduction: 2 to 1. Tax reduction defeats increased defences also 2 to 1. So, improved medical facilities should surely defeat increased defences: yet, counting up the preferences, we see that it is the reverse: increased defences defeats improved medical facilities, 2 to1. We hit inconsistency, given transitive preferences, as in Chapter 1.

The paradoxical claim – from Arrow's Theorem – is that no social welfare principle exists that satisfies a set of innocent, desirable principles such as those mentioned, while ensuring consistency. Majority rule, when ordering preferences, has inconsistency lurking within.

And the Prisoners' Dilemma

The inconsistency above arose, even though each individual's preferences were internally consistent and mutually known. With regard to individual choices, though, we find dilemmas of rational action. Here is the Prisoners' Dilemma in the usual form, where participants are motivated by self-interest. The motivation, though, could be to benefit others; yet, even when so, the dilemma still arises.

The dilemma relies on our separateness. It became a 'prisoners' dilemma' because prisoners, separated from each other, must decide whether to confess to their joint crime. What it is rational for one to do hangs on what his partner-in-crime is confessing elsewhere. A vivid version is a nuclear arms race. We go for the vivid.

Suppose you are a nation, U-nation – and I am a nation, I-nation – and we are at loggerheads, nervous of each other's motives, concerned about national security. You would like to have nuclear weapons as a deterrent, preferably without my having such weapons. I should prefer just the reverse. The second-best option for us both would be for neither of us to waste money going nuclear. The third option is our both spending lots of money on nuclear weapons – somewhat pointlessly. The following is my, I-nation's, order of preference:

Best	I-nation nuclear; U-nation non-nuclear.
Second best	Neither nation nuclear.
Third best	Both nations nuclear.
Worst	I-nation non-nuclear; U-nation nuclear.

For you, U-nation, the best and the worst would be the other way round. In such circumstances, what is it rational for me to do? Well, the reasoning seems straightforward.

If you are going to get nuclear weapons, then clearly that is what I should also do – otherwise I would be in the worst position for me. If you are not going to get nuclear weapons, then I should still go nuclear because that would place me in the best position for me. Either way, I should go nuclear.

I should realize that you, being rational, will be reasoning alike, with regard to your best policy. The result is that we spend lots of money, becoming nuclear, placing ourselves in the third-best position. It would obviously be much better to settle for the second-best position; but how can we achieve that?

Perhaps the answer is simple. We should agree not to go nuclear. But suppose we make a pact, agreeing just that. The dilemma bites again, with regard to keeping the pact. Why should I keep to the agreement? If you intend to break the agreement, then, in order to avoid the worse position for me, it is rational for me to break the agreement. If you intend to keep to the agreement, then again it is rational for me to break the agreement, hence securing my best option. Of course, I realize that this will be your reasoning too.

Paradoxically, our rationality keeps impelling us into the third-best option. We have no way of reasoning to the second-best. Well, we have no way of so reasoning, unless other factors come to the fore, such as trust, which override the preferences. In practice, people do risk trusting each other; and happy results may strengthen the trust. Being trustworthy may bring its own potential rewards. Whatever tale is told, though, somewhere along the line the dilemma resurfaces – because, it seems, we are separate individuals, thinking as each other thinks, but from our own individual perspective.

The Prisoners' Dilemma operates across the terrain of rationality. If you have reason to believe that the other party is highly irrational, then you may need even greater care. We should mention here the Paradox of Deterrence. The ultimate deterrent – Mutually Assured Destruction (MAD) – works, if it works, when parties think the other party is sufficiently irrational to use it. Rationally, it would be crazy to use such a deterrent. So, if you know that you would not use it, how can you rationally form the sincere intention to use it? – a puzzle similar to Chapter 2's Poisoned Chalice. And if I know that you are rational, paradoxically I ought not to fear your using it. So, in a *known* rational world, the ultimate deterrent is, we may paradoxically quip, no deterrent. Of course, the world is not known to be rational; and when rational, prisoners' dilemmas recur.

In the casual sense of 'paradox', a collective decision can paradoxically arise because no one wants to give voice to what, in fact, most or all are thinking. This is the Politeness Paradox. At a large family gathering the mother, thinking she should propose something positive to do, suggests a drive down to Abilene, not mentioning how she would prefer to stay at home. Each individual is polite; each individual nods agreement to the drive. No one in fact fancies the idea at all; but no one wants to sabotage what they take to be the pleasure of others.

Self-interest: acting for free or for a fee?

Taking into account the welfare of others is a significant element in morality. An altruistic act occurs when someone performs an action with the aim of benefiting someone else. The person who acts may incidentally benefit himself as well; but that is not the motivation. Parents rush to save their children; martyrs lay down their lives; and we may simply help someone across the road.

On the surface, people sometimes wittingly act for the sake of others. The Paradox of Altruism questions the reality beneath the surface.

ALTRUISM

When you act to help someone else, you are wanting to do it; so, really, you are satisfying your own want. It is your want that motivates you: and your aim is to satisfy that want. So-called altruistic acts are therefore self-interested ones in disguise.

This line of reasoning often convinces people. With apparent cases of altruism, the response is, for example, 'Well, the mother could not have lived with herself, had she not tried to help her child', or 'You feel good about yourself, a warm inner glow, when you help others;

it's the warm glow that motivates you.' Should we settle for the paradoxical conclusion?

What exactly is the paradoxical claim? Is it that, as a matter of fact, altruism never occurs, but could occur? If so, then we should consider the evidence: the evidence suggests that people do on occasions act altruistically. If the claim, though, is that it is really impossible for anyone ever to act altruistically, then it displays a misunderstanding of altruism. It is ruling that there is a contradiction in a person wanting to act altruistically. Yet why make such a ruling?

A final and quick response is this. Even if we accept the paradox spinners' conclusion, whereby their understanding of 'altruism' ensures that altruism is ruled out, we need then to build a distinction akin to the former distinction between altruism and selfishness – just as we rebuilt distinctions when faced with Descartes' evil genius. We should still need to distinguish between people who act to save the child and help the person across the road, and those people who walk on by. We should still need to distinguish between those people who help for free and those who help for a fee.

*   *   *

The Altruism Paradox emphasizes self-interest; yet, even when self-interested, we often fail to do what is in our self-interest, making mistakes about what that interest is. Further, when no mistakes are made about our interests, we may still resist doing what we ought to do – be that 'ought' telling us what we *morally* ought to do or telling us what it is in our best long-term interests to do.

'I can see the right path, yet I do not follow it.' 'I know that it would be better for me not to have the extra drink, but I cannot resist.' These manifest weakness of will – sometimes known as 'akrasia' and sometimes, and unfortunately, as 'incontinence'.

There are different versions of the Paradox of Weakness of Will. Typically, weakness of will is thought to be a defect; but it need not be so.

If you think that you morally ought to obey the law, and, in the particular circumstances, that means that you would betray your friend, you may 'weaken', remaining loyal to the friend. That could be the right thing to do. Perhaps, once in the hands of the authorities, your friend would be tortured for opposing the regime. That your friendship trumps your respect for the law could manifest a good character. E. M. Forster's different but related reflection comes to mind. 'If I had to choose between betraying my country and betraying my friend, I hope I should have the guts to betray my country.' Of course, there are cases and cases.

Socrates, the philosophical gadfly of fifth-century Athens, argued that no one does wrong knowingly – the Socratic Paradox. He thought virtue to be knowledge. Quite what does that mean? Let us do our best, by applying it to Miranda who is doing her best about herself.

If only Miranda knew – if only she could see clearly – that the excessive drinking and gambling would lead to years of hardship and suffering, then she would resist such activities. Weakness of will is, metaphorically, an eyesight problem. The hardships and sufferings in those years ahead are in the distance: they lack sufficient impact to overwhelm the current transient pleasures for Miranda of the extra whisky and roulette spin. This is one way of trying to explain away the puzzling psychological fact that we sometimes do what we seem to know not to be in our best interests.

We may take the thought radically further. If only we could fully appreciate future pains and pleasures concerning not just ourselves, but also others, then such appreciation – such knowledge – would lead us to be more concerned for the plight of others, for the dispossessed, than many of us are. As it is, though, we think of ourselves as separate and distinct individuals.

We think of ourselves as separate and distinct individuals, separate selves, yet that is curious for, as Chapter 9 discusses, we have little idea of what a self is. The self moves in mysterious ways, but, before losing our 'selves' in serpent windings on the finite self, let us move to those mysterious and divine ways of the grandest and greatest self. Yes, let us soar beyond this human world of puzzles and paradoxes, perplexities and confusions, and enter into a marvellous, transcendent world of – puzzles and paradoxes, perplexities and confusions.

8   Encounters with God –

and his mysterious ways

. . . in which, after an immovable stone proves no stumbling block, God's divine perfections yet create embarrassment, in light of our sufferings, free will and all too human perspectives, from shames and humour to the here and the now.

It is time for God. Before atheists and agnostics scamper free, let us remember that godly paradoxes may pose good arguments against the divine architect. Further, although the paradoxes speak of God, some can be read without religious frills. For example, are the notions of 'knowing everything' and 'being all powerful' paradoxical? In our earlier discussions of infinity and morality, we could have given God, as infinite and all good, a run for his money, there and then.

Here is a further 'furthermore'. We who rest smugly content at perceived absurdities in God should not overlook the motes of paradox in our own life's vision. We have already met chasms, or at least crinkles, in reasoning, rationality and our application of some everyday concepts. In the next chapter, we shall encounter, even embrace, seeming absurdities built deeply within our lives.

Omni this and omni that

Mysteries about God are expected, even praised. Hence, divine perplexities are often undeemed as paradoxes, unless they blatantly clash with some non-divine assumptions. God and gods are delivered to mere mortals courtesy of scriptures, revelations and sermons by those allegedly in the divine know. The deliverances often tell conflicting tales. Revelations offer kaleidoscopic views: they may both charm and depress in their variety, as we turn from one religious sect to another. Casually, we may reflect how paradoxical it is that a loving

God creates a suffering world, offers eternal damnation to many, and demands worship and right living without clarifying what the worship and right living should be – or so it seems. Witness relentless conflicts within even one and the same model of Christianity about the rightness or otherwise of homosexuality, abortion and the role of women.

Happily we avoid here detailed ensnarement in religious texts. We put to one side the web of specific beliefs, attitudes and rituals that constitute a religion. A typical Christian web, for example, has God, an omnipotent being, becoming incarnate; that is, embodied as Jesus Christ on Earth. God seems to become highly limited in mind and body, even being put to death, well, for a while – yet still being God. This is the Christian Trinity: one and the same individual is God, Son and Holy Spirit. What is true of one, though, is not, believers say, true of the others, despite their identity. Søren Kierkegaard, he of the 'leap of faith', sees this as the Absolute Paradox, one for the Offended Consciousness. To be fair, in non-religious life, we have already met problems of identity with Heraclitus' River.

Eager not to tread on the sorrows of those in doctrinal dispute, we stick to widespread beliefs about God, rather than, for example, Trinitarian detail. We ignore puzzles of gods, angels and any pin-dancing. We also ignore the divine Father as a human-shaped being, floating in skies and through clouds, with swirls of greying beard – as portrayed on walls and ceilings of church and chapel.

With the Judaeo-Christian God and the Islamic Allah to the fore, the supreme being is here taken to be all powerful, all knowing, and all good; that is, God is omnipotent, omniscient and omnibenevolent. There are a few more 'omni's, and often also characteristics of simplicity and unchanging. Aligning with tradition, the male pronoun 'he' is used for this being. Two paradoxes, regularly recognized, are the Stone and the Paradox of Divine Foreknowledge. Let us defer Divine Foreknowledge for a page or two.

STONE

God, being all powerful, can make anything. Hence, he can make an immovable stone. Yet if he is all powerful, there can be no stone that he cannot move.

Disquiet about the Stone may be initially quelled by arguing, as Aquinas did, but Descartes did not, that omnipotence is simply being able to do anything that is logically possible and being able to bring about any logically possible states of affairs. Omnipotence does not require being able to beat logical impossibilities into submission, making them possible.

It is not logically possible – and so, not logically possible for an omnipotent being – to draw a round square, to think the unthinkable or to make the number three even. Does this answer the Stone Paradox? Not that quickly, for a round square is logically impossible, but an immovable stone is not – well, not obviously so.

We need to highlight that what an omnipotent being is capable of doing does not involve being able to do what it is impossible *for an omnipotent being* to do. Arguably, this highlight casts little light, for the paradox is making us wonder what an omnipotent being is indeed capable of doing. Now, most beings (to say the least) are not omnipotent; but an omnipotent being, it seems clear, cannot not be omnipotent while being omnipotent – though we may wonder whether an omnipotent being could make himself lack omnipotence such that, for example, a stone he created could not later be moved.

The simple paradox resolution is to accept that an all-powerful being and an immovable stone cannot co-exist. 'An immovable stone is created by an all-powerful being' is self-contradictory. Does the stone or God exist? Religious believers commit to the omnipotent being, rather than the immovable stone. If, though, there is an immovable stone, then an omnipotent being does not exist – and vice versa. However, we are not yet saved from murky waters.

We are not yet saved because, from the impossible co-existence of immovable stone and all-powerful being, we conclude that the latter cannot make an immovable stone. But we could argue in the opposite direction. A being who is all powerful surely could make an immovable stone; to insist that such a being could not also seems contradictory, if an immovable stone is logically possible. Such a being, though, could not then move the stone. So, either 'all powerful' excludes the ability to make immovable stones or excludes the ability to move certain specified stones.

We may generalize the conflict. A being that can do anything cannot co-exist with any beings that cannot have some things done. We could race through a list: if a being can resist everything, know everything, believe everything, conceive everything, then it cannot co-exist with items that are irresistible, unknowable, unbelievable and inconceivable.

If God can resist everything, then he cannot himself possess the power of being irresistible. If God can discover everything, then he can keep no secrets from himself. Care is, though, needed. What is impossible is for God both to discover everything about himself and to fail to discover something about himself. Yet that does not immediately show that he cannot possess the power to discover and the power to hide. What he cannot do is exercise both powers regarding the same matters in all circumstances. There are constraints.

While it may be true that you can do A and can do B, it does not follow that you can do A and B. Maybe God could have created a universe such that suddenly – from tomorrow – all car alarms, leaking MP3-players and drilling equipment cease to make noises that so disturb. It is also true that he could have created a universe in which this happy cessation fails to happen; indeed, sadly, he probably has. He could not, though, have created a universe such that tomorrow the felicitous cessation both does and does not occur. One creation rules out the other.

We shall return to omnipotence, relating to God's other characteristics; but let us now give God's foreknowledge a little spin.

DIVINE FOREKNOWLEDGE

God always knows everything, including therefore everything about what we shall do. If, though, our doings are always known in advance by God, then we are never free agents. Yet we believe ourselves often to act freely. Indeed, paradoxically, it is a common belief that God granted us free will.

We may quickly challenge an assumption. The assumption is that if, for example, it is already divinely known, before you form any relevant intentions, that you will drink champagne tomorrow, then you cannot be free concerning the morrow's drinking. You *must* find yourself drinking champagne. However, the assumption is surely false, unless something further is assumed. The something further is that the foreknowledge only exists because something determines what you will be doing tomorrow champagne-wise – and that something is not under your free choice.

If God knows that Peter will sin, then, yes, it does necessarily follow that Peter will sin, but it does not necessarily follow that Peter will necessarily sin. To note that something necessarily follows is *not* to note that what follows is itself necessary. These are sometimes conflated because we casually say that if you know something, then what you know must be true. That is fine, if it is read as saying that if you know something, then it *must* follow that what you know is true. It is not fine if it is read as saying that anything that you know is a necessary truth; that is, it *must* be true whether you know it or not. That would be a pretty counter-intuitive conclusion. After all, I know that I am writing these words, but presumably there was no necessity that I should write them. You know you are reading these words; but you might not have been reading. This is not, I assume, force-reading.

If the above worries, consider an analogy. If you are thinking something, then it necessarily follows that you exist – but it does not necessarily follow that you necessarily exist. Nothing justifies that second 'necessarily' popping into the story. After all, you do not necessarily exist – though maybe God does. We encountered this thinking matter with Monsieur Descartes in Chapter 6.

The general point is that just because someone – anyone – knows something to be true, it does not mean that what is known is a necessary truth and so could not have been otherwise. Foreknowledge alone is no threat to our acting freely. Of course, if we fail to do whatever was said to be known, then it turns out that it was not known after all.

A different argument is that, for example, thousands of years ago, either it was true that you would be partying tomorrow or it was not true. But whichever it was, that past truth cannot now be changed; hence, if you party tomorrow, you do so necessarily – and if you do not party, that is also necessarily so, necessary non-partying. Paradoxically, therefore, whatever you do, you do necessarily.

This Past Truth Paradox contains a blunder similar to the one exhibited above. Were it indeed a truth 2,000 years ago that you would be partying tomorrow, then it necessarily follows that that is what you will do tomorrow; but it does not necessarily follow that you will necessarily be doing so. Oops – does that mean that what you do tomorrow can change the past? Well, not in any surprising way – for that past truth is about the future. Furthermore, truths are abstract entities, not causes.

The *truth* that the bullet struck his heart did not kill him. What killed him was the bullet's striking his heart. Of course, we could jazz things up. Maybe the bullet's striking his heart did not kill him, but his hearing someone say that the bullet struck his heart gave him a heart attack and killed him. Then it is his hearing a certain claim that is involved in causing his death: the truth of the claim is not the cause.

Despite the above approach towards resolving the Foreknowledge Paradox and similar – a not unusual approach – many people believe that divine foreknowledge and human free will cannot co-exist. The problem motivates some to insist that God is eternal, timeless; that is, not existing in time at all. This contrasts with the belief that God is everlasting, existing in every moment of time – a 'sempiternity'. God's prior knowledge of human actions appears to some as more threatening to freedom than God's timeless knowledge. Either way, though, the knowledge itself is no threat to free will. The threat arises if God's knowledge is somehow grounded in factors outside us, factors that determine what we do; and that threat can exist whether God's knowledge is outside time or within time.

Perfections: omniscience, omnipotence and more

God is the most perfect being. This is a regular understanding of God. Maybe it is why he merits worship. In some way, he is, to quote St Anselm, that being than which nothing greater can be conceived. While we possess an idea of a perfect circle and maybe even a perfectly shaped egg, do we know what counts even as a perfect frog, let alone a perfect being? That is one mystery. Another mystery is why perfection should be tied to greatness, unless limitation is a defect. Is this not, so to speak, being size-ist?

If limitation is a defect, then God just is that which possesses maximal reality – quite whatever that means. With that starting point, perhaps we can see why believers ascribe the characteristics that they do. The 1662 Book of Common Prayer, for example, tells us in Article One, 'There is but one living and true God, everlasting, without body, parts, or passions: of infinite power, wisdom, and goodness: the Maker and Preserver of all things both visible and invisible.'

With God as perfect, possessing maximal reality, we can perhaps grasp how it is better for him to be everlasting or timeless than limited by time, better to have infinite power than finite power, and better to have knowledge than ignorance. It is also better to be all good than limited in goodness. This latter appeals to moral perfection, but the former 'better's lead to perfections in terms of being maximal. It is, though, a moot point why God typically is understood to lack body, even an infinite body. Perhaps there is resort to an argument that body is defective. Now, some bodies are defective – I have intimate knowledge of one – but it is not obvious that bodies are essentially defective. Perhaps the claim is that the body hinders the mind – after all, some bodies are delightfully distracting. Perhaps possession of an unhindered mind – unhindered in various ways – is essential to perfection.

We humans need bodies to gain knowledge of the world. Presumably God, as perfect, possesses direct knowledge, not limited by body. Indeed, he is sometimes spoken of as omnipresent, being everywhere, to account for such directness – and to provide another dimension for his maximal reality. Spinoza, a fine searcher after consistency, known both as 'the god-intoxicated philosopher' and 'the atheist Jew', was radical, ascribing to God not just the attributes of the physical and psychological world but also an infinite number of other, unknown attributes. None of this went down well with his synagogue. He was excommunicated, in fact when a young man, by the Amsterdam Synagogue – and took up lens grinding.

Arguably, God would be limited if other beings could exist independently of him; hence, God is understood as maker and indeed preserver of the universe – and one. Further, God, it seems, is without passions, without sufferings, for they too would constitute defects, though the passionless features sit unhappily with everyday religious belief that God stands in a personal relationship to humans, requiring worship, loving them, pained by their sins, even jealous. God, in his perfection, must, of course, lack all vices and must lack some virtues: presumably he cannot, for example, be courageous – but modest? Being all knowing and all powerful, he is bereft, presumably, of both hope and faith.

Added to these characteristics is the fact of God's existence – a necessary existence, it would seem. If God just happened to exist, then he would be limited in that he might not have existed: it would be chance or external factors that determined his existence. Hence God, unlike human beings, is a necessary existent. Some immediately propose that we have paradoxically understood God such that he cannot exist. This is because it is surely possible that there be no God, but if God necessarily exists, then that lack of God would be impossible; hence, we have a contradiction. Yet we may wonder, of course, how 'surely' it is that God's non-existence must be possible.

Let us stick with a necessarily existent God. We take it that his main characteristics hold of him necessarily. Were God, for example, just to happen to be omniscient, his omniscience would be less than perfect, depending on some chance or contingency. These necessary characterizations of a necessarily existent God bring forth a budget of paradoxes. We could list the Paradox of Omniscience, of Omnipotence, of Omnipresence and so forth. Life being short and our discussion of God confined to a chapter, we unite them as the Paradox of Divine Existence.

DIVINE EXISTENCE

God is necessarily omnipotent, omniscient and omnibenevolent – and necessarily exists. He is indeed the greatest conceivable being, the most perfect being, and creator of the universe. Yet these attributes, singly or in combination, cannot exist; hence, paradoxically, given the nature of God, he cannot exist.

Religious believers reject the conclusion: they try to render God's characteristics consistent. Well, what are the problems? We continue to ignore those puzzles that strike believers only because of particular non-universal doctrinal beliefs – for example, the puzzling clash between God's eternal and unchanging omnipotence and Jesus Christ's crucifixion and resurrection.

We may question the underlying 'greatest' accolade granted to God. Is there a greatest conceivable number? No. Is there a greatest conceivable frog? Well, we are uncertain what to say. Are we talking of size? Perhaps this is where perfection has a grip. Maybe a three-legged frog is more perfect a frog than a two-legged; and a four-legged one is perfect with regard to quantity of legs, a five-legged having gone overboard. With the 'omni' attributes of God there is no going over the top; but if God's features are meant to be infinite, in the sense of limitless, endless, then can God exist? Can the limitless actually exist? The puzzle of the actual infinite was touched on in Chapter 4's discussion of the infinite divisibility of space.

God's omnipotence receives some seeming limitation. It is limited by his nature, by his other properties, unless those properties are limited by his omnipotence. Believers have to choose. For example, is it possible for God to sin? If the answer is 'Yes', protective of his omnipotence, then his omnibenevolence is threatened. If the answer is 'No', then his omnipotence needs restricted renderings.

If God is necessarily omnipotent, then he cannot give up his omnipotence and still be God. If God is disembodied, then he cannot have a drink, go to bed, and wake up with a headache. If God is outside time, or essentially changeless, then this puts a spanner in the works for a whole range of activities, be they mental or physical.

A necessary condition for meriting praise for being virtuous seems to be that the individual did not *have* to be virtuous. If God's nature is necessarily that of being all good – he could not be otherwise – then maybe he neither merits praise, nor, for that matter, does he deserve worship, though the worship may be prudent: recall Pascal's Wager.

Paradoxes also arise with God's being creator of the spatio-temporal world. If God exists outside space and time – and arguably he should, otherwise he would seem to have parts, spatial and temporal – then how could he be omnipresent, present in all places, at all times? Yet, were God to exist in space and time, somehow changelessly and without parts, it is mysterious how he created space and time. Presumably he must be distinct from space and time, in order to create them; but what sense is there in the idea of a creation occurring outside time? How can there be action not in time?

Perhaps space and time are essential properties of God – a view espoused by the seventeenth-century Cambridge Platonist Henry More and later by Isaac Newton. On this view, God exists everywhere and constitutes time and space. This may remind us of a pantheism, where God and the universe are identified as one. In fact, it is panentheism, a sort of 'pantheism plus': God is the whole universe and something more. Talk of God creating space and time may now be understood as space and time being grounded in God's nature. Pantheism and panentheism, of course, take us well away from traditional views of the Divinity.

Let us return to tradition – and to omniscience. If God is omniscient, then he knows every true proposition, and so must know a limitless number of propositions. For example, he must know with regard to any even number that it is even; but there is an infinite number of such numbers. We – mere humans – know that they are all divisible by two, but God should have specific knowledge of each particular number, despite there being no end to them. Bearing in mind Zeno's Paradoxes, if space and time are continuous, then, when I cross the room, God maybe should know for an endless number of traversals at which time I started to move through each one.

Suppose we can make sense of a collection, albeit infinite, of all truths such that God knows every one: we need, then, to expand that set with the additional truth that God knows that he knows all of them – and then expand that expanded set because he should know that he knows all of that expanded set's propositions. Are we not spinning off endlessly?

Focusing on the idea of *all* truths, suppose there is a set of *all* truths. The set of its subsets is larger, as shown in Chapter 3 with Cantor's Paradox. So, the number of truths about all those subsets – for example, concerning which subsets contain which truths – must exceed the set of all truths. But that is impossible; we hit a contradiction. Perhaps God could be understood as knowing an ever-expanding number of truths, but this sits unhappily with God's being unchanging.

God's features generate paradoxes. In one way or another, we hit against limits of what, in some way, is meant to lack limits.

God and humanity: embarrassments and evils

Moving on from the somewhat abstract, there are puzzles concerning God's knowledge of those things that we, mere finite humans, know. Human that we are, limited in time and space, we have knowledge of shyness, temptations, mistakes and sensations. I experience embarrassment, am tempted by the wine, become aware of a mistake, or sense a tingle in my toe. Not being all seeing, I fail to foresee the joke's punchline, only slowly wake up to a pun, and remain baffled by paradoxes. I know what it is to be surprised, to laugh, to spot incongruities, and to miss solutions. God presumably lacks such knowledge. Paradoxically, in a manner of speaking, his greatness restricts his greatness – arguably and paradoxically, this should be something of an embarrassment for the greatest.

A vast amount of our human knowledge rests on how things stand in relation to ourselves. There is knowledge that I have concerning me, concerning what is near and far from me and what is here. This is indexical knowledge, knowledge that I have from my particular perspective, my particular position. If Flora knocks her head and sees some stars, she knows that she is seeing stars and may also know that she does not know who she is. Perhaps God could know that Flora knocked her head and saw the stars, but he could not – could he? – possess the knowledge that Flora possesses when receiving the starry vision, no longer knowing that she is Flora. God could not have the knowledge that Flora has when regaining awareness that she is Flora.

Time presents distinct puzzles. We humans know of past, present and future happenings. We may look forward to the future; we may regret the past. If God is everlasting, existing in the whole of time, yet unchanging – or outside time, in a changeless timelessness or atemporal eternity – how can he possess knowledge of the past and future as past and future? Perhaps he grasps the idea of events in a series, perhaps even of the before/after direction in time, but he would not thereby know of events *changing* from being in the future to the past. Possibly his timeless knowledge could have dates built within: for example, 'Spinoza is excommunicated on 27th July 1656' would be grasped as holding eternally; but there would be no knowledge of that excommunication *now* being past.

We are lax. Could God grasp even timeless or everlasting truths that contain timed locations? Appreciation of events having dates, and being before some other events and after yet others, may well require a sense of past, present and future.

With regard to God and Puzzles of Divine Indexical Knowledge, it is often a mystery how we could ever tell what could be so, let alone what is so.

*   *   *

Turning our attention to God's being all good – his omnibenevolence – we encounter a classic puzzle, given voice in Plato's *Euthyphro* dialogue, well over 2,000 years ago, namely, that of how goodness stands to God. Here is one way of posing the *Euthyphro* Puzzle:

> Does God command the good because it is good – or is the good good because God commands it?

If God comands the good because it is good, then that suggests that the good exists independently of God's command; so goodness does not depend on God. If, though, the good is only good because God commands it, then, it seems, *whatever* God commands would be good – hardly impressive grounds for praising God for his goodness. Whichever way we turn, we have a problem. A resolution could be the identification of God with goodness itself, yet how could goodness itself (quite whatever that means) be, or be combined with, omnipotence, omniscience and a concern for mankind?

With God's goodness in the spotlight, the sufferings, pains and hopelessnesses – the evils – in the world come shrieking at us. We hit a paradox that should strike all believers in the Judaeo-Christian-Islamic God. It is one that ensures that many people cannot be believers. It can be put very simply.

EVIL

God is all good and all powerful, yet considerable evil, gratuitous evil by way of unnecessary suffering, exists in the world. Therefore, either God is not all good or is not all powerful.

The conclusion contradicts the basic common belief of Jews, Christians and Muslims – a paradoxical result for these believers. Indeed, the world's unnecessary sufferings form a springboard for arguing that God as all powerful and all good cannot exist.

The paradox hangs on the existence of *gratuitous* evils, unwarranted, unnecessary evils. Doubtless, life would be bland and boring – and unrecognizable as life – were there neither struggles in achieving, nor failures to be met. In the world, though, there are many sufferings, pains, distresses that appear highly unwarranted and, allegedly, caused by an omnipotent, omnibenevolent God. Christians sometimes note a specific biblical example; namely, God's treatment of his servant Job. The Paradox of Job draws attention to the sufferings, undeservedly placed upon him by God – yet God is meant to be good and just.

'What seems to be evil is not really evil: we would see this, were we possessed of the perspective of eternity.'

This wildly optimistic response to the evil problem could receive a wildly pessimistic reply that, equally, perhaps what appears good is not really good – and the world is the work of the Devil.

There are various wriggles designed to make intelligible God's omnipotence and omnibenevolence as compatible with the world's sufferings. Being essentially omnipotent and omnibenevolent, God, it has been claimed, must have made the best possible world: any evils are, somehow, essential to the best. A related thought is that for goodness to exist, there must be some evils; just as for tallness to exist, there must be shortness. As previously explored, God's omnipotence does not demand performance of the impossible.

Even were goodness to require evils, that would leave unexplained the vast quantity of unnecessary evils, unnecessary sufferings. Further, it is not at all clear that for items to be good, there must exist some evils, though it is true that certain goods require evils. In order to manifest the virtue of compassion, some individuals need to suffer. One suspects that those who suffer would value not suffering – over suffering albeit with compassion. Further, if goodness logically requires some evil, then, if it is possible for God not to have created a world, then in such circumstances God could not be good, for there would be no evils. This is God's Goodness Puzzle.

Sometimes it is said that for humans to be *aware* of the good/evil distinction, good and evil must both exist. Again, this would not justify the quantity of evil: presumably, just one speck of evil would need to be put on parade. In any case, we could learn the good/evil distinction through fiction, not reality.

The most common story, aimed at resolving the Evil Paradox, acknowledges that God could indeed have created things differently, with the world empty of pointless evils. However, were the world guaranteed evil free in this way, it would lack creatures with free will, containing instead robots who always perform the good. Robots necessarily possess less value than free agents – or so it is assumed. Hence, God created individuals with free will, individuals free to perform bad deeds as well as good – and sadly often they go for the bad. Further, free will, evils and goods are essential for humans in their character development; it may lead to their eternal salvation.

The above defence – the Free Will Defence – at best explains those evils caused by humans acting freely; namely, the moral evils. It leaves unexplained those evils, natural evils, caused by non-human events such as earthquakes. Another explanation would be needed to justify those natural evils. The Defence also casts some doubt on God's value. Is God free to choose whether to perform good deeds? If he possesses such freedom, then, it seems, he must be capable of doing bad things. Some religious believers may be unhappy with that divine capacity. If he lacks such freedom, then he merits the robotic tag, robotic on a pretty grand scale. Either way, there is the Puzzle of God's Free Will. In the next chapter, we see an 'either way' problem for human free will.

If God is a necessary being whose characteristics are necessary, then it seems as if the created world and its sufferings necessarily flow from him. If sense can be made of God having freely created this world, this world of free agents, and if God is omniscient, then he would have known what the free agents would do. After all, we have already established that free will is not incompatible with fore-knowledge. In view of his foreknowledge, why did God not create a world of humans whom he knew would freely act well rather than badly? It is no good response to insist that the beings would not then have been acting freely, for the Free Will Defence accepts that God created *this* world in which, it is claimed, we often act freely.

To the complaint that the world is not better, it is no good response that the complaint implies that God ought to have created the best possible world, but there is no best possible. The complaint is simply that he could have created a world with less unnecessary suffering than this, though paradoxically, if there is no best possible, then that complaint could always be made, but with differing degrees of justification. It is, furthermore, no good response to say that he cares for *us* – and with a different world, we would not have existed. Indeed, that is so; but think of those other beings, more worthy if of good character, who would have existed instead of us.

Despite factors such as the above, millions of people believe in an all-powerful, all-good God. Paradoxically, though, the evils in the world – and the various religious explanations – could be revised to defend belief in an all-powerful, all-evil Devil. The Evil Paradox would be transformed into the Goodness Paradox. Given the Devil as creator of the world, how come there is so much good? Well, a free will defence could be used, maybe with the other religious explanations, but all flipped over, in order to justify belief in the omnipotent devilish divinity.

*   *   *

Linking God, religion and morality leads many believers to perform good deeds because of the carrot of heaven and their personal salvation, despite some religious teachings rightly insisting that this is highly inappropriate motivation. It is inappropriate because it undermines the goodness of the individual's character. A moral motivation typically is aimed at benefiting others for their sakes – not others as means to one's own heavenly ends.

When we aim to be good, whether on religious grounds or not, puzzles arise. For a flavour, a digression is worth engaging.

RAKEHELL

The good man, when he does something bad, should surely feel shame, remorse and regret. Yet in feeling shame, he shows himself not as bad as the shameless man, thus paradoxically detracting from his shame, and making himself feel a little better. Feeling a little better about himself at feeling ashamed, may yet generate a new level of shame; but being aware of that, he may spiral into another level of feeling pleased with himself – and so on.

Given the obscurity of the term 'rakehell' – for a dissolute man, a libertine, a rake – perhaps the puzzle would be better labelled the 'Paradox of Shame'. 'Rakehell', though, retains a certain charm.

There is nothing odd about having different levels of feelings and emotions, beliefs and desires. You may yearn for some cigarettes, yet also yearn to lack such yearnings. Further, there is the fact of human psychology that, if we reflect on our psychological states, such as feelings or emotions, we are usually less directly involved in them, reducing their intensity. If we attend to our feelings of shame as being appropriate, we are distracted to some extent from feeling ashamed. Analogously and paradoxically, focusing on a pain can help to reduce the painfulness. Disanalogously though, a pain – to be a pain – must be felt; but to be ashamed does not require constant awareness of a feeling of shame. So, being distracted is not key to the puzzle, once it is read in terms of being ashamed rather than just the feeling of being ashamed.

The Rakehell suggests a spiralling problem. We cannot, so to speak, catch the full extent of our wickedness about which to be ashamed. Once we seem to have clasped it, its immensity reduces a little; and this is because we have the merit of being ashamed. Simply in being ashamed we necessarily reduce our wickedness; we are thereby a little bit better. Yet we may be ashamed at that, ashamed at reducing our wickedness in this way, thus spiralling us into new levels of shame – but then further reductions in wickedness.

Reflection on our psychological states can pose such puzzles, but reflection is not necessary. Consider the Masochist Puzzle: the masochist receives satisfaction from pain and humiliation – yet that satisfaction may be thought to reduce the suffering a little. We may argue that the true masochist, paradoxically, does not even want the satisfaction resulting from the suffering. Dissatisfaction gives satisfaction that yet gives dissatisfaction – and so on.

Returning to reflection, some virtues are not undermined by our knowledge that we possess them. We may be generous, kind and courageous, and know that we are generous, kind and courageous. Some virtues, though, such as humility and modesty, may require our ignorance of our possession, if we possess them. To put it paradoxically – the Modesty Paradox – if we know we are modest, then we are not.

If Mona is modest, obviously she ought not to brag about it and ought not to overestimate her achievements. Suppose modesty requires that she should underestimate her achievements, or at least place them in perspective, diminishing their importance. If she deliberately underestimates, then that smacks of dissembling, false modesty rather than modesty; she needs to be playing down her achievements naturally, not as a modesty project. Recall the first/third-person distinction within Moore's Paradox of Chapter 2. We may rightly think of Mona that she is modest and, hence, plays down her achievements; but maybe Mona cannot rightly think, 'I'm modest and, hence, I play down my achievements.'

* * *

We digressed from God, though the virtues of ignorance would, pretty plainly, be necessarily absent from God. Once the understanding of God is modified, to explain how his characteristics are consistent – how his knowledge, goodness, power must be understood or restricted in certain ways – then we probably have less reason to believe in such a god, or he becomes so abstract that it is bizarre to think of his caring about the world and deserving worship.

Here, Tertullian's Paradox deserves mention. Tertullian, around AD 200, when objecting to those Christians who insisted that God's incarnation involved contradictions, declared that the Son of God was born and then died and 'just because it is absurd, it is to be believed; and he was buried and rose again; it is certain because it is impossible'. Possibly Tertullian was arguing, following Aristotle (albeit in exaggerated language), that something highly unlikely would not be reported, unless it happened. There remains though, the paradox that God is in many ways incomprehensible, his relation to the world being a mystery.

Religious believers often readily grasp at the mystery, the incomprehensibility, of the divine, sometimes implying that their words about the divine take on different meanings from the everyday. The meanings, they say, cannot be assessed by human standards of reason and good sense. People should learn to live with the divine paradoxes, with divine mysteries. They may even sustain faith; they show the vast distance between God's greatness and humanity's weakness. Of course, all this is baffling, if the claim really is that the words we use to describe God have different meanings. What meanings? Why, then, use the words we do? We may as well describe God as short, dusty and bicycle-like.

Many of us would regard the Tertullian line as yielding to irrationality and superstition, to 'hocus-pocus', a term deployed by Maynard Keynes of religion. Many of us would respect, instead, the contrasting line of those believers, for example the fourteenth-century Jewish philosopher Gersonides, who insist that religious doctrines need to be understood in accord with the demands of reason. Yet that need not rule out the significance of symbols and rituals in our lives.

Atheists – and I write as one – dismiss as absurd the claim that there is God's eternal presence at Jerusalem's Western Wall – the Wailing Wall – where the world was founded, its centre; but that does not justify the belief that the wailing rituals are pointless and lack value in the lives of religious Jews. After all, those of us who believe in no afterlife may yet place flowers at a grave; we do not think the deceased or the decaying corpse delights in the scent.

Yes, our understanding needs to accord with reason, but some of our actions may reasonably enough – and paradoxically – be without reason. Some things, we just do. Further, having seen throughout this book how reasoning gets us into trouble, we should embrace some caution, some humility, regarding how far reason and experience can take us, when seeking to iron out inconsistencies. We meet some un-ironed concepts – and we travel a rocky and human terrain – in the next chapter, where we turn to puzzles at humanity's centre.

9 Encounters with *our* mysterious ways –
love, luck and life

. . . in which we meet a bad man, yet also a good man just as bad; question our freedom and our selves; engage with Sleeping Beauty and those who do not exist – and, with music and paintings in mind, we ask, 'What is it that we love when loving?'

Our paradoxical journeying has seen reason and rationality running out of control. It is time to face concepts at the heart of life and death, concepts of responsibility, free choice, the self. They are concepts that, upon reflection, are seemingly as paradoxical as concepts of the divine. They possess features of absurdity, even magic.

MORAL LUCK

If I am rightly to be held morally responsible for a deed, the deed should surely be within my control; yet I am frequently held morally responsible – praised or blamed – for many things not remotely within my control. Indeed, what is truly within my control?

The paradox underlines, yet also undermines, how we see ourselves in everyday life – and how, arguably, we must see ourselves.

Praising or blaming people for having performed good or bad deeds rests uneasily with the thought that what they did was a matter of luck, of chance, or resulted from causes prior to their birth. Moral luck has a paradoxical feel. Bernard Williams, originator of the term a few decades ago, thought it an oxymoron. To see the paradox coming into view, let us peel away layers of supposed accountability. Peeling an onion, we may find what seems to be a centre; with this moral peeling, we reach only a nothingness, a nothingness that the existentialist philosopher Jean-Paul Sartre paradoxically embraced

'I can't help myself' – peeling the onion

Mr Badman is a bad man. Although married to an adoring wife and proclaiming his fidelity, he has sexual liaisons with a swathe of girls. He becomes angry easily and has at times struck down his better half. He once was so careless when driving that he hit a small girl, killing her. Mr Badman is a liar, a wife-beater and killer – a morally bad man and, under various jurisdictions, would be in prison. Contrast him with Mr Goodman who is none of these things, being faithful, having neither beaten his wife, nor hit a child when driving. (This is, by the way, no reference to Nelson Goodman, creator of Grue.) A little reflection leads us to see how Goodman could be incredibly similar to Badman, except Badman is unlucky, Goodman lucky.

Goodman pursues the girls, but the girls are untempted. Goodman takes swipes at his wife: she skilfully ducks; he misses. Goodman drives carelessly, but no child ever runs in front.

It is no paradox that we prefer some people to others: the careful driver to the bad, the loving partner to the unloving, the good golfer to the poor. The paradox concerns what justifies our showering moral accolades on some and condemnations on others – when the relevant differences reside in factors outside their control, 'without' their control. When voyaging, we may prefer calm seas to choppy; but we do not praise seas for being calm or blame them for being choppy.

In the cases cited, Badman initiated actions that led to the unhappy results. Badman points out that Goodman initiated similar actions, yet – through luck, through lack of good looks, or whatever – failed to generate the unhappy results. So, it is paradoxical and unfair that Badman is blamed whereas Goodman is not.

We may resolve the problem here by arguing that both are equally blameworthy. Peeling off the luck of the results, we are driven to the basic actions performed. Goodman drove carelessly, took swipes at his wife, and tried to chat up the girls. He may, though, even without doing any of these things, be morally as bad as Badman. Peel off the basic actions – for we need to look at intentions.

Goodman's intentions may be no better than Badman's. If he intends to hit his wife, yet things intervene preventing even the raising of the hand, is he not as morally bad as the man who strikes out and misses – and as morally bad as Badman who strikes out and hits? If he lusts after the nubile young ladies, is he not as bad (if bad it be) as the man who chats them up and fails – and as morally bad as Badman who chats and seduces?

Ought we to peel away even the intentions? Consider a revised Goodman: he *would* intend to use his chat-up line, but lacks the intention – only because there are no girls around. He *would* at times intend to beat his wife – but he has no wife. The simple point is that circumstances, to some extent at least, are matters of luck and partially explain our intentions. Peeling our onion of responsibility, it looks as if we ought to peel off actual intentions, aiming our moral assessment at individuals' characters, dispositions, what they would do, were opportunities to arise – even if they will not arise and are thus 'counterfactual'.

For a vivid example, reflect upon how exceptionally lucky we readers of this book probably are, though not necessarily in reading this book. We are thought of as pretty decent people – very, very different from those 'monsters' running the concentration camps in Nazi Germany or brutally putting down protestors, be they in Zimbabwe, Burma or China. Yet suppose we were in those situations, needing to feed our families, scared of opposing governmental authorities, perhaps swept along by surrounding fervour and frenzy. Are we so smug, so confident, in our characters? Would we really stand up and be counted, refusing to join in the repressions, refusing to take jobs as guards in Auschwitz-Birkenau? Would we even recognize the moral horror surrounding us?

More peeling, though, is required. This is because, whatever our character, our dispositions, our possible intentions, are not they all, in a way, out of our control? We did not choose our character. We had no say in our genetic make-up and upbringing. So, after this peeling, what is left? What is left of *us* – of *me*?

*   *   *

There is no core 'me', it seems, that can be rightly held morally responsible. The puzzle is the Paradox of Free Will, bedecked in recent finery. The matter is not so much that of 'control', for, of course, we do control things – even a thermostat manages that – but of what we can freely choose to control. When we praise or blame people for what they do, the usual implication is that they are free agents. They can choose what to do; they can do otherwise than what they do. Yet, asks the paradox, can they really?

The paradox extends beyond morality. Most generally, it is the Appraisal Puzzle, including puzzles of 'glory luck' and 'skilful luck'. Whether people are winning gold medals, writing symphonies or passing examinations, that they are able so to do, and actually are doing so, depends on many factors about which they lack free choice. 'There's glory for you!' we may say, echoing Lewis Carroll's Humpty Dumpty, as the Nobel Prize winners collect their prizes. There was the luck, for example, of a mould growing, a mould that Alexander Fleming happened to notice, leading to the penicillin discovery. There are the lucks of education, brain power and determination. Whether the baseball player, footballer, the racing driver, do well depends, in part, on the gust of wind, the crick in the knee, the slip of the finger. True, successful golfers, when told how lucky they are, may ironically respond, 'Yes, the more I practise, the luckier I get' – but the keenness to practise has ultimately resulted from factors over which they had no choice.

The Appraisal Puzzle rests on our appraisals presupposing that the individuals in question *freely* controlled what they did. Appraisals, though, can merely hang on what is or is not achieved. They may indeed be valuable ways of encouraging further desired activity; they may be causal carrots to generate certain behaviour. Praise the salesman and he may sell even more. Oil the machine and it will run more efficiently. Whether people *deserve* praise, though, requires the praiseworthy acts to be under their free control, directly or indirectly.

There is, by the way, a traditional puzzle – let us deem it the Puzzle of the Virtuous – regarding whether people are more virtuous if they experience temptations for wickedness and overcome them, or more virtuous if they lack all such temptations. Why do people merit moral credit for self-control, if there is, so to speak, nothing to control? As Plato pointed out, if a man is blind, he cannot claim the moral strength not to feast his eyes.

A landmark murder case in the United States involved Clarence

Darrow defending two wealthy, well-educated students, Leopold and Loeb. Darrow argued that their actions resulted from hereditary and environmental factors. Speaking of Loeb – or was it Leopold? – he proclaimed, 'He was not his own father; he was not his own mother; he was not his own grandparents . . . He did not make himself.'

FREE WILL

If we act of our own free will, we possess the ability to do otherwise than what we do. Increasingly, though, there is evidence that our actions result from past causes, such that we could not now have done otherwise. Yet, were such causes lacking, our actions would be random rather than free. Hence, paradoxically, either way we lack free will.

Either way – with our actions determined or undetermined – appears incompatible with free will.

I choose to lift my arm – and I lift. The movement was caused by certain types of electrical impulses in certain nerves and muscles caused by certain neural changes, all no doubt with long names with which only neurologists and anatomists are familiar. The causal chains presumably can be traced back in time. Indeed, recent excitement occurred when experiments showed that some neurological changes leading to such movements occurred before the conscious choices to make the movements. (Should the existence of prior causes have been surprising?) There is no room, it seems, for a free decision to move my arm, for I – this mysterious *I* – could not have done otherwise, given the causes.

However, would things be any better regarding 'free', had my arm or my choice or my will been uncaused, undetermined? The events would then seem to be random. Freely willing, choosing, acting, are not matters of things happening randomly. The paradoxical conclusion is now reached. Our understanding of free will – free choice, free decision, free action – makes such freedom logically impossible. There is no third way.

Presenting these very thoughts – these logical insights, words and wisdom (!) – as the truth may be undermined, if the thoughts are solely the result of causes or chance. Neither causal chains nor chance-landings of dice ensure hitting the truth. Further, were we to see other people as causally determined or random in their choices and behaviour, we should treat them as akin to trees rocked by gales, bees attracted by pollen, or shuffled cards being dealt at gaming tables. Arguably, there would be no scope for praise and blame, admiration and resentment – save as means of affecting their future behaviour. True, we do sometimes see people – even ourselves – as driven by external forces or acting randomly; but this is exceptional, when we are treating people as ill, deranged or brainwashed.

There is no third way, I said earlier – but, fallible as I am, maybe that is mistaken. When we act freely, we often give reasons for what we do. You raised your arm. Why? The reason is unlikely to mention changes in the brain. Rather it will be, for example, because you wanted Anthea's attention, or needed to pay the bill, or was stretching for a book. When the gun is pointing at you, do you act freely in handing over your money? You have a reason for handing, but would prefer not to hand; you could choose a risky fight or flight instead. Perhaps these thoughts point to free will, choices, decisions, actions, being matters of our having reasons for what we do, reasons that involve our wants and worries, hopes and fears – and reasons that may sometimes show our actions as to some extent free, to some extent not.

This compatibilist approach – making free will as much compatible with randomness as with determinism, note – requires considerable refinement. Sometimes we would prefer not to have certain desires and yearnings. Alcoholics who want a drink and get what they want may well not want to be alcoholic. They have good reason for losing their drinking wants. There is a second-order want concerning the first-order want for a drink.

In presenting this compatibilist approach, the common identification of reasons with causes is resisted. This is wise resistance, for we may evaluate a person's reasons as good and bad, but we do not evaluate causes in this way. Mystery, though, pervades the relation between reasons and causes or, indeed, the lack of causes. Perhaps the mystery may be reduced a little, if reasons are not viewed as entities competing with causes. Rather, reasons involve the dimension of interpreting and judging and context – seeing actions in a certain light to understand them. The mystery becomes how to relate that dimension to the neural. Whatever the relation, whether a hand movement is a matter of doodling, practising a signature, writing a shopping list, depends on context and what else the person does.

Whether people are acting freely depends on their various reasons and desires, and with which ones – first order? higher orders? – they identify. Yet a slave may identify with his slavery, some Muslim women with the burqa and some Westernized girls with the scanty – but do they thereby do so freely?

'I am not free to choose my desires and those with which I identify; I am not free to choose which reasons strike me as most powerful.'

This is the common retort to compatibilist approaches. The retort is motivated at the metaphysical level by the paradoxical pull of wanting to be a pure subject with no pre-formed character, no desires – and yet, as such a subject, choosing what to do and being responsible for the choices. It is an impossible dream – or nightmare. The subject, the self, is reduced, metaphorically, to nothing. And that lands us even deeper in the paradoxical mire.

*   *   *

Before we turn explicitly to the self, here are a couple more thoughts on free will.

When I think I am freely choosing, can I in fact consciously believe that the choice I shall make is already causally determined by events unknown to me, by prior neural changes in my brain? Perhaps I can, yet paradoxically that still leaves me with having to choose what to do. Further, if I am told what someone has predicted I shall do, may I not then choose to do something different? We are raising the Contrary Choice, Prediction, Paradox, or remembering how contrary was Miss Mary of the nursery rhyme, the Mary, Mary Paradox.

If the causal deterministic picture is true, then scientists, in principle (and Chaos Paradox ignored), could predict what Mary will do on the basis of her brain states and the world's impingings. If, however, she learns of their prediction, then she could surely choose to do otherwise – and hence could falsify their predictions. Now, suppose that she is the scientist who makes the predictions: she self-predicts on the basis of neural evidence. Whatever she is led to predict, may she not then choose to do otherwise?

Awareness of a prediction can be a factor relevant in making the prediction. We may picture Mary as a cat chasing her own tail. After she pops into her calculation her awareness of what is predicted, the resultant new prediction spills forth; but her awareness of that new prediction now needs to be entered into the calculation. The puzzle may remind us of the player's reasoning, when thinking through what to do in Newcomb's Problem.

Taking into account how *others* take into account your taking into account occurs in Prisoners' Dilemmas – and in the Dr Psycho Puzzle. You eat an apple and then are told by Dr Psycho that he had injected it with a fatal poison – or had not. If the apple has been poisoned, then you should drink the antidote medicine available, despite its nasty taste, for it counteracts the poison and all will be well. If the apple has not been poisoned, then certainly do not drink the medicine: when it has no poison to counteract, it kills. Dr Psycho gleamingly comments, 'You don't really need to worry, for I only poisoned the apple if I foresaw that you would drink the medicine. If I predicted you would choose not to drink, then no apple poisoning occurred.' He adds, wandering off, leaving you to stew, 'As you know, I am a good predictor.'

The puzzle raises various questions: as it stands, without more details, rationality alone cannot tell you what you ought to do, as we have found with many paradoxes. Moving on from the good doctor, there is often a vague feeling in the air that, given time, science can solve all our problems. There could be pills for everything – to stop us smoking, to improve our memory, to lower our desire for food, to make us feel attracted to certain people, and so forth.

We would still need the desire to make the relevant changes in, for example, eating, smoking, sexual preferences, study or whatever. 'Ah, no problem,' comes the scientists' reply, 'we have a pill for you to take, so that you want to change.' Well, you would still need to decide whether you wanted the desire to change. At each level, a pill may be proffered to generate the want in you, yet there is always the further factor of whether you want that want, whether you want to change and develop in certain ways.

The Pill Puzzle above raises again problems about the 'you' or 'I'. Some people dislike pills and potions: they are external chemical interferences – yet have we any clear idea what counts as external here? Ourselves and our choices relate not just to how we are now, and what counts as within and outside us, but to how we *shall* be. That raises the question of what makes an individual the same person, the same self, over time.

'Will it be me?' – and Sleeping Beauty

Many tales have filled many pages, displaying perplexities of the self, deep perplexities, for a lot hangs on whether an individual is – or is not – me. Well, a lot hangs on it for me.

SELF

I think of myself as an enduring entity, persisting through time; yet what is it that persists? The body? The body, including the brain, undergoes radical changes; it seems that I can even make sense of myself moving into a new body. The mind? Well, presumably that is the stream of consciousness, with memories, thoughts and intentions, but that too can be altered or blocked, yet *I* would continue to be. There seems to be nothing that the continuing self can be.

Religious belief sometimes offers the immaterial soul as solution, the soul immune from the physical network of decay, a soul with potential for eternal life. The introduction, though, of such a mysterious entity is no help in determining what makes me *me*.

To illustrate some self perplexities, here are two typical tales of everyday philosophical, thought-experimental life, based on deliverances of Bernard Williams.

First tale

Lilly is locked in the lilac room; Polly in the peach room. They know that tomorrow one locked inhabitant will be tortured, the other receiving vast wealth and set free. Neither are masochists; both are monetarily motivated and self-interested. They are clear for what they hope. Lilly hopes that the individual in the lilac room – she, Lilly – will receive the money; Polly hopes the opposite.

Here is the next step. They learn that before the morrow comes, they will be put to sleep and operated upon. Happily the operations' details need not concern us. Suffice it to say that their minds are to be switched. Suffice that to mean that all the psychological states, the thoughts and memories, the hopes and intentions, the character traits and dispositions of Lilly will end up holding of Polly's brain and body, and vice versa. Before this is rejected as phantasy, let us remember that more and more psychological states are found to be grounded in states of the brain. What matters for our identity seems to be the configurations, intensities and types of neural firings rather than the brain's material stuff. A metaphor often used is that minds, the psychological states, are more like software than hardware. The software that makes up Lilly's psychology and consciousness of self could be transferred to another person – well, maybe.

After the operation, when the Polly-body (so to speak) wakes up in the peach room, she will say things such as, 'Ah, I've survived the operation; I'm Lilly.' She will have Lilly's memories, beliefs and intentions. She may reflect how odd it now feels, looking down and seeing the Polly-body, particularly if it transpires that the body turns out to have a wooden leg, or for that matter that Polly was a cross-dresser. There could well be changes quickly occurring in Lilly's mentality, in such circumstances. The Lilly-body will, of course, be voicing itself as now being Polly.

Here is the key question. Before the operations, when Lilly and Polly are told what will happen, what should they request, regarding which post-operative individual receives the money?

After a little musing, it seems obvious to Lilly, sitting in the lilac room, that she now wants the individual in the peach room to be given the wealth tomorrow, and the individual in the lilac room to receive the torture. If that indeed happens – and let us assume that it does – then the peach room individual will be speaking in terms of 'I am Lilly, so pleased that I'm getting what I wanted, so relieved I am not being tortured.'

The above tale is a vivid and contrived reminder that a person seems to be the same person when there is continuity of the psychological states. After all, are not psychological states, memories, hopes, sense of self, what make me *me*?

Putting that conclusion to the back of our minds for the moment, now try this, a second tale.

Second tale

Suppose you are locked in the lilac room, told that you will be tortured tomorrow. You dread the morrow. Would things be any better if you learn that, while you sleep, before the torture, your mind is to be wiped of all memories and beliefs and so on? You would still experience the horrendous painful experiences tomorrow, even though not knowing who you are. Would it help, were you told that you would receive a set of beliefs and seeming memories making up a coherent life, yet not your own? You would still be undergoing the painful horrors tomorrow.

The tale continues. The source of the new 'memories', beliefs and hopes and so forth, would seem irrelevant to what you undergo tomorrow – as would what happens to your set of psychological states when wiped from your brain. Hence, also to learn that, in fact, your new psychological states derive from an individual in the peach room, who will receive your old psychological states, would be irrelevant to the torture *you* undergo tomorrow. You do not look forward to the morrow because – despite all these psychological changes – you expect to be suffering the pain tomorrow, here in the lilac room.

The two tales

A moment's reflection shows that we have the same happenings in the second tale as with the first, yet different intuitions regarding outcomes. Think of yourself as Lilly. In the tale's first presentation, it seemed that you would be in Polly's body in the peach room tomorrow, not experiencing the lilac room's torture. In the second presentation, you see yourself as remaining the individual in the lilac room, suffering badly.

The sagas can be abbreviated to the following dilemma. I do not look forward to torture tomorrow. Should I hope, then, that this body is not tortured, whatever my psychological states; or should I hope that whichever body carries my psychological states should not be tortured?

Neither 'continuity of body' nor 'continuity of psychological states' seems essential to me. May I not still be me, even though inhabiting a different body *and* with a completely different set of thoughts and memories? The Paradox of the Self thus becomes the Puzzle of the Vanished Self. It has the bizarre – and nonsensical outcome – that we (!) could be perpetually undergoing such changes, yet unable to tell. It becomes an idle supposition. In any case, a fallacy is committed, in reaching the vanished self.

Just because, if true, I can survive without continuity of body and I can survive without continuity of psychological states, it does not follow that I can survive without either. Just because I could live without getting married and could live with being married, it does not mean that I could live neither married nor unmarried. Recall Chapter 5's Theseus' Ship. A ship could survive as the same ship if consisting largely of the same components, or if performing the same function with the same ownership, yet it would not survive if failing all these conditions.

Perhaps what makes me me over time is either physical or psychological continuity. Yet even this suggestion hits buffers when we reflect on the possibility of replications and divisions. Surely I am *this* individual here; any replications will be just that: replications. Further, I cannot readily make sense of myself dividing, such that *I* am over here, yet also *I* am over there – be that division occurring because my consciousness stream splits or because my brain is divided.

*   *   *

Troubles about the relationship between me and the here and now are within the Sleeping Beauty Paradox, even though its explicit puzzle is one of probability. Arguments still rage.

SLEEPING BEAUTY

Beauty is soon to be drugged and put to sleep. What then happens – and she knows this – depends on a fair coin's random spin. If the coin lands heads, she will be woken just one morning, randomly chosen, during the coming ten years, and after an hour returned to sleep. If the coin lands tails, she will be woken every morning of the coming ten years, each for an hour, though she will be unable to remember any previous awakenings within the game. The game ends after the tenth year when she is woken, her memory restored. Whenever she is woken, she remembers everything about the game's set-up. The puzzle is, whenever she is awake during the game, ought she to think it more likely the coin landed tails?

To sum up, if the coin has landed heads, then she wakes up once – obviously not remembering any prior waking. If the coin has landed tails, she wakes up 3,652 times, never remembering any other awakenings during the game. Speaking roughly, tails for Total Possible awakenings – the Tails Total sequence of events happening – and heads for the Hardly Any, Hardly Any being just the one awakening.

It is a 50:50 matter whether the coin lands tails, so it is a 50:50 matter whether Beauty is in the Tails Total sequence. Yet, whenever she is awake during the game, even though she has no new information, ought she not to think it far more likely that she is in the Tails sequence? She may argue in the following way, when awake during the game:

That this awakening happens to be just the one awakening that results from heads coming up is so unlikely. This awakening is far more likely to belong to the 3,652 awakenings of the Tails Total.

Behind the paradox lurks the question of what makes an awakening experience for Beauty *this* experience rather than *that*. Beauty, it seems, cannot distinguish when in the game.

Suppose, as the result of a random mechanism, some external observers are allowed to gaze at Beauty just one morning throughout the whole ten years. They see her on no other morning and do not know which way the coin came down. Suppose that, on this one occasion when they gaze, she happens to be awake. Were Beauty in the Heads Hardly sequence, that would be an incredible coincidence, for in 3,651 mornings of that sequence she would always be asleep. Surely, the observers should conclude that it is far more likely that they are seeing Beauty in the Tails Total sequence.

The external observers spot an unlikely coincidence, making it rational to argue that tails came up. It is difficult to see what coincidence Beauty can spot. There is no coincidence for her in, on the one hand, happening to be awake and, on the other hand, noticing that it is *this* morning, for *this* morning for her is indistinguishable from any other waking morning.

Controversially, I maintain, therefore, that whenever Beauty is awake, she has no reason to think it is more likely she is in the Tails sequence rather than Heads. Were she to place bets when awake, it would, though, be rational for her to bet on Tails. This is because, if under Tails, she would be placing 3,652 bets and winning, whereas if under Heads, she would be placing only one bet and losing.

Life, luck and love

Most of us value life – well, at least human life. One immediate paradox is the casual way in which we accept that we exist. It is so incredible that I exist, given the trillions of chances against it. Indeed, the inspirer of the Sleeping Beauty Paradox, Arnold Zuboff, argues that Sleeping Beauty can guide us to see that all experiences are really *my* experiences. There is, then, no unlikelihood in these experiences happening to be *mine*. Zuboff's intriguing, though bizarre, position has consequences for our treatment of 'others'; they are not really other. Chapter 7 has already engaged some ethical dilemmas in viewing ourselves as distinct, separate individuals.

Even though we do see ourselves as distinct individuals, centres of consciousness, most of us accept that it is wrong to kill someone. Zooming into detail, most of us judge killing someone to be harmful. Question: how has the deceased individual been harmed?

One answer is the loss of life for that person. Possibly that explains why an octogenarian's death is usually viewed as not as bad as a teenager's. We feel that the young person has suffered a greater loss – though, recalling the infinity paradoxes, both have paradoxically thereby lost equinumerous infinite years ahead.

Consider the Repeated Firing Puzzle. I fire two shots and kill Cristabel. The first bullet strikes her brain, killing her immediately. The second bullet lodges in her heart: it would have killed her, had she not already died because of the first bullet. I argue that I did no serious harm. Bearing in mind what the second bullet would have done, the first bullet merely caused Cristabel the loss of one second of life – hardly serious. The second bullet, of course, did not kill her. This paradox urges the response that my firings constituted one combined harmful action. We saw some actions, when uncombined, generating puzzles with the Innocent Murderers.

If the wrongfulness of killing lies in the loss of life, then we have the Abstinence Puzzle. Few people believe that abstaining from sexual intercourse is morally wrong; yet in their abstinence they are causing loss of life to the children who otherwise could or would have been created. So, surely that is morally wrong. True, they cannot name the children or pick them out. True, they do not know for sure whether, on any particular occasion, conception would have occurred; but, on many occasions, it is likely.

We cut through this paradox with a thought from a certain Henry Salt, a humanitarian reformer: individuals can be harmed only if they have the foothold of existence. Yet that moves the puzzle along. What sort of existence? The answer has consequences for the moral assessment of abstinence, contraception, abortions and infanticide.

Many people think that the fertilized ovum should be protected because of its potential. On this view, a teenager, Lucy, for example, possessed a foothold on existence through the existence some years earlier of the fertilized ovum from whence Lucy developed.

We may question, though, why fertilization is taken as key. After all, the spermatozoon and the ovum, when separate, must have possessed the potential to become the fertilized ovum – otherwise, how else would it have come about? Were mere potential key, the Abstinence Puzzle would loom again. Development into a person, though, is gradual. How far an item is along the developmental line to personhood is surely an important factor in determining the degree of rightness or wrongness in preventing further development.

WRONGFUL LIFE

Suppose you have a choice between conceiving a child now, one who will be disabled, and conceiving a child later, one who will have a flourishing life. Your child will be better off if you wait; yet the child you considered conceiving now would not then exist at all. So, she could be better off to have been born. Yet suppose that she is born and she argues she ought not to have been born. Could her non-existence have been better for her?

HARMING THE DEAD

Assuming that death is annihilation, death cannot be a harm for you. This is because you are not in existence to undergo any harm. Further, there seems no justification for respecting the dead for their sakes. You cannot respect someone who does not exist.

When harms occur, the individuals need to exist to undergo the harms – well, so we may think. We may be thinking rightly, but we need careful thought, at least about timing.

Before you exist, things may be done that bring harms to you – when you do exist. Drug-taking before conception, smoking during pregnancy, may have consequences for a child when born. It is in the child's interests, even before conception, that would-be mothers do not act in certain ways. Once the child exists, then it may bring an action against its parents for not protecting its interests prior to existence. A child who never gets to existence lacks any foothold for such an action.

The Wrongful Life Paradox, working on these matters, highlights how a would-be mother may be correctly advised to conceive a child later than planned – in the interests of the child. Yet, as seen, that temporal delay would result in a different child; so the delay fails to give a better life to the child who is not brought into existence. Indeed, it prevents that child's existence. Harms are identity dependent: there needs to be an identifiable individual in existence who is harmed. Delaying the conception benefits *a* child, but not the child who otherwise would have been. The expression 'the mother's child' could have designated either.

The related puzzle is whether a child born, maybe with a lifetime of severe pain ahead, could argue that it ought not to have been born. How can we compare its life now with how it – it? – would have been without life? Some proclaim that there should be rejoicing whenever the gift of life is bestowed; but that assumes that life must always be better than no life. That is not an obvious truth – though, of course, we need life to be in a position to judge that we would prefer not to have received the gift.

Turning to death, despite death being the loss of life, some paradoxically conclude that it cannot be a harm, and that no events after death can harm the deceased. The background assumption is that death is genuine annihilation. Epicurus, in third-century BC Athens, taught in the Garden, aiming to remove the fear of death, a fear which is an obstacle to happiness. His pithy comment was, 'When death is there, we are not; when we are there, death is not.' We should no more care about our future non-existence than we care about our prenatal non-existence, our non-existence before birth.

Whether there is symmetry between prenatal and posthumous non-existence is doubtful. We can readily make sense of our lives continuing longer than in fact they will. But it is doubtful whether we can make sense of our lives starting centuries earlier – and their still being *our* lives. What sense can you make of its being you, with all the experiences of, say, someone living on the land, in poverty, in sixteenth-century England?

Harms must be experienced harms, insist some. Hence, as the deceased do not exist, they have no experiences; therefore they undergo neither harms nor benefits. Yet people are harmed when betrayed, even if they never discover the betrayal and even if their prospects, love and life are otherwise unaffected. Modest Mona has her privacy violated by being peeped upon by a peeping Tom, even though it is never revealed to her what she has unwittingly revealed to Tom. 'How can such events be harms, if the person never finds out?' Well, were they to find out, they would be distressed – and not necessarily distressed at finding out, but at what they find out about.

This suggests that what they find out about is harmful and would be so, even if undiscovered.

Suppose we accept that harms need not be experienced to be harms: we may still be captivated by the picture that the individual must exist in order to be harmed. True, the unconceived child does not exist when some harmful deeds are done, but eventually she comes into existence and suffers the harms. Now, while it is true that the deceased did exist, actions occurring after their death are not going to affect those past lives.

The argument should not convince. Why we respect an individual's corpse, his will, his last wishes – when we do – could be for our own benefit, but many of us recognize that we are doing these things for that person's sake, the one who is deceased. We can justify the recognition by the following point: had – *per impossibile* – the deceased discovered our kicking his corpse, ignoring his will, mocking his life, then he would have been distressed. By mistreating the corpse and so on, we are not harming some ghostly deceased figure; we are harming the person who once lived.

To return to the graveyard mentioned at the close of the previous chapter, when we leave flowers at the graveside, we may be showing our esteem for the person who once lived – and not showing it for the show to the living.

We can, it seems, have justifiable concerns about non-existent people, so long as at some time in the future or past they exist. In the next chapter, we touch on how we are sometimes wrapped up in the lives of permanent non-existents, for example, characters of fiction.

*   *   *

Throughout this chapter, we have been hitting bafflement about the self. We may be attracted by mysterious comments such as Wittgenstein's 'The subject does not belong to the world but it is a limit of the world.' The indexical features – the I, the here, the now – are as mysterious for me as they are apparently incomprehensible for God. I can no more point at my 'self' than, as we saw earlier, God can point at the here and now. The self seems a magician's illusion.

Before we lapse into either mystic mumbles or soul-filled silence, let us spin into love, for love is an everyday paradoxical occurrence. It leads to talk of sparkles, rainbows and soarings, and being meant for each other. Love, desire and lust are directed at particular (lucky?) individuals – this particular man or that particular woman. Larry declares that it is solely Ludmilla whom he loves; and that love is more than skin deep. Yet, we may have awareness of manipulations and chance factors involved. Larry may have followed Scott Fitzgerald's recommendation, 'Don't marry for money – go to where the money is, then marry for love.'

There are immediate paradoxes. How can 'true' love be love at first or immediate sight? How does love affect the lovers' perceptions of each other? We explain why Larry overlooks Ludmilla's many blemishes by saying that his perception is distorted by his love; yet we may explain his love by saying how he overlooks her blemishes. This circular movement undermines any explanatory value. Let us, though, focus on what it is that Larry loves.

LOVERS

Larry loves Ludmilla – yet Larry's love of Ludmilla must be because of her various characteristics. If so, then ought not Larry also to love anyone else who has those characteristics? Does he not really love anyone like Ludmilla, rather than Ludmilla in particular?

Larry's love rests on his experiences and knowledge and beliefs concerning Ludmilla; and they rest on Ludmilla's qualities – physical, emotional, intellectual and so forth. He may adore her smile, her walk and talk; he may value her kindness, her cuteness, her flick of the hair.

We could list away: he loves her because she has qualities F, G, H and so on. Once we have the list, the paradox presents. Larry loves a Ludmilla type rather than this particular or token Ludmilla. (The type/token distinction was encountered in Chapter 3.) If someone else comes along with Ludmilla's qualities, Larry should love her just as well.

'No, only *this* Ludmilla!' Larry insists. We then ask, 'Well, what is it about this Ludmilla?' If an answer is given, then we may be able to add it to the F, G, H list – and off we go again. The list gets blocked in two different ways – unless our questioning leads Larry to realize that he does not really love Ludmilla, or would indeed settle for any Ludmilla look-alikes when Ludmilla is out of town.

One block is, 'I love Ludmilla because she is Ludmilla' – but that is no explanation at all. It may be a deferral, with Larry thinking that some other qualities must exist. It may, though, be more of a commitment to *this* individual here – which leads to the second block.

The second block has a story told about how and where they met. Love develops through a joint causal history of intertwined lives. That causal history cannot now be repeated: it ties Larry to this particular Ludmilla here. Although Ludmilla's qualities are repeatable, in the sense that other items could have those qualities, Ludmilla herself cannot be repeated. She is irreplaceable as far as Larry is concerned – well, for the moment. Larry is a particular, enmeshed with a particular.

Many items in our lives are readily replaceable; and we approve of such. We replace the computer, the dishwasher, maybe even the cat. We do not mind which particular item we have of the type, so long as of the right type. That glass of wine or this? No matter, so long as they are same size, quality˙ and cost. Yet, most people think differently about friends and lovers, about wives and husbands – and about cats. They are not treated solely as items of a certain type.

The irreplaceability stance applies to certain inanimate objects. Heirlooms form obvious examples; but a curl of hair, a worn dressing gown – an ancient Volvo named 'Silver Streak', to give a personal example – can be 'irreplaceable', even if the proposed replacements are indistinguishable from the originals, be they new or shabby.

The replaceable/irreplaceable distinction has bearing on contrasts between music and paintings. We value this particular painting – the original. But with the music, we listen to different performances of the score. We are not usually devotees of one particular performance, though occasionally we are. You may value listening to Handel's *Agrippina*, whether it be Monday's performance or Tuesday's, whether it be in Zurich, London or New York. Indeed, there is a particular puzzle here – His Master's Voice Puzzle. We really do hear someone's voice and singing on the 'phone, on the recording, or via the internet, yet we do not so readily agree that we really saw the person or painting, if only seeing a photograph of the person or painting.

Paintings and repeatability – replications, copies – give rise to the Paradox of Forgery. Why is a forgery less valued than the original? There are answers in terms of the importance of the historical connections, or the disvalue of the deceit. Yet many art historians claim to see something in the fakes themselves: in some way, it is claimed, their intrinsic qualities are inferior. A few fakes, though, have deceived the experts for decades – and no doubt a few still do. So, it is paradoxical that, when fakes, when copies, cannot be distinguished from originals by the quality of painting, experts still find them aesthetically less satisfying than the originals.

Returning to love, as you look across the room at the one whom you love, do you love that person as a painting hanging in a gallery – or as a symphony that may be played in different cities? Does your being in love with Mehitabel mean being in love with the original that you met last week, last month or last year – or being in love with any Mehitabel who is being played in the town where you happen to be?

Be it falling in love, moral character or winning games grounded in skill – contingencies, serendipity, luck, good or bad fortune, enter into the story, as we have seen. Machiavelli wrote of a leader's glory depending in part on Fortuna – on *Miss* Fortuna, for Fortuna is a woman needing to be beaten. Placing the historical sexism and metaphorical abuse to one side, Machiavelli reminds us that, however much we plan, however hard we try, we ought neither to assume that success will come our way nor to assume that success ought so to do. The Machiavellian reflection may nourish a humility, a humility to be welcomed in these times of endless babble about what people – often, well-heeled people – have a right to expect, be they investors, home owners or offspring eager to inherit.

Harold Macmillan, the British Prime Minister, knew of Miss Fortuna. What ran policy? 'Events, dear boy. Events.' Events, events outside our control, largely determine the pathways, straight or meandering, of our lives, our loves and lovers, of our glory or otherwise. Indeed, what we deem to be our very selves, what we sense as within our control – these conceptual conjuring tricks that shape our lives – result from events outside, well outside, 'our' control. Events build us, batter us and, eventually, break us.

Events, dear boy. Events.

10   When to stop

. . . in which, after handling life's meaning, we find that Nirvana eludes us, the biggest bang possible is missing, and time and language appear fragile; so, we turn to fiction and logic – and realize that the tortoise requires us to stop – well, eventually.

A tale is told of a young man searching for the meaning of life. He has heard tell of a wise old woman who lives in the remotest of mountains, who is as wise as wise can be. She knows the meaning of life. So, the young man goes in search, encountering struggles, exhaustion and immense dangers. He crosses continents, climbs mountains, swims lakes, leaps ravines, perspires in jungles, freezes in icy wastes – and after months and months of devoted journeying, he finds the wise old woman, the wise old woman who knows the meaning of life. She sits quietly, warming herself by some burning logs, her craggy face lit by flickering flames. After respectful words and knowing silences, the young man, impatient for the conclusion to his quest, blurts out, 'O wise woman, wise woman who knows the meaning of life, tell me. What is the meaning of life?'

The wise old woman looks thoughtful, her face now half in shadow. She stretches her eyes at the distant stars, her craggy brow furrowed. The young man feels a whole universe of understanding within her gaze. Eventually comes a whispered reply, 'Life is a fountain.'

'Life is a fountain?' The young man cannot contain his anger. 'I've walked the Earth. I've crossed oceans, hacked through jungles, risked body and soul – just to be told that life is a fountain?'

The wise woman remains calm, unperturbed, and stares into his eyes, 'So, it's not a fountain. Whatever you say . . .'

*   *   *

We treat the meaning of life as highly important. We want our lives to be meaningful, to matter, and that seems to require that they have a point. Many people seek an answer of the form, 'The point of life is ___' with the gap filled by something sufficiently point-worthy. The Puzzle of Meaningfulness is that the gap can never be filled. The wise old woman makes that point by being casual about the point.

Many people, believing that an external meaning or point to life is seriously needed, look to gods or God: without divine presence and eternity, our lives, with their stresses, strivings and distresses, are pointless. Other people just get on with their lives: they do not cry out for anything external to the meaning, purposes and points that they find within their lives and the lives around them.

Apart from introducing the Meaningfulness Puzzle – to which we shall return – the point of raising this point about points is to show that one man's paradox, puzzle or perplexity, is sometimes another man's piece of cake. What strikes some people as an amazing and disturbing conclusion, amazes and disturbs others not at all. One man's paradox may even be another man's blank stare. This can be because what impresses some people as obvious starting points of paradoxical pathways are, for others, utterly baffling.

There are many paradoxes lurking within the depths of physics and mathematics, yet they are so arcane, requiring specialist knowledge, that they are rarely encountered by non-specialists. True, scientific paradoxes occasionally hit the headlines: this is usually when imaginative illustrations are presented. People can become fascinated by Einstein's Twins Paradox, its starting point being relativity theory's implication that travelling very fast, near the speed of light, slows down time. Let one identical twin remain on Earth, while the other twin journeys at high speed into space; on her return she will be younger than the Earth-resident twin. That is paradoxical enough, but the further paradox is that, from the perspective of the journeying twin, the Earth-resident twin is speeding; so ought she not to end up younger?

For some scientists, some theories of time raise the time-travelling possibility, with the resultant Time-Travel Paradox of how, it would seem, you could travel into the past, shoot your parents before you were born; and hence you would fail to exist to do anything, let alone to embrace time-travelling.

Schrödinger's Cat is another vivid illustration of scientific paradox, this one using the apparent indeterminacy of decay regarding a small piece of radioactive substance over, say, one hour. A live cat is hidden away in a box and unobserved. Whether the cat during the hour is dead or alive hangs on whether radioactive decay has occurred; but that, according to one theoretical interpretation, is indeterminate until aforementioned cat is observed. Hence, paradoxically, it seems as if the cat must be in an indeterminate state, neither dead nor alive – or maybe both? – until observed.

These are paradoxes for philosophers of science to handle by examining the theories and concepts for coherence and clarity – after all, 'observer' presumably excludes the cat, but not because it is asleep or lacks sufficient perceptivity. 'Observer' marks a certain interference.

We typically expect evidence and success, or otherwise, of predictions to be relevant, though some theories, such as those of many universes and strings, may be exceedingly remote from experimental possibilities. It is worth remembering that scientific theories tend to be transient and meet with revision, even rejection. We should also remember that, whether uttered by eminent scientists or not, a contradiction remains a contradiction. There are also philosophical questions concerning, for example, whether scientists' theoretical entities – electrons, neutrons, Higgs bosons – have an existence and reality, as do tables and turnips, or whether they should be viewed as fictions, useful tools or instruments for making predictions.

Despite the vast success of the mathematical-based scientific enterprise, some caution is well advised when reading scientists' popularizations – with paradoxical, indeed contradictory claims. For example, Peter Atkins, an Oxford Professor of Chemistry, comments, 'At the time before time, there is only extreme simplicity. There is really nothing . . .' Later, he adds, 'In the beginning there was nothing . . . There was no space, nor was there time, for this was before time. The universe was without form and void. By chance, there was a fluctuation, and a set of points, emerging from nothing . . .'

Yet whatever is meant by 'time before time', by 'a universe without form and void', and by a 'fluctuation' from, or of, nothing?

Stephen Hawking, Cambridge's Lucasian Professor of Mathematics, writes of the 'beginning of time' and the possibility of a 'unified theory bringing about its own existence', yet he also suggests that theories exist only in the mind, being just useful models for describing observations.

Cosmology is not the sole source of paradoxical scientific claims. Richard Dawkins, former Oxford Professor of the Public Understanding of Science, argues that gene selfishness usually gives rise to selfishness in human behaviour (with 'selfishness' being used in different senses), that our biological nature offers little encouragement towards altruism; yet, also, that culture and learning allow us to fight such selfishness. Paradoxically, it seems, culture and learning enter the frame as independent of our biological nature. That is as mysterious as religious talk of souls standing outside the physical world; so, clarification is needed.

Scientists have the credibility of major successes in understanding the world, so maybe they merit forgiveness if they lapse, perhaps through excitement, into obscure or contradictory tales. Some 'postmodernist' writers deserve little understanding. Indeed, understanding is often the problem with much of what they write.

When Jean Baudrillard publishes a work entitled *The Gulf War Did Not Take Place* he no more means it literally than Dawkins does with *The Selfish Gene*. Paradoxical titles are forgiven, if ultimately explained; yet, within some texts of, for example, Baudrillard, Irigaray, Kristeva and Lacan, there is a seeming and unexplained paradoxical erudition – we may bravely risk the technical term 'nonsense'. For example, Lacan, giving an equation, announces that the erectile organ is equivalent to the square root of minus one. Irigaray tells us that Einstein's $E = mc^2$ is a sexed equation, privileging 'the speed of light over other speeds that are vitally necessary to us'. It is too depressing to cite more detailed examples. Just because sentences are baffling, obscure and paradoxical, it does not mean that there is something deep to fathom.

Philosophical writings, of the analytical variety, can also be obscure because of topic or presentation or the writer's own confusion: see, for example, McTaggart's Paradox below. No doubt many passages in this book display obscurities of my confused thinking – and this sentence itself could generate a puzzle akin to the Preface Paradox. Most philosophical paradoxes – apart from a few logical ones – possess, though, the great advantage of being highly accessible, dealing with everyday concepts such as those of motion, rationality and saying that something is false. The paradoxes often address very simple, overwhelmingly obvious beliefs, yet reach exceptionally unobvious conclusions, even contradictions. As we run through some further paradoxes – some light, some deep – we review some paradoxical features already encountered.

Frustrations and failings

Life's meaning, as we saw at the beginning of this chapter, requires life to have a point – according to some thinkers. 'The point of A is B', we may say. 'Ah', they shake their heads, 'but what is the point of B?' 'C', we reply. 'Not good enough,' they say, 'for what is the point of C?' Some pop in God as the answer; but if the question of 'What is the point?' is legitimate, then it too should be asked of God.

If, for something to be meaningful, it must possess an external meaning that is itself meaningful by possessing a further external meaning, then we shall be forever frustrated and inconsolable. But that is only because we have set ourselves a logically impossible demand, a demand that, in a sense, demands nothing – for there is nothing that could possibly satisfy the demand. Impossible tasks often feature in paradoxes. We met some impossibilities arising with the Poisoned Chalice's offer, with the demand to resolve what to do in the Newcomb game, and what to believe in the Surprise Examination. We saw how concepts, when applied to motion, can generate an endlessness; yet, to the frustration of Zeno, we rightly accept that we really do move our legs and walk, and move our tongues and talk. We sought to find an error in Zeno's application of endless division. Here are some further seeming frustrations.

NIRVANA

Tired of this world of suffering, I may follow a Buddhist path.

I must overcome all selfishness to attain peace, yet my seeking such peace is, it is said, a selfish act.

If Nirvana is only to be achieved when all selfish motivation is gone, then allegedly it is impossible to achieve for those who seek it, for seeking anything for oneself is a selfish act. Steps can be taken. Buddhist monks, bodhisattvas, can detach themselves from the 'red dust', from earthly desires, but Nirvana remains elusive, if that is what they seek. Possibly the paradox distorts what is meant by 'self-lessness': we saw such a distortion in the Paradox of Altruism.

A related picture, derived from Mahayana Buddhism, depends on the individual's aim being the salvation of all mankind – the Greater Vehicle – rather than just his own. None shall be saved until all are saved. The bodhisattva is a paradigm, a centre at peace. He has attained enlightenment in this world, but he cannot pass to Nirvana alone for, to do so would be selfish, leaving the rest of mankind behind. This frustration, though, involves no impossibility built into the conditions: all mankind could attain enlightenment together in one go – well, in theory.

We need not remain on the edge of another world for frustrations. People often notice that seeking happiness is not the best way of achieving happiness. Resolution of this Happiness Puzzle is possible by focusing on specific goals: individuals, looking back later on, may realize that some happiness had been attained. The possibility of happiness contrasts with a forthcoming impossibility of avoiding flying missions:

CATCH-22

'The catch specified that a concern for one's safety in the face of dangers that were real and immediate was the process of a rational mind. Orr was crazy and could be grounded. All he had to do was ask; and as soon as he did, he would no longer be crazy and would have to fly more missions.'

Joseph Heller's well-known catch frustrates, for no one, sane or insane, can avoid the flying missions. The catch rules out as impossible someone being both insane and also requesting being grounded. An ancient tale that involves such frustration by one argument, yet satisfaction by another, relies on a contract's conditions being dubiously applied to a situation not explicitly catered for by the contract:

LAWYER

Euathlus, an impoverished student, received legal training from the
silver tongue of Protagoras. The deal was that Protagoras would
receive his fee, once Euathlus won his first court case. Euathlus,
after his studies, turned away from the law, favouring politics
instead. He won no cases because he took on no cases. Protagoras,
irritated, sued Euathlus for the fee.

Each party argued that he was onto a winner. Protagoras argued that
if he, Protagoras, won, then the court was ruling that his wayward
student should pay. If he, Protagoras, lost, then Euathlus would have
won his first case – and so should pay.

Euathlus argued the reverse. Euathlus argued that if he lost the
case, then obviously he, Euathlus, would not need to pay – for he had
only to pay when he won his first case. If he, Euathlus, won the case,
then the court would be ruling that he should not pay. Either way,
according to the Euathlusian reasoning, he should not pay.

The pattern may remind us of the Liar, where a liar speaks the truth
if and only if he is not speaking the truth. We may try to squash the
Lawyer into a contradiction – namely, that Euathlus should pay if,
and only if, he should not pay. More expansively, one version, with
Euathlus having lost the case, would be: Euathlus should pay (by court
order) if, and only if, he should not pay (according to the contract).

This paradox seems to overlook the fact that court judgements are
made at a particular time. Arguably, overlooking the temporal element is at the heart of Chapter 7's Self-Amendment Paradox. With
temporal element to the fore, the Lawyer can be resolved. Protagoras
should lose the case – after all, Euathlus has not yet won a case – but,
with that ruling, Euathlus is now a winner, and so Protagoras is then
indeed owed his fee. If necessary, he could sue Euathlus for the
money and, this second time round, win.

The Lawyer bemuses because two conflicting criteria for judgement – the contract, the court – are merged, resolution seemingly
impossible. Catch-22, Meaningfulness and Nirvana set conditions,
ensuring that desired outcomes were impossible. Puzzles also exist,
though, about the possible.

Camels, scales – and the non-existent

The impossible, of course, does not exist; indeed, it cannot exist. Round squares cannot exist. In previous chapters we saw how some (mis)characterizations of free will and altruism made them impossible. Many things that are possible do not exist – but they could exist. Dodos no longer exist, but circumstances could have been such that some dodos still exist. Maybe you lost at roulette the other day, but your chosen numbers might have come up. Paradoxically, states of affairs that do not exist – non-existents – are sometimes highly relevant in our understanding of what does exist. We saw the alleged relevance of the non-existent when we noted the moral force of 'What if everyone were to do likewise?' – even though everyone's doing likewise fails to occur.

Consider: you see the bus coming. Is it worth running to try to catch it? What you need to know is not whether the bus will stop, but whether it will stop *if* you run. The driver could be malicious, someone who speeds up, when he sees people running. Flipping the tale into the past, you may be interested in knowing whether the bus would have stopped, had you run. That interest involves a counterfactual – a state of affairs that is counter to the fact; a state of affairs that does not exist. In our everyday thinking, we often hold such counterfactuals to be true or false. 'Had you had another drink, you would have been unfit to drive.' That statement, on occasions, may be true, even though it concerns the non-existent state of your having that additional drink.

Puzzles quickly arise with counterfactuals – the Puzzles of Counterfactuals. Let us take an Iraqi example. The former US President, George W. Bush, ordered the invasion of Iraq. Suppose someone more ruthless to have been President, say, Napoleon: we would then be tempted by the counterfactual claim, 'Had Napoleon been US President, he would have used nuclear weapons.' That manifests a plausible line of thought. Yet here is another plausible line. 'Had Napoleon been President, he would have used horses and muskets.' The example shows that, when we assess counterfactuals, we need to be clear what is permitted into the supposition.

Counterfactuals are involved in our understanding of causality and laws of nature. Suppose that the twenty cats in the cattery are all black. You have a gloriously white cat. With regard to colour, you would have no worries about boarding your white cat at the cattery; you have no reason to believe that the cattery turns cats' fur black. Now, were the cattery filled with starving cats, you would reasonably hesitate whether to let your lovely white fluffy creature holiday there. The cattery's owners, no doubt, failed to go in for feline feeding. The first scenario speaks of an accidental connection; the second of a causal connection. The difference seems, in part, to rest on truths concerning 'What would happen *if*'.

With causality in mind, we introduce two further puzzles, one of the large, one of the small. We start with the small: it re-visits a matter left hanging in Chapter 5's Sorites.

'The straw that broke the camel's back' – well, it is a saying – may do just that. The straw may be the last straw. Let us ignore what the camel may or may not notice. We ignore, so that it is clear that the impending puzzle does not solely relate to how physical changes affect psychology. We may reasonably doubt whether the camel's skeletal-muscular system would register the weight of a single straw; yet, at a certain point, a single *extra* straw makes all the difference. Is not that puzzling?

People may think not. They may, with a superior air, observe, 'It only puzzles those unaware of the fallacy of composition, outlined in Chapter 5.'

Well, let us consider the matter in a little more detail. Some scales with a rusty mechanism respond – the pointer moves – only to weights, say, of at least a pound. Place one apple on the scales: no pointer movement. Place another, and another, and another – still no movement. One apple causes no movement – it seems. Yet that is not true, for when we place the fifth, the pointer springs to life and registers a pound weight. What are we to say?

Perhaps each apple's weight affects the spring which affects the pointer; but now we have questions concerning how the spring affects the pointer and how the apple affects the spring. Suppose the apples are chopped into teeny pieces, must we say that each teeny piece, however small, makes a change in the spring's tension, yet these small changes in tension initially make no change in the pointer's location? Must each straw cause a small change in the camel's backbone? It is odd to answer 'Yes', yet we appear compelled sometimes to do so to explain the effects. After all, it would be more puzzling were an additional straw never to break the camel's back or always to do so. If the former, the camel could carry any weight, however heavy; if the latter, the camel could carry no weight at all.

The Puzzle of the Camel and Scales has us thinking that, if the whole affects the camel and the scales, then parts of the whole, however small, must sometimes individually affect the camel and the scales – yet our empirical observations do not readily show that to be true. It looks as if we impose on the world the assumption that teeny parts must, in some cases, make changes – physicists may speak of forces of the teeniest apple parts affecting the tension – yet sometimes only the accumulation of the changes makes a subsequent change: witness, for example, the pointer's movement or lack of such.

Further reflection on causes and effects leads us to the large. This is the Puzzle of Time-Taking. A cause is usually understood as an event that is sufficient to bring about an effect. We need to qualify by adding, 'given the surrounding conditions'. Lighting the match caused the explosion – well, given that the chemicals were dry, oxygen was present and so forth. So, perhaps it is better to say that it is because of the presence of all those conditions and the lighted match that the explosion occurred – otherwise there would have been no explosion. Those factors in total were sufficient to bring about the explosion. Now, here is the reasoning into puzzlement.

TIME-TAKING

The lighted match and surrounding conditions caused the explosion. When did the explosion occur? The answer may be 'a split second after the lighting'. What, then, accounts for that split-second duration? It looks as if another causally relevant event is required for the explosion. The 'When?' question, though, can be asked repeatedly, until the answer refers not to a time after the last causally relevant event, but to a simultaneity of that causal event and explosion. The reasoning applies generally. Paradoxically, the conclusion is that all effects must have occurred at the same time as their sufficient causes first presented.

What we think of as a single complex chain of causes and effects over time would have to be one instantaneous big bang – everything in that particular chain all at once – a big bang far bigger than the biggest bang in physicists' wildest dreams. Its effects would be squashed into it.

Perhaps we need to conclude from this puzzle – and the Camel and Scales – that we sometimes slip into pressing onto the world an understanding of cause and effect that fails to apply. Earlier, we saw how the concept of infinity was wrongly pressed onto the world, generating Zeno's paradoxes. Of course, such comments do not explain what is the correct way, the most consistent way, of pressing such concepts – itself a pressing question.

Time and star-making

Causation is paradoxical, and so is time. McTaggart – 'John McTaggart Ellis McTaggart', a splendid name – a Cambridge philosopher of the early twentieth century, argued that time is an illusion. 'You mean, I didn't have breakfast before afternoon tea?' would be asked by G. E. Moore whom we met earlier, in Chapter 2. McTaggart, however, did mean that – thus granting the world McTaggart's Paradox.

McTaggart distinguished between two different ways of describing events time-wise. There is the A-series which orders events in terms of being future, present, past; that is, of events that will happen, are happening, and did happen. There is the B-series which orders those events in the temporal before/after relation.

According to McTaggart, the A-series is essential to time, for only the A-series involves change. Events ordered in the B-series' before/after manner remain eternally in their particular position. Socrates died before Plato died: that B-series relation, of Socrates' death before Plato's, never changes. However, with the A-series descriptions, at one time Socrates' death was in the future, then it changed to being in the present – and now it is well in the past. The need to allow for change is the reason why some philosophers doubt whether an object, such as Heraclitus' river (met in Chapter 5), should be thought of as four-dimensional, consisting of a lot of temporal stages, with only one temporal stage seemingly 'present' at any given moment.

Consider a poker, red at one end, black the other. That alone does not suggest change in time. For such change, we need the poker, for example, to have been black in the past and red in the present and future, perhaps through heating. If the A-series is essential to time – and hence to the B-series' before/after relation – then McTaggart's argument, about to be given, may establish time as illusory. Of course, it leaves puzzling how our experiences seem to be in time and seem to be of events occurring in time. For example, remembering embarrassments differs from expecting them. There was a similar problem for Zeno: even if movement is illusory, our experiences still seem to involve movements. McTaggart's argument for time's unreality sometimes receives support with regard to the A-series: the A-series is contradictory. Such supporters, though, sometimes argue that sense can be made of the B-series as a temporal series, independently of the A-series.

The A-series is rejected by McTaggart because virtually every event, such as Socrates' death, possesses the contradictory combination of being future, present and past. The swift reply is that Socrates' death, for example, *was* in the future, *was* later in the present, and *is* now (and has been for some time) in the past. McTaggart, though, raises a similar challenge about these more complex 'dual temporal' states, arguing that they too possess the incompatible A-series properties. Consider Barack Obama's presidential election. It possesses the incompatible properties of being past in the present, and past in the past (for some of the past), yet also being future in some of the future. We may respond that Obama's election, for example, being future in some of the future was in the past. But McTaggart raises the question again, now concerning such 'tri-temporal' states as Obama's election's being future in some of the future in the past – and so on.

The argument's plausibility is obscure, but worries about the A-series and its consistency are understandable. Here is a more accessible A-series puzzle:

PRESENT

It is commonly believed that the future does not exist – after all, it is in the future. Similarly, the past does not exist: it is in the past. So, how can the present exist? If it has any duration, then some of it is in the past or future; so, we are compelled to think of the

present as a boundary lacking duration. Yet how can that be?
How can we live in a boundary? And how can there be an existent
boundary between two non-existent parts?

This temporal puzzle, a puzzle of disappearing times, leaves us reeling
– and leaves time with no time. We may be tempted to give up on the
A-series, of future, present, past. We may seek to make do with the
B-series alone. Ignoring the problem of alleged 'no change' within the
B-series, the B-series fails to capture the idea of something happening
now. There is no present in the B-series world – merely some events
simultaneous with others, or before, or after. Muse on the universe
millions of years ago, prior to conscious beings existing: even though
events gave way to other events – the before/after description having
application – none was in the future, present or past. That surely is
paradoxical.

Once again we are enmeshed within the general puzzle of how our
concepts apply to the world. Many people readily accept that some
concepts lack worldly application independently of human interests
and desires. Whisky is not nice or nasty 'out there', independently of
human tastes. When Johnny insists that Talisker whisky is nice, he
displays *his* taste and fancy. Some people understand aesthetic judgements in a similar way: whether an item is beautiful, refined, dainty,
depends in part on human sensitivities. Some bring even more
judgement areas into the realm of partial dependency on minds: for
example, heat, sounds and colours. Grass's greenness is not 'out
there', but results from human observers interacting with the grass's
uncoloured constitution. Putting to one side the great scope for
muddled thinking here, we may be tempted to embrace the whole
world, by similar argument, as dependent on us.

STAR-MAKING

We notice the constellations in the sky. Those groupings are
imposed by us. They depend on what we find natural to notice and
bring together. The sky's stars would have been grouped differently by different creatures. Yet what of the stars themselves?
Do they not depend on how we tend to group various masses?

The puzzle is whether the world, independently of us, is already carved into objects; or whether we do the carving.

Our commonsense belief is that planets, oceans and trees existed before consciousness existed. The paradoxical conclusion of Star-Making is that the way that the world is carved – the planets, oceans and trees – depends on the concepts deployed; and they depend, in part, on what comes naturally to us, on our interests and needs. Without those concepts, there is just – what? In the eighteenth century, the great German philosopher Kant spoke of things in themselves, the noumena, which we cannot penetrate. In the twenty-first century, Donald Rumsfeld, the not-so-great former American Defence Secretary, spoke of the known unknowns – and the unknown unknowns. There are indeed such; on this matter Rumsfeld was unfairly mocked.

Any substantial answer about what exists independently of us seems necessarily to involve imposing our human concepts. The paradoxical conclusion, though, need not be that there were no animals, oceans and solar systems before human beings. After all, talk of the past is also, on this view, an imposition of a human concept onto the world – and that concept is such that we do make sense of objects and events prior to human existence. If we step outside our concepts, we ought not to be surprised at the lack of any conception of the world.

We appear to be battling at boundaries of thought. The picture that generates the battle presupposes the concept of being human and the existence of other people star-gazing. Were the puzzling reasoning correct, *I* should question whether the existence of other people, for example, hangs on my own use of the concept of a person. I should question both the coherence of the concept of 'a consciousness other than mine' and, if the concept is coherent, how I know that there are other subjects of consciousness, other minds. Yet the 'I' seems as much a magician's conjuring trick as 'you' and the 'mind-independent world'.

Wittgenstein spoke of pictures sometimes holding us captive. In putting forward the Star-Making Puzzle, we have the picture of 'us' already carved from the world, in some way separate. Many concepts, though, presuppose that we move around the world, interacting with items already present and independent of us. Our concepts in the main are not divorced from a world of unknown objects; and we are not divorced from each other.

Relevant here is Wittgenstein's rejection of the possibility of a private language, a language in which paradoxically only I can know the meanings of my words. Many people think this to be so with sensation words such as 'pain' and 'ache'. Can anyone else know what a pain is for me – and what, indeed, I mean by 'pain'? If the answer is 'No one', then we may wonder how we were ever taught use of the word 'pain', and how lucky it is that we often use such terms seemingly appropriately. Arguably, the response to this Puzzle of Privacy is that a language to be a language requires a community of speakers. Words such as 'pain' and 'ache' do not secure meaning from some private and privileged pointing within.

Fancy flights and regimentations

The Star-Making Puzzle may be useful in reminding us of our distinctive viewpoint on the world. This receives further voice from the question, 'What is it like to be a bat?' However much we may learn of bats' nervous systems, their perception – how the world strikes them – remains elusive. Women and men, similarly, can find each other elusive

When reflecting on how the world strikes bats and us, we step outside our own perspective – or, so it seems. 'Enmeshed within our human perspective' can be highlighted by tales of our being plugged into virtual-reality machines, unable to tell that we are. We may then wonder how the world really is. We encountered an early version of this with Descartes' evil genius.

We can indeed step outside our lives – moving from within, to without – taking a wider view. This gives rise to a clash: the Puzzle of Absurdity. Our lives possess considerable significance for us. Think how concerned we can become about the first greying hair, the possible slight at work, whether she will turn up for the date. Yet, adopting a more detached viewpoint, such concerns are unimportant. From the viewpoint of the universe, humanity is but a speck: the importance that we give to whether our lipstick is smudged becomes the teeniest of specks within that speck. The universe is cold and uncaring.

We deploy a picture that lapses into error. The universe is not something that cares or does not care; and there can hardly be a viewpoint without a viewer with viewing characteristics. Yet many of us cannot help lapsing into sensing absurdities about the significance we give our lives. A seeming absurdity that keeps many of us going is fiction.

FICTION

We can have feelings and emotions about items that do not exist, for we may believe that they do exist. For example, you fear her infidelity, yet she may be faithful. You are frightened by a spider, yet there is no spider: it was a trick of the light. More puzzling is that we can fear and admire characters in fiction – in plays, operas, novels – even though we know full well that the characters do not exist; they are not real.

The Paradox of Fiction is the absurdity of emotional involvement with the non-existent known by us to be such. We grow distressed by some of the novel's characters, excited by others, and even fall in love with the heroine or hero. Some people worry about how characters' lives develop after the stories end. Audiences may hope that the play's heroine marries or that justice prevails.

Although we know that the characters are non-existent, perhaps within the theatre we genuinely believe in their existence, deceiving ourselves; yet, were that true, why do we not, for example, rush from our seats to prevent the 'murder' on stage or shout out the assassin's whereabouts? Presumably it is not shyness.

With such paradoxes involving emotional and psychological states, perhaps we should simply accept, 'human that we are', that we do respond in these ways. After all, if we merely imagine something nasty happening to Aunt Agatha, we may be distressed – though we know full well that we are but imagining. Why we behave in such ways may have interesting explanations, but there exist, it seems, no deep paradoxes here – just some surprises.

Surprisingly, indeed, our human psychology may lead us to embrace the disturbing. Some people cannot help worrying about distressing scenarios: they may even worry about seeming to have no worries – a self-fulfilling Puzzle of Worry. 'What have I forgotten that I should be worrying about?' There is the Paradox of Horror. People seek out horror movies in order to be scared. Although they know they are in a cinema, they feel tingles of fear. We may be on the edge of suspense, even when seeing the thriller for the tenth time – the Paradox of Suspense. A similar case arises with the Puzzle of Humour. Some of us find the same joke, frequently repeated, still funny. I write as a connoisseur.

A wider question lurks. Why and how do we enjoy fiction, stories, plays, ballet, opera? We sometimes speak of their truthfulness, of learning from them. We may sense meaning and eternity being explored in some music; try, for example, Charles Ives' *Unanswered Question*. We may sigh at Keats' line, 'Beauty is truth, truth beauty'. Metaphors abound – and poems often display paradox, melding discords and contradictions. In Donne's 'The Canonization' we are told about love. 'Wee can dye by it, if not live for love.' Love may lead us to relinquish the world. Yet, while we value the imaginative and fancy – the magical indeed – we cannot help but impose some rigours of reasoning. Without regimentation of good argument, life would be chaotic; yet there are cases and cases, degrees and degrees.

*   *   *

Logicians, we may quip, are lovers of regimentation. They uncover structures in arguments. Some structures guarantee valid arguments; others do not. Arguments are deductively valid when it is impossible for the premisses to be true, yet the conclusions false. That ensures that from truth, we at least stay on the path of truth – an excellent aim, one distorted by Sorites. Liar-type paradoxes arise, if we create self-referential arguments as in Pseudo-Scotus or the Validity Paradox.

A medieval logician, Pseudo-Scotus ('pseudo' because his writings were erroneously ascribed to John Duns Scotus), was interested in arguments such as, 'This very argument is valid; therefore, Shakespeare was female.' Of course, I popped in the Shakespeare example. The argument would be invalid only were it possible for its single premiss to be true and conclusion false. What if the premiss is false? Well, for determining validity, we just need to consider what would be so, were that false premiss true – the importance of a counterfactual again.

Is the argument invalid? Its premiss is 'This very argument is valid', so, it is impossible for the premiss to be true and the conclusion false. Therefore, the argument is valid, and its premiss is true. Hence – paradoxically – its conclusion must be true. Its conclusion could, of course, be anything: Afghan hounds are Martians in disguise, triangles have four sides, and, next month, a wild, passionate affair with a charming millionaire lord or lady will be overwhelming you.

As with the Liar – and the Truth-Teller – we may rule the Pseudo-Scotus out of court on the basis that there is nothing that determines the content of the premiss. Curry's Paradox may be handled in a similar way. The paradox is that from the premiss, 'If this conditional proposition is true, then the Moon is made of cheese – or whatever' we may, by some simple moves, validly conclude that the Moon is made of cheese – or whatever. These paradoxes rely on illegitimate uses of self-reference.

Unfortunately, there remain non-self-referential ways in which validity leads to unhappy paradox.

STRICT IMPLICATION

For a deductive argument's premisses to imply the conclusion – for the conclusion to follow from or be entailed by the premisses – it must be impossible for the premisses to be true, yet the conclusion false. Therefore, as a contradiction cannot be true, a contradiction as premiss paradoxically implies any proposition. Further, anything implies a necessary truth as a conclusion – for a necessary truth cannot be false.

The paradox may seem worrying, yet it concerns relations between abstract propositions. In contrast, in the everyday, we give arguments to justify what we assert and how we act, making use of evidence and common assumptions. Our everyday involves more than the abstract.

It would be absurd wittingly to assert a contradiction – true, there may be special cases when financial incentives are on offer. Typically, we do not knowingly use contradictions as premisses from whence to draw any conclusion. Further, if we recognize propositions as necessarily true, then we recognize their truth as not depending on just anything. Hence, we would not seek to support them by 'just any' premisses, though we may offer other necessary truths as support. The regimentation that can be useful in the abstract is not thereby always helpful in actual reasoning, here on Earth.

Logicians speak of material implication. A proposition p materially implies q so long as it is not the case that p is true and q false. Paradox arises when material implication is taken to capture what is essential to our ordinary use of 'If . . . , then . . .' conditional propositions – for we should have to accept both the following as true, 'If squares have five sides, then Obama is not President', and 'If squares have five sides, then Obama is President.' They would be true because the 'If' clauses, the antecedents, are false – but, of course, five-sided squares have no sway regarding Obama's constitutional status.

The assumption that conditional propositions are correctly analysed as material implications can seem helpful in dealing with Carroll's Barber Shop Paradox (distinct from the Barber Paradox). Yes, this is the fascinating and fascinated Revd Charles Lutwidge Dodgson, the sometime Mr Lewis Carroll, author of *Alice in Wonderland*, student of Christ Church, Oxford, in the nineteenth century.

BARBER SHOP

Three gentlemen, Allen, Brown and Carr, run a barber shop. One of them is always present in the shop, scissors at ready. Allen never goes out alone; he only ever goes out with Brown. So, if Allen is out, then Brown is also out. That seems to ensure the following is false: if Allen is out, then Brown is in. But we know that one barber always remains in the shop; so, if Carr is out, then if Allen is out, Brown is in. Hence, on the hypothesis that Carr is out, we are landed with the false consequent 'then' clause, namely, 'If Allen is out, then Brown is in.' So, paradoxically, it seems that Carr can never go out.

Something has gone wrong, for, of course, when Allen is in, Carr is free to sally forth. Although it is true that if Allen is out, then Brown is also out, that does not contradict the claim that if Allen is out then Brown is in – if these conditionals are treated as material implications. This is because when it is false that Allen is out, both conditionals are true, given their antecedents, the 'If' clauses, are false.

A problem with using material implication as the puzzle's escape route is that, when material implication is used to analyse counterfactual conditionals, it ensures that all such conditionals are true. This is because counterfactuals' antecedents are counter to fact and hence false. The Barber Shop has true counterfactuals such as: were Carr to be out, then were Allen to be out, Brown would (have to) be in. As Allen does not go out without Brown, were Carr to be out, then Allen would be in. The truth of such counterfactuals, though, does not rest on their being material implications. 'Had you imbibed, you would have been unfit to drive' (see p. 175) – that is true, but not because you did not imbibe.

Logicians also formalize propositions concerning moral duties. Such deontic logic usually has the rule that if you ought to do something, then you ought to do what is logically implied by that something. If you ought to feed the goats, then, if Grace is one of the goats, you ought to feed Grace.

GENTLE MURDER

If you commit a murder, then you ought at least to do it non-violently; that is, without the victim suffering. Let us refer to that as 'gently'. If you ought to commit the murder gently, then it follows that you ought to commit the murder. After all, you cannot murder gently without murdering. Yet, you ought not to murder. We have a contradiction.

The paradox rests on a mistake: perhaps the mistake results from the desire for regimentation. A quick thought is to challenge the premiss that if you ought to do something, then you ought to do anything logically implied by that something. You ought to say sorry for having bored her. Arguably, that implies that you bored her – but we do not think that you ought therefore to have bored her.

There is another mistake. Consider an analogy. If it is raining, then the pavements are wet. This sets a sufficient condition for the pavements' wetness – namely, the raining condition. Now, *if* you murder, then you ought to murder gently. This sets a condition for murdering gently – namely, that a murder take place. The condition, though, is not that you ought to murder – but what you ought to do, *if* you do murder. This may still leave uneasiness, for it may then be argued that therefore, *if* you do murder, you ought to murder gently; and so, if you do murder, then you ought to murder.

The paradox's unhappy conclusion may be resisted by understanding the correct starting point not as, 'If you murder, then you ought to murder gently.' Rather, the truth is, 'What ought to be so is that, if you murder, then do it gently.' By analogy, consider a distinction dealing with necessities, made in Chapter 8. 'Necessarily, if I am thinking, then I exist.' That is true. What is not true is, 'If I am thinking, then I am a necessary existent.'

When to stop

Explanations must come to an end – somewhere. The problem is, where? Wittgenstein famously recognized that at times one must just stop and say, 'This is simply what I do.' We reach bedrock; the spade is turned.

A paradox, introduced and dismissed by Wittgenstein, arguably illustrates the spade turning. The paradox, highlighted by the brilliant American Saul Kripke, can be viewed as pushing Grue to an extreme. Controversy rages over Kripke as interpreter of Wittgenstein; consequently the paradox is sometimes attributed to a mythical Kripkenstein.

WITTGENSTEIN'S PARADOX

What is it about my use of terms, such as 'add' or 'green', that determines how I intend to use them in the future? Whichever way I use them could be made out to accord with future uses, uses which I intended and meant 'all along' – or so it seems. If so, paradoxically, nothing fixes what I mean by any term.

We may – perhaps a little misleadingly – think of ourselves as following a rule, when using a meaningful word. The rule sets what counts as right and wrong uses of the term in future. After all, typically we intend to use a term, such as 'green', with the same meaning as before. A commonsense belief is that usually I know what I mean when I use a word; but what is it that I know – and what constitutes my meaning one thing rather than another? There is, the paradox suggests, no fact that determines what counts as my future use being in accord with my current use. The paradoxical conclusion is that all language use is meaningless – which, of course, defeats this linguistic expression of the paradox. If the argument is right, we are truly in the inexpressible and cannot express that we are; indeed, we cannot be taken there by any good argument.

Consider the word 'add' or 'plus'. My use is such that, if told to add 68 to 57, I should answer 125. That is the right answer; yet what fixes *my* use of 'add' such that 125 was the right answer, given *my* understanding of 'add'? My use of 'add' – what I intended – perhaps was such that I ought to have delivered a different answer.

Suppose a child seems to grasp the notion of odd numbers by being given the examples of 3, 5, 7, 9. She is asked to carry on with the series in 'the same way'. She may think that 'the same way' is shown by repeating the numbers 3, 5, 7, 9 rather than by continuing with 11, 13, 15 *and so on.*

Suppose a different case:Sophie has correctly identified numerous numbers as odd, up to one million. 'I surely do know what an odd number is,' she says. Yet how does Sophie's use of 'odd' determine what she will deem odd when given large numbers previously unmet?

The history of our use of any terms does not fix what we mean to do in the future. The mantra 'and so on, in the same way' leaves things open regarding what strikes us as 'the same way'. Maybe we feel that there should be rails stretching out into future uses, to keep us true to the meanings – or to enable us to recognize when we have gone off the rails, into some new meanings. Yet such rails do not exist.

Are there some psychological states or mental images present *now* that determine our future use? It would seem not – and even if there were, they could be interpreted in different ways. Perhaps we possess a disposition to behave in certain ways when told to add numbers – even trillions of unknown ones – but what ensures that that disposition would have us using 'add' in accord with what we meant? Further, frail creatures that we are, we may be disposed to make mistakes with large numbers.

Arguably, the paradox arises because it seeks the impossible. It seeks something more than the fact that, when we behave in a certain way in the future – 'adding' numbers; spotting items that are green – we can often recognize that that is what we intended. Explanations must come to an end.

Explanations must indeed come to an end – and it is nearly time to stop. Our 'stop' is a wonderful puzzle from Lewis Carroll. It is the Paradox of Valid Inference. It has the tortoise – let us make him our 'Mr T' – getting Achilles and all of us into a muddle – well, a muddle if we are blind to the thought that sometimes we just must stop.

Let us strip away some colour and animation, simplifying proceedings. Mr T challenges Achilles to justify his claim that a particular conclusion validly follows from some premisses. To set the background, our Achilles has argued thus:

Premiss 1   All philosophers deserve respect.
Conclusion C   Zeno deserves respect.

This alone seems far from valid; the conclusion fails to follow from the premiss. Mr T is right to expect something more. Achilles is happy to oblige. He adds:

Premiss 2   Zeno is a philosopher.

'There, Mr T, you must now accept the conclusion, since you accept both premisses as true,' says Achilles proudly.

Mr T scratches his shell, unsure. Yes, he accepts the premisses, but why accept the conclusion? Achilles, now a little tetchy, explains, 'Look: if all philosophers deserve respect and if Zeno is a philosopher, then it follows that he deserves respect.'

'Ah,' says Mr T surprisingly quickly, 'that sounds like another premiss: please add it into the argument.' Achilles obliges.

Premiss 3   If Premiss 1 and Premiss 2, then C.

'Yes,' says Mr T, 'I shall accept all three premisses, but . . .'

'No "but",' interrupts Achilles, with a triumphant tone. 'You must now accept the conclusion. If you do not, logic will grab you by the throat and . . .'

'I'm still not certain about all this,' replies Mr T.

'Try hard,' says Achilles, increasingly exasperated. 'If premisses 1 and 2 and 3, then C must follow.'

'Ah, another premiss, I do detect,' detects Mr T, 'Please write it down as Premiss 4.'

Thus the tale continues potentially endlessly – for the answers are endless, if we seek to placate Mr T. The ever-increasing number of premisses form the first elements of an endless series. Following the rule of 'First add a corresponding "If . . . , then . . ." conditional as an additional premiss in whatever latest argument is proposed', in order validly to reach a sought conclusion, ensures no conclusion is validly reached. However many conditionals of a finite number are added, there remains an endless number to add – and so, it seems, no conclusion is validly reached. Recall Zeno's Traversal Challenge.

The attempted solution often put forward to Mr T's Deduction Challenge is that the challenge mistakenly demands premisses, when all that is required is a valid rule of inference, a rule being no premiss. This attempted solution is exposed to a revised challenge, revised in that 'rule' now replaces 'premiss'. The challenge demands a further rule to justify use of the earlier rule.

To dissolve the Deduction Challenge we need to resist Mr T's repeated demands for something more. Sometimes, an argument of the form 'P1: therefore C' is valid, with nothing more needing to be said. A simple example, ambiguities apart, is 'This animal is a vixen: therefore, this animal is a fox.' This is valid for it is impossible for the premiss to be true with the conclusion false.

Sometimes, by insertion of a further premiss, an invalid argument can be seen as a casual way of expressing a related valid argument. Here is an example. The Queen requested Descartes' attendance: therefore Descartes attended. This invalid argument could be transformed into the valid: the Queen requested Descartes' attendance; whatever the Queen requests, happens: therefore Descartes attended.

The argument that all philosophers deserve respect and Zeno is a philosopher, therefore Zeno deserves respect, simply is a valid argument – full stop.

Various particular arguments are valid. It is because we identify features common to certain groups of various valid arguments that we are able to display valid *forms* and *rules* of argument. It is often a mistake, though, to insist that there must be some general form or rule behind what we do that justifies what we do.

*   *   *

Many paradoxes arise because we keep on going, keep on going for too long. In Samuel Beckett's works, there occurs the mantra, 'I can't go on; I'll go on.' That is a contradiction, formal logicians may say – yet we know the feeling. We want to reason things through more and more closely, seeking to have everything explained, be it the bat's perspective, the right judgement in a moral dilemma, or the meaning of life. Yet we can also recognize that there are times when we just have to stop – in reasoning, justifying, explaining, and in life.

That stopping time has almost arrived, for while this book could be greatly improved, with its contents clearer, proposals deeper, and its style far more elegant, deadlines have been reached and crossed, the head droops, the mind slows, and eyelids close. I must stop. The empirical world intrudes upon abstract reasoning, as we have seen with paradoxical tales stretching from the Ass of Buridan to Zeno's infinite dealings. But, one more thing – the Puzzle of Non-Existence.

Human lives stop. Perhaps the greatest surprise – the greatest paradox – is not just that we exist, but that we once did not exist, and in due course shall not exist. We may lapse into confusion, when seeking sense of the world lacking our presence. We know it will happen, yet we usually steer clear of the immensity to us – the overwhelming immensity – of our finitude and non-existence. One's non-existence can weigh heavily. For me, my non-existence is paradoxical – and yours for you.

What can the world be like without me? In a sense, it seems obvious what it will be like; yet, in a sense, it may baffle. What we shall be without is, though, no more baffling than what we, every day, live within, conjuring with magical concepts. It is no more baffling than the persisting self, of what it is to be me, and what it is to choose freely. It is no more baffling than our spending much of our time losing ourselves – losing ourselves in thought, in music, in fiction; in work, in play, in others. In the absurdity of life . . .

Paradoxically, many of us are most fulfilled when we are lost to ourselves – lost, often, in simply experiencing the world, no reasoning at all.

And yet . . .

'The difficulty here: is to stop.'

Appendix 1
Further reading

Structurally inappropriate though it is, I cannot resist drawing attention first to Lewis Carroll's phantasies, of 1865 and 1872 respectively, *Alice in Wonderland* and *Through the Looking Glass*. See the edition, with notes by Martin Gardner, *The Annotated Alice* (London: Allen Lane, 2000). Gardner and also Raymond M. Smullyan provide entertaining collections of logical puzzles – for example, the latter's *What is the Name of this Book?* (Harmondsworth: Penguin, 1981).

Valuable reference works are Michael Clark, *Paradoxes from A to Z*, 2nd edn (London: Routledge, 2007), and Glenn W. Erickson and John A. Fossa, *Dictionary of Paradox* (Lanham, MD: University Press of America, 1998). The latter has wider coverage, but the former is more accessible in various ways. Another good source, albeit forcing paradoxes into moulds, is Nicholas Rescher, *Paradoxes: Their Roots, Range, and Resolution* (Chicago: Open Court, 2001). For a more informal, distinctive and entertaining intertwining, try William Poundstone, *Labyrinths of Reason* and *Prisoner's Dilemmas* (New York: Anchor, 1988/1993).

Detailed studies of core paradoxes are R. M. Sainsbury, *Paradoxes*, 3rd edn (Cambridge: Cambridge University Press, 2009), Stephen Read, *Thinking about Logic* (Oxford: Oxford University Press,1995) and Doris Olin, *Paradox* (Chesham: Acumen, 2003), all with comprehensive references. Roy Sorensen has many thought-provoking and engaging works, often with original paradoxical variants: note his *Blindspots* (Oxford: Clarendon, 1988) and *A Brief History of the Paradox* (New York: Oxford University Press, 2003). An older good work is J. L. Mackie, *Truth, Probability and Paradox* (Oxford: Clarendon Press, 1973).

Adrian Moore offers a fine and accessible – and finite – work on both infinity's history and its paradoxes in *The Infinite*, 2nd edn (London: Routledge, 2001). Readers seeking the classical and erudite could wisely dip into Richard Sorabji, *Time, Creation and Continuum* (Ithaca: Cornell University Press, 1983). For some morality paradoxes, go for Saul Smilansky, *Ten Moral Paradoxes* (Oxford: Blackwell, 2007).

Lighter enjoyment, introducing philosophy more generally, is Robert M. Martin, *There are Two Errors in the the Title of this Book* (Peterborough, Ontario: Broadview, 2002); also, Colin Radford, *Driving to California: An Unconventional Introduction to Philosophy* (Edinburgh: Edinburgh University Press, 1996). Clear background material is in Robert Audi, ed., *The Cambridge Dictionary of Philosophy*, 2nd edn (Cambridge: Cambridge University Press, 1999). For summaries of recent philosophers mentioned in the text, see Stuart Brown, ed., *The Dictionary of Twentieth-Century Philosophers* (Bristol: Thoemmes Continuum, 2005).

For internet lovers, there is the valuable Stanford Encyclopedia of Philosophy, freely available at http://plato.stanford.edu; and links to various philosophy pages and podcasts should be available at: www.petercave.com.

I discuss some paradoxes in more detail elsewhere. Many others, of course, discuss them in even more detail, with greater insight and clarity; but should readers be interested in more of my take, here are the references. Indeed, a small number of this book's paragraphs derive from some of the articles below, with kind permission.

For Placebo and Self-Fulfilling Paradoxes, see 'Too Self-fulfilling', *Analysis* 61.2, 2001. For Newcomb and Surprise, 'Reeling and A-Reasoning: Surprise Examinations and Newcomb's Tale', *Philosophy* 79 (310), 2004. For some Sorites' arguments, '"About" Puzzles, Muddles and First Person Inferences', *Philosophical Investigations* 29.1, 2006. For Machiavelli Puzzles, Moore and more, see 'Humour and Paradox Laid Bare', *The Monist* 88.1, 2005. For Zeno's Achilles and Carroll's Valid Inference, 'With and Without End', *Philosophical Investigations* 30.2, 2007. For yet more on Moore, Newcomb, Toxin and Surprise, see, co-authored with Laurence Goldstein, 'A Unified Pyrrhonian Resolution of the Toxin Problem, the Surprise Examination, and Newcomb's Puzzle', *American Philosophical Quarterly* 45.4, 2008.

Modesty should forbid, but now fails. For lighter vein Peter Cave, with some overlap to the paradoxes here, see the collections of perplexing philosophy puzzles, namely, *Can a Robot Be Human?* – hereafter *Robot* – and *What's Wrong with Eating People?* – hereafter *Eating* – (Oxford: Oneworld, 2007/2008). For God, ethics and life's meaning, see my *Humanism: A Beginner's Guide* (Oxford: Oneworld, 2009).

A book, of course, cannot directly convey the understanding and meaning that may be given to life, its paradoxes, incongruities and absurdities, through theatre, music and art. These days many musical tasters are available on Spotify and YouTube, from Christina Pluhar and Philippe Jaroussky's jazzed-up Monteverdi, stumbling within love, to Richard Strauss's opera *Salome*, with its obsessions and lusts, to John Adams' opera *Doctor Atomic*. The latter presents Oppenheimer's 'dirty hands', when testing the first atomic bomb, and his plea for redemption through John Donne's 'Batter my heart'. Links should be available at my webpage: www.petercave.com.

Appendix 2

Notes, sources and references

Preface

Twentieth-century philosophy, for the first half, was dominated by three Cambridge thinkers: Bertrand Russell, G. E. Moore and then Ludwig Wittgenstein. We meet all three in our paradoxical journey – and also Frank Plumpton Ramsey, a highly influential, brilliant young man who died in 1930, when aged 26. John Maynard Keynes – he originally wrote on probability – the world-famous economist, was a leading member of the circle, a circle that included the secret society the Apostles, centring on Trinity College and King's College. Keynes was also part of the Bloomsbury Group. Later on, we encounter some non-philosophers associated with the group – in the form of the novelist E. M. Forster and the poet Rupert Brooke.

For the Keynes' quotation on pretence, see his (1921) p. 427. The young Keynes was said, by Russell, to be the cleverest man he had met. The anguished genius, Wittgenstein, his life and philosophy, are well explored in McGuinness (1988) and Monk (1990). McGuinness (2008)'s collection of letters shows the relationship between the key philosophers here. Brief outlines of their lives and work are in Brown (2005). Philosophy as assembling reminders is from Wittgenstein (1953), §127.

Chapter 1: Welcome to the rational irrational

For paradox classifications, see Quine (1966), Olin (2003) and Smilansky (2007). A useful introductory background on logic is Goldstein et al. (2005).

Newcomb's Problem was first delivered to the philosophical world by Robert Nozick: see his paper in Rescher et al. (1969). The history and analysis of Buridan's Ass is in Rescher (2005). Spinoza, in his posthumously published *Ethics*, 1677, speaks of the ass as being truly assine – and man likewise, were he to behave in such a way. I thank Angela Joy Harvey for the ass's doggerel. For more on Newcomb and Buridan, see Chapter 2's references. Newcomb here is from Goldstein and Cave's (2008).

Mele and Rawling (2004) provides rationality and decision topics, and contains Roy Sorensen's 'Paradoxes of Rationality', which discusses Money Pump, St Petersburg Paradox and much more. The St Petersburg became so called because Nicolaus Bernoulli's brother, Daniel – the brothers were Swiss mathematicians – published it in the St Petersburg Academy 1738 proceedings. The Charitable Trust is from Landesman (1995): see also Moller (2006). Donald Davidson reflects on how we make irrational behaviour rational in his 1982 paper 'Paradoxes of Irrationality', now in Davidson (2006). Binmore (2009) looks at expected utility.

The Bottle Imp can have us reasoning step by step through pennies and pounds, cents and dollars. Martin Hollis (1986) offered a Train of Thought Puzzle, with similar step-by-step reasoning. It can be presented as you and I each having chosen a card from a pack numbered 1 to 100, ignorant of each other's number. A third party has seen our cards; she informs us that we cannot determine, just by reasoning, who has the higher number – and she leaves the scene of forthcoming anguish.

We each reason that the other cannot have card numbered 1 – otherwise he could work out who has the higher – hence, that number can be discarded from our reasoning. Next stage is the thought that, therefore, the other cannot have card numbered 2, otherwise he would know who has the higher – thus, that number can be discarded. And so on.

The puzzle is often likened to Chapter 2's Surprise. However, for the train of thought to work, we each need to know of the other, at each discarding stage, that he does not have that number; yet we cannot possess that knowledge, for we both know that, somewhere along the line, we shall be holding the card that reasoning paradoxically rules out. Matters would be different were we, at each stage in the reasoning, to declare, 'Yes, I do not have that number', when true.

Chapter 2: Too clever by one half
The title is, I believe, a quip by Ted Honderich in a review of a Bernard Williams book.

Sainsbury (1995) is a good start for Surprise and Newcomb. We could give Surprise variants in terms of the past and memory. More complicated moves, including a 'glimpse' version, are in Williamson (2000). The Poisoned Chalice deploys Kavka's Toxin Paradox: see Kavka (1987). Munchausen is from Sorensen (2000). Sorensen also produces Surprise variants in his (1988), including Indy which uses features of Surprise and Toxin combined.

Moore's Paradox is in Moore (1993) and Wittgenstein (1953) II.x; see also McGuinness (2008) for Wittgenstein's letter 316, and Green and Williams (2007) for developments. Austin – John Langshaw Austin – introduced 'performatives', found in his posthumous (1962), with some characteristic dry humour. In view of his name, he entitled one lecture series *Sense and Sensibilia*.

A common structure to these paradoxes is examined in Goldstein and Cave (2008). For more on the Machiavelli Puzzles and Placebo, see my papers cited in 'Further reading' (p. 194). Also, for Placebo, see Smullyan (1988). Bernard Williams casts an erudite and wide eye over truthfulness in his (2002). Sartre on self-deception – 'Bad Faith' – is in his (1957).

Russell's view of Moore's truthfulness and integrity was no aberration. Moore was a great influence on the Bloomsbury Group and its ethics: see Keynes (1949).

Linking to perspective puzzles, here is a reported tale about Wittgenstein by F. R. Leavis – see Rhees (1981) – albeit with modified wording by me. After his first meeting with W. E. Johnson, the established logician assigned to teach him logic, Wittgenstein said, 'He could teach me nothing.' Johnson said, 'I could teach him nothing.' Think how different the meanings were. Johnson's work merits scrutiny: see Brown (2005) and Johnson (1921–3).

Chapter 3: Lather, rinse, repeat

Sainsbury (1995) and Read (1995) offer clear discussions of both Liar and Russell. For emphasis on infinity, but also some set theory paradoxes, for example, the Burali-Forti Paradox involving the set of ordinals, see Adrian Moore (2001). Ramsey's stance is in his (1931), where the redundancy theory of truth is also promoted, presumably encountered through his King's College Cambridge logician colleague, W. E. Johnson: see Johnson's (1921–3), vol.1.

Regarding the Liar, truth-bearers and Russell, an enjoyable presentation is Goldstein (1999). Berry's Paradox is called thus because Russell derived it from G. G. Berry, a librarian at the Bodleian. Yablo's use of infinite sequences is in his (1993). Disquotational is from Quine (1987), a work which is an enjoyable mish-mash of topics, written in Quine's distinctive and entertaining style – well worth dipping into. Quine and others have attributed greatness to Frege: Quine writes, for example, 'Logic is an old subject, and since 1879, it has been a great subject', 1879 being the publication year of Frege's *Begriffsschrift*. Liberated Secretaries is reported, as Sec Lib, in Chihara (1979). Chihara attributes it to Frank Cioffi who encountered it in a film.

The original Russell, together with other paradoxes, is in his (1903). In 1913 P. E. B. Jourdain suggested the 'calling card' example. Graham Priest defends dialetheism: detailed, advanced and wide-ranging work is (2002). For advanced discussion on abstract entities and sets as abstractions, see Lewis (2001).

For the Liar's history, see Spade (1988). Buridan's interest in insolubilia is in his (1982). Buridan anticipated some recent self-referential puzzles, for example, the Seducer. Buridan's Bridge, the Bridge Puzzle (a subsequent version is in Cervantes, *Don Quixote*), is the following. In order to cross the bridge controlled by Lord Plato, Socrates' next statement must be true, otherwise Socrates will be thrown into the waters. Socrates says, 'You are going to throw me in the water.' Plato is now stuck: what Socrates said is true if, and only if, it is false.

Chapter 4: Infinity: without end, without beginning

For a fine introduction and comprehensive survey concerning the many infinity paradoxes, see Moore (2001). Bernadete (1964) is the source of Gods and Spaceship – and many variants.

Zeno's Stadium is obscure, but maybe seeks contradiction by assuming that space and time are composed of discrete atoms. Consider two lines of three such atoms, lined up,

A1   A2   A3
⇕   ⇕   ⇕
B1   B2   B3

Suppose that the A line moves one atom distance to the left and at the same time and speed the B line moves one atom to the right. A3 is now lined up with B1, even though paradoxically at no stage did A3 line up with B2, or B3 with A2. For some classical scholarship, see Barnes (1979) and Sorabji (1983).

Expressly for Zeno and related paradoxes, including the Trojan Fly devised by A. K.

Austin, is Salmon (1980). Thomson's Lamp, with responses, are in Salmon (1970); see also Russell (1903) and Mazur (2007). Some of my critical comments of the 'mathematical ignorance solution' are cheekily directed at Clark (2007).

My flea received its first outing in Cave (2007), noted in 'Further reading' (p. 194). Clark (2008) raises some puzzles of logic's application. Bandit occurs in *Robot* (2007), but for detail, expansion and Cambridge changes, see Ruben (1999) and Weintraub (2003). The quip about messages without poles is from the splendid Wisdom (1965) pp. 133–4.

Chapter 5: Heaps and haze, colours and clocks
A good comprehensive essay collection (though no easy read) on Sorites is Keefe and Smith (1997): note too Sorensen (2001). Wiggins, also difficult, looks at identity in his (2001) – and see Williamson (2000) for the Magoo example, from whence 'pigeons' derives. Geach (1972) raises relevant matters and his (1980) gives the 1,001 cats. For clouds, see Unger (1980). Saul (2007) discusses Superman. Goldstein (2000) tells of the frog and in (2002) wisely urges us to refuse the Yes/No concerning Pierre.

For a persuasive approach, concerning heap versions of soritic arguments, stressing the importance of hesitation and resistance, see Hanfling (2001). For earlier comments on Sorites and the fallacy of continuous questioning, see Neville Keynes (1906) pp. 371–2. Neville Keynes was father of Maynard, Maynard bringing global fame.

Mathematical induction, by the way, proceeds by proving, for example, that if a proposition holds true for any number n, then it also holds true of $n + 1$ – and also proving that the proposition does, indeed, hold true of a base case, say, 1. The proposition must then hold true of 2, 3, 4 – and so on. The numbers fall as a column of dominoes may fall, as the first one knocks down the second, the second the third – and so on.

For knights and grains, see my 'About' in 'Further reading', and Wittgenstein (1974), I, §1.1. Note his (1953), 1. §120: 'When I talk about language (words, sentences, etc.) I must speak the language of every day. Is this language somehow too coarse a material for what we want to say? *Then how is another one to be constructed?* – And how strange that we should be able to do anything at all with the one we have!'

The caveat about reasoning and *modus ponens* relates to an example by McGee (1985) – the *Modus Ponens* Puzzle – discussed in, for example, Goldstein et al. (2005). Here is my less historical example. Suppose two animals and one bird are racing – a gazelle, a sloth and a secretary bird. You have excellent reason to think the gazelle will win and the sloth will come last, the bird coming second. You are, though, committed to the belief: If an animal wins, then if the gazelle does not win, then the sloth will. You also believe that an animal will win. Hence, it looks as if you should believe that, if the gazelle does not win, the sloth will win. Yet given your background beliefs, you are far from believing that – and rightly so.

Chapter 6: Ravens, lotteries, medical matters
Inductive problems are in Sainsbury (1995), a good starting place for Hempel's Ravens and Goodman's Grue. Hempel's original article appears in (1965): see also his (2000). For a clear defence of inductive reasoning, see Hugh Mellor's paper, 'The Warrant of

Induction' at: http://sms.cam.ac.uk/media/19261, also in Mellor (1991). For some practical oddities, muse upon how some financial regulators insist that past fund performance is no guide to future performance, while permitting advertising of past performances – or consider investors and investment managers who think they know when a share is under- or overvalued, yet know no more than the rest of the market. There are intriguing controversies here concerning the Random Walk Hypothesis: to get started, try Malkiel (2003).

Grue, introduced in 1954, is best seen in Goodman (1965). A 1946 paper raised the puzzle with the predicate, concerning marbles, 'drawn by Victory in Europe Day and is red, or is drawn later and is non-red'. The word 'gruebleen' first appeared in 1939 with James Joyce's *Finnegan's Wake*. Bertrand Russell also raised puzzles of manufactured classes: see his (1948). For a gruesome collection, see Stalker (1994), and note Israel (2004).

The epistemic paradoxes concerning fallibility and lotteries and the like are discussed in detail in Olin (2003). Probability's straightforward errors abound; for example, see Monty Hall, cited in many places – e.g. *Robot* (2007). Some troubling probabilities include Bertrand's Chord, see Shackel (2007), and Two Envelopes. In the latter, you randomly select one of two sealed envelopes. Each envelope contains money, but one contains twice as much as the other. Whichever envelope you have, should you take the opportunity to switch? Paradoxically – and fallaciously – the answer is 'Yes', for suppose there is x amount in your envelope, then if you switch you are equally likely to secure an additional x, or lose just half x. But . . . See Clark and Shackel (2000).

Descartes is everywhere, so to speak – his evil genius famously appears in the first of his six *Meditations on First Philosophy*, published in 1641. For more on conscious assent and contradictory beliefs, see my 'Humour and Paradox Laid Bare', cited in 'Further reading' (p. 194). The rarer Harman's Paradox is in Harman (1973); and see Sorell (1981). How should we respond to evidence? Well, let us turn to John Maynard Keynes again. 'When the facts change, I change my mind. What do you do, sir?'

Chapter 7: Morality and politics

For attacks on relativism, see Nagel (1997). Saul Smilansky (2007), an honorable exception to the paucity of books explicitly on moral paradoxes, is my source for some blackmail examples – Smilansky stresses what here is termed 'Blackmail Stage II' – and for the Perfect Punishment, called 'Non-Punishment' by Smilansky. Clark (2007) seems to recognize only the Stage I slighter problem. The Divestiture Paradox appears in Cahn (2007). A wonderful collection of the dubious is Katz (1996). Glover (1975) is clear and good on the 'Why vote?' question and more. Innocent Murderer, from *Robot* (2007), does the rounds under various guises; I think I first met a version in a Lewis Carroll collection. For causation and counterfactuals, see Lyon (1967). For detailed discussion on Self-Amendment, see Peter Suber on-line: www.earlham.edu/~peters/writing/psa/index.htm. Sainsbury (2009) now has a chapter on moral paradoxes.

Prisoners' Dilemmas feature a lot in Olin (2003); for Deterrence, see Kavka (1987). Popper (1945), vol. 1, ch. 7 notes, raises the various freedom/democracy paradoxes. Weakness of will receives discussion and references in Mele and Rawling (2004).

Systematic work on voting and elections started with the eighteenth-century Jean-Charles de Borda and – to give his full name – Marie Jean Antoine Nicolas Caritat, Marquis de Condorcet, encyclopédiestes. For a survey, see Black and Newing (1998). See also Sen (1970) on collective decision-making; the theorem's eponym is Kenneth J. Arrow. The Politeness Paradox, as the Abilene Paradox, is from Harvey (1988).

Forster's two cheers are from his (1951). Forster, also associated with Bloomsbury Group, being at King's with Keynes and so on, was a humanist, argued loudly for freedom of speech and more quietly for the repeal of laws prohibiting homosexual activities. He spoke in strong defence of D. H. Lawrence's *Lady Chatterley's Lover*.

Chapter 8: Encounters with God

For godly matters, excellently surveyed, see Everitt (2004). A good collection, including godly defences, is Copan and Meister (2008). An outspoken defender of traditional Catholicism, yet also eminent logician, is Peter Geach: see both of his (1977). For a humanist perspective on God, religion and meaning, yet celebrating absurdities, see my (2009). Aware of religion's dangers and *Euthyphro*, humanists promote goodness without God.

Closely argued work on divine foreknowledge is Zagzebski (1991). Grim (1991) uses Cantor in questioning God's omniscience. For the Rakehell and related, see Moran (2001). See also Flanagan (1996). A 1955 discussion of Tertullian's Paradox is in Williams (2006). Lighter works are Pickover (2001) and Cahn (2007).

'Sympathy for the Devil' appears in *Robot* (2007) – as does more on motivation and heaven seeking. *Eating* (2008) looks at a particular argument for God's existence, namely the ontological argument.

Spinoza vigorously sought to understand religious claims consistently. He spoke of 'God or Nature' and refused to anthropomophize – or fish-ize – God. A work discussing his excommunication is Nadler (2001). For Spinoza's honest simplicity, Leibniz's worldliness and their interaction, see Stewart's lively (2005). The quip concerning flowers at the grave originates, I think, from G. K. Chesterton.

Rupert Brooke perhaps puts us – or God – in our place. His splendid poem 'Heaven' has 'Fish say they have stream and pond, but is there anything beyond?' Reflecting on their heaven of 'unfading moths, immortal flies, and the worm that never dies', we meet: 'and when in that heaven of all their wish, there shall be no more land, say fish'.

Chapter 9: Encounters with *our* mysterious ways

Moral luck, death, harm, put in appearances in Williams (1981) and Nagel (1976) – Nagel's papers are more accessible. For courtroom arguing, see Darrow (1957). Altham and Harrison (1995) provides papers on Williams and his reflections. A good general collection of metaphysical essays is Sider, Hawthorne and Zimmerman (2008).

Puzzles involving the self abound. Some influential discussions from late twentieth-century philosophers are Williams (1973) and Parfit (1984), the latter especially for Wrongful Life. For a taste of Salt, see Salt (1989). The Wittgenstein 'limit of the world' is from (1922), 5.632; and see Valberg (2007).

A recent reflection on Sleeping Beauty, referencing other papers, is Jenkins (2005). More papers are in the pages of the philosophy journal *Analysis*, 2009. For Zuboff's distinctive view on such matters, see his (2000) and my *Eating* (2008). Soble (1990) has love's perplexities. Neill and Ridley (2002) covers fake art.

With Wrongful Life in mind, when reflecting on what makes sense, try Sophocles, 'The most blessed are those not to have been born'.

Chapter 10: When to stop

The 'meaning of life' tale does the rounds in different versions. For some Buddhist puzzles, see Danto (1976) and, for Tao, Smullyan (1977). Nagel (1976) discusses absurdity and 'What is it like to be a bat?' The question originated from Timothy Sprigge.

Science quotations are from Atkins (1981) pp. 99, 119; Hawking (1995) pp. 135, 155, 192–3; and Dawkins (2006) pp. 2–3, 332. Postmodernist dangers and pseudo-science, including the text's examples, are in Sokal and Bricmont (1998) and Sokal (2008). I hasten to add that Dawkins' work, usually splendidly written, is not remotely akin to universal relativism and the fashionable nonsense of some postmodernists. Dawkins, in fact, regrets his rogue sentence, 'Let us try to teach generosity and altruism, because we are born selfish.'

For the Euathlus tale, see Diogenes Laertius (1938), also Carroll (1977), where labelled, 'Antistrephon' or 'The Retort'. For counterfactuals, see Goodman (1963); for 'bus' example, see Watling (1992). An introductory survey is in Read (1995), where validity, material implication and paradoxes such as Curry's are also examined. It is controversial to claim that counterfactuals are capable of truth and falsity. Ramsey (1931) is highly influential for some current analyses of counterfactuals, also of causation and theories. For essays on Ramsey's work, see Lillehammer and Mellor (2005) and www.fil.lu.se/sahlin/ramsey.

For Camels and Scales, I guess we need more physics. Russell seemed to recognize the puzzles. Time-taking occurs in *Robot* (2007). McTaggart's argument for the unreality of time – and a defence by Mellor – are in Le Poidevin and MacBeath (1993). The Star-Making Puzzle derives from Goodman: see McCormick (1996).

G. H. von Wright is father of deontic logic. A recent work formalizing puzzles is Forrester (1996). Fiction paradoxes are in Yanal (1999) and Neill and Ridley (2002). For poetical paradoxes, see Cleanth Brooks (1968).

On Wittgenstein's Paradox, Wittgenstein writes, 'This was our paradox' (1953), §201: note the past tense – and see §§138–242, which then move into the private language argument. For the controversial take, see Kripke (1982) and Miller and Wright (2002). Lewis Carroll's tortoise is from his (1895), reprinted in his (1977), which also contains Barber Shop. Mr T appears in my *Eating* (2008). Valberg (2007) addresses the paradox of our death; and my work on humanism (2009) has a chapter on life's mish-mash of absurdities, from opera to self.

Opera – an absurd art form – can yet sweep us away from ourselves, with the kaleidoscope of orchestra, singing, acting, narrative, metaphor, lavishly presented. We can be lost in the opera, yet, paradoxically, not lost at all. A mesmerizing recent opera, with Arjuna and Krishna present, is Philip Glass's *Satyagraha*, directed by Phelim McDermott for the English National Opera, London, and the Metropolitan Opera, New York (2007). For a chamber piece that captivates, enfolding listeners in a mystical eternity, try Messiaen's *Quartet for the End of Time*, written in 1941, when Messiaen was interned in a prison camp. And – well . . ,

Wittgenstein (1967), §314, tells of the difficulty to stop.

Appendix 3

Paradoxes purveyed

The following lists the paradoxes in this book, without the word 'paradox' or 'puzzle' tediously added. Page references are to central discussions only; the General Index, under the relevant topic, may mention more. The perplexities that are considered classic philosophical paradoxes – and recent paradoxes that have generated considerable interest – are in bold. I have asterisked paradoxes that receive reasonable discussion, even resolution, here, or are variants of ones with such – or are ones with simple resolution. 'Classic', 'considerable' and 'reasonable' all indicate some soritic haziness. While a few paradoxes have names now enshrined, many appear differently labelled by different authors, sometimes depending on example deployed. Hence, some names below point to the same text, where the paradox is discussed under a key name, but with the different names registered. There is charm in such nomenclature muddles – well, there can be.

Bibliography

Altham, J. E. J. and Harrison, Ross, eds (1995) *World, Mind and Ethics: Essays on the Ethical Philosophy of Bernard Williams*. Cambridge: Cambridge University Press.

Atkins, P. W. (1981) *The Creation*. Oxford: W. H. Freeman.

Audi, Robert, ed. (1999) *The Cambridge Dictionary of Philosophy*, 2nd edn. Cambridge: Cambridge University Press.

Austin, J. L. (1962) *How To Do Things With Words*. Oxford: Oxford University Press.

Barnes, Jonathan (1979) *The Presocratic Philosophers*. London: Routledge.

Benardete, José Amado (1964) *Infinity: An Essay in Metaphysics*. Oxford: Clarendon.

Binmore, Ken (2009) *Rational Decisions*. Princeton: Princeton University Press.

Black, Duncan and Newing, R. A. (1998) *Committee Decisions and Complementary Valuation*, rev. 2nd edn. Dordrecht: Kluwer.

Brooks, Cleanth (1968) *The Well Wrought Urn*, rev. edn. London: Dobson.

Brown, Stuart, ed. (2005) *The Dictionary of Twentieth-Century British Philosophers*. Bristol: Thoemmes Continuum.

Buridan, J. (1982) *John Buridan on Self-Reference*, trans. and notes by G. E. Hughes. Cambridge: Cambridge University Press.

Cahn, Steven (2007) *Puzzles & Perplexities: Collected Essays*, 2nd edn. Lanham, MD: Lexington Books.

Carroll, Lewis (1895) 'What the Tortoise Said to Achilles'. *Mind* 4.

—— (1977) *Symbolic Logic*, ed. William Warren Bartley, III. Hassocks: Harvester.

—— (2000) *The Annotated Alice*, 2nd edn with notes by Martin Gardner. London: Allen Lane.

Cave, Peter (2007) *Can a Robot Be Human? 33 Perplexing Philosophy Puzzles*. Oxford: Oneworld.

—— (2008) *What's Wrong with Eating People? 33 More Perplexing Philosophy Puzzles*. Oxford: Oneworld.

—— (2009) *Humanism: A Beginner's Guide*. Oxford: Oneworld.

Chihara, Charles (1979) 'The Semantic Paradoxes: A Diagnostic Investigation'. *The Philosophical Review* 88.4.

Clark, Michael (2007) *Paradoxes from A to Z*. London: Routledge.

Clark, Michael and Shackel, Nicholas (2000) 'The Two-Envelope Paradox'. *Mind* 109.

Clark, Stephen R. L. (2008) 'Deconstructing the Laws of Logic'. *Philosophy* 83.1.

Copan, Paul and Meister, Chad, eds (2008) *Philosophy of Religion: Classic and Contemporary Issues*. Oxford: Blackwell.

Danto, Arthur C. (1976) *Mysticism and Morality*. Harmondsworth: Penguin.

Darrow, Clarence (1957) *Attorney for the Dammed*, ed. Arthur Weinberg. New York:

Simon and Schuster.

Davidson, Donald (2006) *The Essential Davidson*. Oxford: Clarendon.

Dawkins, Richard (2006) *The Selfish Gene*, 30th anniversary edn. Oxford: Oxford University Press.

Descartes, René (1996) *Meditations on First Philosophy* (1641), trans. John Cottingham. Cambridge: Cambridge University Press.

Diogenes Laertius (1938) *The Lives of Eminent Philosophers*. London: Heinemann.

Erickson, Glenn W. and Fossa, John A. (1998) *Dictionary of Paradox*. Lanham, MD: University Press of America.

Everitt, Nicholas (2004) *The Non Existence of God*. London: Routledge.

Flanagan, Owens J. (1996) *Self Expressions: Mind, Morals and the Meaning of Life*. Oxford: Oxford University Press.

Forrester, James Wm (1996) *Being Good and Being Logical*. Armonk, New York: M. E. Sharpe.

Forster, E. M. (1951) *Two Cheers for Democracy*. London: Edward Arnold.

Geach, Peter (1972) *Logic Matters*. Oxford: Blackwell.

—— (1977) *Providence and Evil*. Cambridge: Cambridge University Press.

—— (1977) *The Virtues*. Cambridge: Cambridge University Press.

—— (1980) *Reference and Generality*, 3rd edn. Ithaca, NY: Cornell University Press.

Glover, Jonathan (1975) 'It Makes No Difference Whether or Not I Do It', reprinted in Peter Singer, ed. *Applied Ethics* (1986). Oxford: Oxford University Press.

Goldstein, L. (1999) 'A Unified Solution to Some Paradoxes'. *Proceedings of the Aristotelian Society* 100.

—— (2000) 'How to boil a live frog'. *Analysis* 60.2.

—— (2002) 'Refuse Disposal'. *Analysis* 62.3.

Goldstein, L., Brennan, A., Deutsch, M., and Lau, J. (2005) *Logic*. London: Continuum.

Goldstein, L. and Cave, P. (2008) 'A Unified Pyrrhonian Resolution of the Toxin Problem, the Surprise Examination, and Newcomb's Puzzle'. *American Philosophical Quarterly* 45.4.

Goodman, Nelson (1965) *Fact, Fiction and Forecast*, 2nd edn. Indianapolis: Bobbs-Merrill.

Green, Mitchell and Williams, John N., eds (2007) *Moore's Paradox: New Essays on Belief, Rationality, and the First Person*. Oxford: Clarendon.

Grim, Patrick (1991) *The Incomplete Universe*. Cambridge, MA: MIT.

Hanfling, O. (2001) 'What Is Wrong With Sorites Arguments?'. *Analysis* 61.1.

Harman, Gilbert (1973) *Thought*. Princeton: Princeton University Press.

Harvey, Jerry B. (1988) *The Abilene Paradox and Other Meditations on Management*. Lanham, MD: Lexington.

Hawking, Stephen (1995) *A Brief History of Time*. London: Penguin.

Heller, Joseph (1961) *Catch-22*. New York: Simon & Schuster.

Hempel, C. G. (1965) *Aspects of Scientific Explanation and Other Essays*. New York: Free Press.

—— (2000) *Selected Philosophical Essays*, ed. Richard Jeffrey. Cambridge: Cambridge University Press.

Hollis, Martin (1986) 'More Paradoxical Epistemics'. *Analysis* 46.4.

Israel, Rami (2004) 'Two Interpretations of "Grue": Or How to Misunderstand the

New Riddle of Induction'. *Analysis* 64.4.

Jenkins, C. S. (2005) 'Sleeping Beauty: A Wake-Up Call'. *Philosophia Mathematica* (III) 13.

Johnson, W. E. (1921–3) *Logic*, vols 1–III. Cambridge: Cambridge University Press.

Katz, Leo (1996) *Ill-gotten Gains: Evasion, Blackmail, Fraud, and Kindred Puzzles of the Law*. Chicago: University of Chicago Press.

Kavka, Gregory (1987) *Moral Paradoxes of Nuclear Deterrence*. Cambridge: Cambridge University Press.

Keefe, Rosanna and Smith, Peter, eds (1997) *Vagueness: A Reader*. Cambridge, MA: MIT Press.

Keynes, John Maynard (1921) *A Treatise on Probability*. London: Macmillan.

—— (1949) *Two Memoirs*. London: Rupert Hart-Davis.

Keynes, John Neville (1906) *Studies and Exercises in Formal Logic*, 4th edn. London: Macmillan.

Kripke, Saul (1982) *Wittgenstein on Rules and Private Language*. Oxford: Blackwell.

Landesman, Cliff (1995) 'When to Terminate a Charitable Trust?'. *Analysis* 55.1

Le Poidevin, Robin and MacBeath, Murray, eds (1993) *The Philosophy of Time.* Oxford: Oxford University Press.

Lewis, David (2001) *On the Plurality of Worlds*. Oxford: Blackwell.

Lillehammer, Hallvard and Mellor, D. H., eds (2005) *Ramsey's Legacy*. Oxford: Oxford University Press.

Lyon, Ardon (1967) 'Causality'. *The British Journal for the Philosophy of Science* 18.1.

Mackie, John (1973) *Truth, Probability and Paradox*. Oxford: Clarendon Press.

Malkiel, Burton G. (2003) *A Random Walk Down Wall Street*, 8th rev. edn. New York: W. W. Norton.

Martin, Robert M. (2002) *There are Two Errors in the the Title of this Book*. Peterborough, Ontario: Broadview.

Mazur, Joseph (2007) *The Motion Paradox*. New York: Dutton.

McCormick, Peter J., ed. (1996) *Starmaking*. Cambridge, MA: MIT.

McGee, Vann (1985) 'A Counterexample to Modus Ponens'. *Journal of Philosophy* 82.

McGuinness, Brian (1988) *Wittgenstein, a Life: Young Ludwig, 1889–1921*. London: Duckworth.

—— (2008) *Wittgenstein in Cambridge: Letters and Documents 1911–1951*. Oxford: Blackwell.

Mele, Alfred R. and Rawling, Piers, eds (2004) *The Oxford Handbook of Rationality*. Oxford: Oxford University Press.

Mellor, D. H. (1991) *Matters of Metaphysics*. Cambridge: Cambridge University Press.

Miller, A. and Wright, C., eds (2002) *Rule-Following and Meaning*. Chesham: Acumen.

Moller, Dan (2006) 'Should We Let People Starve – For Now?'. *Analysis* 66.3.

Moore, A. W. (2001) *The Infinite*, 2nd edn. London: Routledge.

Moore, G. E. (1993) *G. E. Moore: Selected Writings,* ed. Thomas Baldwin. London: Routledge.

Monk, Ray (1990) *Ludwig Wittgenstein: The Duty of Genius*. London: Jonathan Cape.

Moran, Richard (2001) *Authority and Estrangement: An Essay on Self-knowledge*. Princeton: Princeton University Press.

Nadler, Stephen (2001) *Spinoza's Heresy*. Oxford: Clarendon.

Nagel, Thomas (1976) *Mortal Questions*. Cambridge: Cambridge University Press.
—— (1997) *The Last Word*. Oxford: Oxford University Press.
Neill, Alex and Ridley, Aaron, eds (2002) *Arguing about Art*, 2nd edn. London: Routledge.
Olin, Doris (2003) *Paradox*. Chesham: Acumen.
Parfit, Derek (1984) *Reasons and Persons*. Oxford: Clarendon.
Pickover, Clifford A. (2001) *The Paradox of God and the Science of Omniscience*. New York: Palgrave.
Popper, Karl (1945) *The Open Society and Its Enemies*, vols I–II. London: Routledge.
Poundstone, William (1988) *Labyrinths of Reason*. New York: Anchor.
—— (1993) *Prisoner's Dilemmas*. New York: Anchor.
Priest, Graham (2002) *Beyond the Limits of Thought*. Oxford: Clarendon.
Quine, W. V. (1966) *The Ways of Paradox and Other Essays*. New York: Random House.
—— (1987) *Quiddities*. Cambridge, MA: Harvard University Press.
Radford, Colin (1996) *Driving to California: An Unconventional Introduction to Philosophy*. Edinburgh: Edinburgh University Press.
Ramsey, F. P. (1931) *The Foundations of Mathematics and Other Logical Essays*, ed. R. B. Braithwaite. London: Kegan Paul.
Read, Stephen (1995) *Thinking about Logic*. Oxford: Oxford University Press.
Rescher, Nicholas (2001) *Paradoxes: Their Roots, Range, and Resolution*. Chicago: Open Court.
—— (2005) *Scholastic Meditations*. Washington, DC: Catholic University of America Press.
Rescher, N., Davidson, D. and Hempel, C. G., eds (1969) *Essays in Honor of Carl G. Hempel*. Dordrecht: Reidel.
Rhees, Rush, ed. (1981) *Ludwig Wittgenstein: Personal Recollections*. Oxford: Blackwell.
Ruben, David-Hillel (1999) 'Act Individuation: The Cambridge Theory'. *Analysis* 59.4.
Russell, Bertrand (1903) *The Principles of Mathematics*. London: Allen & Unwin.
—— (1948) *Human Knowledge: Its Scope and Limits*. London: Allen and Unwin.
Sainsbury, R. M. (2009) *Paradoxes*, 3rd edn. Cambridge: Cambridge University Press.
Salmon, Wesley C., ed. (1970) *Zeno's Paradoxes*. Indianapolis: Bobbs-Merrill.
—— (1980) *Space, Time, and Motion: A Philosophical Introduction*. Minneapolis: University of Minnesota.
Salt, Henry (1989) *The Savour of Salt*, eds George Hendrick and Willene Hendrick. Fontwell: Centaur Press.
Sartre, Jean-Paul (1957) *Being and Nothingness*, trans. Hazel E Barnes. London: Methuen.
Saul, Jennifer (2007) *Simple Sentences, Substitution, and Intuitions*. Oxford: Clarendon.
Sen, Amartya K. (1970) *Collective Choice and Social Welfare*. San Francisco: Holden-Day.
Shackel, Nicholas (2007) 'Bertrand's Paradox and the Principle of Indifference'. *Journal for the Philosophy of Science* 58.
Sider, Theodore, Hawthorne, John, and Zimmerman, D. W., eds (2008) *Contemporary Debates in Metaphysics*. Oxford: Blackwell.
Smilansky, Saul (2007) *Ten Moral Paradoxes*. Oxford: Blackwell.
Smullyan, Raymond M. (1977) *The Tao is Silent*. San Francisco: Harper.

—— (1981) *What Is the Name of This Book?* Harmondsworth: Penguin.

—— (1988) *Forever Undecided.* Oxford: Oxford University Press.

Soble, Alan (1990) *The Structure of Love.* New Haven, CT: Yale University Press.

Sokal, Alan (2008) *Beyond the Hoax: Science, Philosophy and Culture.* Oxford: Oxford University Press.

Sokal, Alan D. and Bricmont, Jean (1998) *Intellectual Impostures.* London: Profile.

Sorabji, Richard (1983) *Time, Creation and Continuum.* Ithaca, New York: Cornell University Press.

Sorell, Tom (1981) 'Harman's Paradox'. *Mind* 90.

Sorensen, Roy (1988) *Blindspots.* Oxford: Clarendon.

—— (2000) 'Faking Munchausen's Syndrome'. *Analysis* 60.2.

—— (2001) *Vagueness and Contradiction.* Oxford: Oxford University Press.

—— (2003) *A Brief History of the Paradox.* New York: Oxford University Press.

Spade, Paul Vincent (1988) *Lies, Language and Logic in the Late Middle Ages.* London: Variorum.

Spinoza, Benedict de (1985) *Ethics* (1677) in *The Collected Writings of Spinoza*, trans. Edwin Curley. Princeton: Princeton University Press.

Stalker, Douglas, ed. (1994) *Grue! the New Riddle of Induction.* Chicago: Open Court.

Stewart, Matthew (2005) *The Courtier and the Heretic: Leibniz, Spinoza, and the Fate of God in the Modern World.* New Haven, CT: Yale University Press.

Unger, Peter (1980) 'The Problem of the Many'. *Midwest Studies in Philosophy* 5.

Valberg, J. J. (2007) *Dream, Death, and the Self.* Princeton: Princeton University Press.

Watling, John (1992) 'The Importance of "If"', in *A. J. Ayer: Memorial Essays*, ed. A. Phillips Griffiths. Cambridge: Cambridge University Press.

Weintraub, Ruth (2003) 'The Time of a Killing'. *Analysis* 63.3.

Wiggins, David (2001) *Sameness and Substance Renewed.* Cambridge: Cambridge University Press.

Williams, Bernard (1973) *Problems of the Self.* Cambridge: Cambridge University Press.

—— (1981) *Moral Luck: Philosophical Papers 1973–1980.* Cambridge: Cambridge University Press.

—— (2002) *Truth and Truthfulness.* Princeton: Princeton University Press.

—— (2006) *Philosophy as a Humanistic Discipline.* Princeton: Princeton University Press.

Williamson, Timothy (2000) *Knowledge and its Limits.* Oxford: Oxford University Press.

Wisdom, John (1965) *Paradox and Discovery.* Oxford: Blackwell.

Wittgenstein, Ludwig (1922) *Tractatus Logico-Philosophicus*, trans. C. G. Ogden and F. P. Ramsey. London: Kegan Paul.

—— (1953) *Philosophical Investigations*, trans. G. E. M. Anscombe. Oxford: Blackwell.

—— (1967) *Zettel*, trans G. E. M. Anscombe. Oxford: Blackwell.

—— (1974) *Philosophical Grammar*, trans. A. Kenny. Oxford: Blackwell.

Yablo, Stephen (1993) 'Paradox without Self-reference'. *Analysis* 53.4.

Yanal, Robert. (1999) *Paradoxes of Emotion and Fiction.* Pennsylvania: Pennsylvania State University.

Zagzebski, Linda Trinkaus (1991) *The Dilemma of Freedom and Foreknowledge.* New York: Oxford University Press.

Zuboff, Arnold (2000) 'The Perspectival Nature of Probability'. *Inquiry* 43.

General index

Appendix 3, Paradoxes Purveyed, lists the paradoxes, referencing the central discussions. The references are repeated here, but usually, where possible, within the topic areas. Where clarity is not challenged, the terms 'paradox', 'puzzle' and 'example' are omitted.

Please note that references in **bold** are to chapters.